by rebecca walker

Black White and Jewish:
Autobiography of a Shifting Self

edited by rebecca walker

To Be Real:
Telling the Truth and
Changing the Face of Feminism

praise for
what makes a man

"Read it to revive your belief that the human species, both sexes included, may actually be capable of evolving."

—Barbara Ehrenreich

"*What Makes a Man* was inspired by Rebecca Walker's eleven-year-old son's commenting, 'Maybe girls will like me if I play sports.' The statement starts Walker ruminating about the paths that have been laid out for American boys. Hence, she has assembled this collection, which offers alternative modes of manhood to, and cautionary tales about, the American male. There is Jarvis Jay Masters's vivid, well-written description of prison life . . . David Coates's exploration of his sensitivity in 'This Is My Story' . . . one on being gay . . . on being a stay-at-home dad . . . on trying to be selfless, one on overcoming a violent father, one on overcoming a tough, pig-butchering mother. There is a portrait of a voodoo grandfather . . . a little illustrative lecture on setting boundaries for boys and a hopeful essay about finding kindness and peace within, and radiating it out."

—San Francisco Chronicle

"In this literate essay collection, Walker brings together male and female writers to ponder the male figure in its various poses: ill, robust, young, aged, confident, emotionally spent. The result is a book that portrays masculinity as a fluid mosaic, giving added resonance to contributor Caitríona Reed's claim that 'the Navajo have at least forty-nine gender designations.' Elsewhere, humor writer Bruce Stockler, in 'No Means No,' uses agile diction to portray the frenetic schedule and social stigma attached to being a stay-at-home dad—for four children, including triplets. And Meri Nana-Ama Danquah, in an essay that uses narrative twists to surprise readers with thoughtful analysis, ambivalently describes Ghana, a country where men link pinkies while chatting in bars because Ghanaian society accepts the display of physical affection between male friends. . . . The anecdotes and insights will keep readers engaged."

—Publishers Weekly

"[Walker's] agenda is ambitious . . . to break through the whole array of remaining barriers to a higher quality of life."
—*U.S. News & World Report*

"Walker . . . has put together a timely and profound anthology. One wonders what changes could occur in our society if such texts were read and openly and sensitively discussed among boys and girls who are on the verge of entering the limiting spaces we call 'manhood' and 'womanhood.' Walker's introductory essay offers poignant and insightful observations about our reactions as parents, children, and peers to the process of becoming a 'man.' Other striking pieces include a mother's questions about her three-year-old son's insistence that he's a girl; a man's reflections on his childhood and the experiences, role models, and expectations that shaped him; a privileged young black man's life of trying to fit in while remaining true to his belief in peace over violence; and a transsexual's search for self beyond stereotype. Walker has done society at large a great service by bringing forth these voices, these views. Now if only society will listen."
—*Booklist*

"Their articles treat gender-related themes like sex, power, and violence from a variety of viewpoints and styles, ranging from novelist Martha Southgate's moving struggle to come to terms with her son's gender confusion in 'My Girlish Boy' to film-maker Michael Moore's *(Bowling for Columbine)* satirical tirade against the male sex as an enemy of Nature in 'The End of Men.'"
—*Library Journal*

what makes a man

22 writers imagine the future

edited by

rebecca walker

riverhead books

New York

THE BERKLEY PUBLISHING GROUP
Published by the Penguin Group
Penguin Group (USA) Inc.
375 Hudson Street, New York, New York 10014, USA
Penguin Group (Canada), 10 Alcorn Avenue, Toronto, Ontario M4V 3B2, Canada
(a division of Pearson Penguin Canada Inc.)
Penguin Books Ltd., 80 Strand, London WC2R 0RL, England
Penguin Group Ireland, 25 St. Stephen's Green, Dublin 2, Ireland (a division of Penguin Books Ltd.)
Penguin Group (Australia), 250 Camberwell Road, Camberwell, Victoria 3124, Australia
(a division of Pearson Australia Group Pty. Ltd.)
Penguin Books India Pvt. Ltd., 11 Community Centre, Panchsheel Park, New Delhi—110 017, India
Penguin Group (NZ), cnr Airborne and Rosedale Roads, Albany, Auckland 1310, New Zealand
(a division of Pearson New Zealand Ltd.)
Penguin Books (South Africa) (Pty.) Ltd., 24 Sturdee Avenue, Rosebank, Johannesburg 2196,
South Africa

Penguin Books Ltd., Registered Offices: 80 Strand, London WC2R 0RL, England

PRINTING HISTORY
First Riverhead hardcover edition: March 2004
First Riverhead trade paperback edition: February 2005
Riverhead trade paperback ISBN: 1-59448-068-0

The Library of Congress has catalogued the Riverhead hardcover edition as follows:

What makes a man : 22 writers imagine the future / edited by Rebecca Walker.
    p.   cm.
  Includes bibliographical references.
  ISBN 1-57322-269-0
  1. Men. 2. Boys. 3. Fathers. 4. Masculinity. I. Walker, Rebecca, date.
HQ1090.W473   2004   2003066789
305.31—dc22

PRINTED IN THE UNITED STATES OF AMERICA

10   9   8   7   6   5   4   3   2   1

For Solomon and Jovan,
and the beautiful ones not yet born

Anthologies are full of challenges. I bow deeply to Joan Miura for her help transcribing and securing permissions, and also to Wendy Weil for getting this book landed in the first place. Much respect and gratitude to the Riverhead team, including Marilyn Ducksworth, Liz Perl, Dick Heffernan, Leslie Schwartz, Bonnie Soodek, Sadeqa Johnson, Marysarah Quinn, and Marc Haeringer. I am, as always, grateful to the ever-supportive Susan Petersen Kennedy, and my brilliant and cherished editor, Amy Hertz.

contents

what makes a man

putting down the gun
rebecca walker

THE IDEA FOR THIS BOOK was born one night after a grueling conversation with my then eleven-year-old son. He had come home from his progressive middle school unnaturally quiet and withdrawn, shrugging off my questions of concern with uncharacteristic irritability. Where was the sunny, chatty boy I dropped off that morning? What had befallen him in the perilous halls of middle school? I backed off but kept a close eye on him, watching for clues.

After a big bowl of his favorite pasta, he sat on a sofa in my study and read his science textbook as I wrote at my desk. We both enjoyed this simple yet profound togetherness, the two of us focused on our own projects yet palpably connected. As we worked under the soft glow of paper lanterns, with the heat on high and our little dog snoring at his feet, my son began to relax. I could feel a shift as he began to remember, deep in his body, that he was home, that he was safe, that he didn't have to brace to protect himself from the expectations of the outside world.

An hour or so passed like this before he announced that he had a question. He had morphed back into the child I knew, and was lying down with a colorful blanket over his legs, using one hand to scratch behind the dog's ears. "I've been thinking that maybe I should play sports at school."

"Sports?" I replied with surprise, swiveling around and leaning back in my chair. "Any sport in mind, or just sports in general?"

A nonchalant shrug. "Maybe softball, I like softball."

I cocked my head to one side. "What brought this on?"

"I don't know," he said. "Maybe girls will like me if I play sports."

Excuse me?

My boy is intuitive, smart, and creative beyond belief. At the time he loved animals, Japanese anime, the rap group Dead Prez, and everything having to do with snowboarding. He liked to help both of his grandmothers in the garden. He liked to read science fiction. He liked to climb into bed with me and lay his head on my chest. He liked to build vast and intricate cities with his Legos, and was beginning what I thought would be a lifelong love affair with chess.

Maybe girls would like him if he played sports?

Call me extreme, but I felt like my brilliant eleven-year-old daughter had come home and said, "Maybe boys will like me if I stop talking in class." Or my gregarious African-American son had told me, "Maybe the kids will like me if I act white."

I tried to stay calm as he illuminated the harsh realities of his sixth grade social scene. In a nutshell, the girls liked the jocks the best, and sometimes deigned to give the time of day to the other team, the computer nerds. Since he wasn't allowed to play violent computer games—we forbade them in our house—he was having trouble securing his place with the latter, hence his desire to assume the identity of the former. When I asked about making friends based on common interests rather than superficial categories, he got flustered. "You don't understand," he said huffily. "Boys talk about sports, like their matches and who scored what and stuff, or they talk about new versions of computer games or tricks they learned to get to higher levels." Tears welled up in his eyes. "I don't have anything to talk about."

He was right; until that moment I had had no idea, but suddenly the truth of being a sixth-grade boy in America crystallized before me. My beautiful boy and every other mother's beautiful boy had what essentially boiled down to two options: fight actually in sport, or fight virtually on the computer. Athlete, gladiator, secret agent, Tomb Raider. The truth of his existence, his many likes and dislikes, none of them having to do with winning or killing of any kind, had no social currency. My son could compete and score, perform and win, or be an outcast or worse, invisible, his unique gifts unnoticed and unharvested, the world around him that much more impoverished.

That night I went to sleep with several things on my mind: the conversation I planned to have with the head of my son's school about the need for a comprehensive, curricular interrogation of the contours of masculinity; the way girls find themselves drawn to more "traditional" displays of masculinity because they are more unsure than ever about how to experience their own femininity; and the many

hours and endless creativity I would have to devote to ensuring that my son's true self would not be entirely snuffed
out by the cultural imperative.

And then there was the final and most chilling thought
of all:

A bat, a "joy stick." What's next, a gun?

It occurred to me that my son was being primed for war,
was being prepared to pick up a gun. The first steps were
clear: Tell him that who he is authentically is not enough;
tell him that he will not be loved unless he abandons his
own desires and picks up a tool of competition; tell him that
to really be of value he must stand ready to compete, domi-
nate, and, if necessary, kill, if not actually then virtually, financially, athletically.

If one's life purpose is obscured by the pressure to conform to a generic type and other traces of self are ostracized
into shadow, then just how difficult is it to pick up a gun,
metaphoric or literal, as a means of self-definition, as a way
of securing what feels like personal power?

"Sissy, wuss, freak, fag, bitch, punk, pussy, homo, queer."

If I didn't get it that night, I got it after talking with all
of the men who were willing to write or share their stories
for this book: There is a war being waged on boys, and it
starts before they are even born. It is a war against vulnerability, creativity, individuality, and the mysterious unknown.
It is a war against tenderness, empathy, grief, fear, longing,
and feeling itself. It is a war against wholeness and psychological integration. In its determination to annihilate the
authentic self, it is a war against peace.

Over the last two years every man I know shared his own version of the same basic story: a few years filled with wonder and freedom cut short by the subtle and not so subtle demands of being a man. In what seemed like a moment but what was actually a slow buildup over time, an insidious and deceptively gradual occupation of psychic territory, young men were expected to change, to follow spoken and unspoken cues: don't feel, take control, be physically strong, find your identity in money and work, do not be afraid to kill, distrust everything that you cannot see. Don't cry.

This war against what is considered feminine that is wounding our sons and brothers, fathers and uncles, is familiar to women, but now we see that it is killing the other half of the planet, too. But instead of dying of heartache and botched abortions and breast cancer and sexual trauma and low self-esteem, this half is dying of radiation from modern weaponry, suicidal depression, and a soul-killing obsession with the material. This half is dying of prostate cancer and heart attacks and workaholism and an overwhelming sense of failure, of missing something exceedingly important that they cannot name.

What many men today are missing is themselves, the complex and unique experience of self that has been rerouted and suppressed in the name of work, war, and the arduous task of "being a man." This mandate to repress or obliterate anything and everything expansive or off the grid has defined generations, so much so that most men cannot even perceive the extent to which they have been robbed. Those men who have managed to survive more or less intact, the artists, healers, teachers, philosophers, and monks,

are the ones with the most harrowing tales. Having challenged the status quo, they enjoy more freedom, but carry
gruesome battle scars.

The good news is that things are changing as more and
more men begin to interrogate debilitating notions of masculinity, and to break away from conventional social scripts.
In an effort to support and bolster this developing consciousness, and also to have something to hand to my son
when he comes of age, I offer this collection of essays,
mostly by men but including a few by women, all trying to
deepen our collective humanity by daring to imagine what
the world would be like if men decided to put down the
gun, and women decided to let them.

These essays cover a lot of ground, moving from war to
peace and from fear to love, excavating each stop along the
way: sex, privilege, friendship, family, marriage, work. Con-
tributors unearth the themes of their lives as they struggle to
make sense of the disturbing legacy of masculinity they all
share, and as they struggle to move from two-dimensional
"men" to multidimensional beings.

In the process of reconfiguring what makes a man, some
of the writers here put down actual guns while others de-
militarize their souls by coming to understand what, emotionally, has been taken from them. In this vein, Douglas
Rushkoff writes brilliantly on the limitations of partnership
based on the pornographic model, and David Coates skill-
fully reveals a life numbed by privilege and materialism.
Malidoma Somé, in an excerpt from his amazing autobiography, writes about the profundity of the ancient bond between grandfather and grandson, and Choyin Rangdrol, an

African-American lama in the Tibetan Buddhist tradition, reveals the indestructible inner peace common to all beings that only needs recognition to be enjoyed.

There are also women in these pages, women struggling to disarm their own internalized masculinity. Tajamika Paxton does this in the loving arms of her newly disarmed father, and Martha Southgate, when confronted with her son's insistence on wearing a tutu and calling himself a girl, does this by seeing not one but two therapists to gain perspective on her "girlish boy." Caitríona Reed, herself once a man in body but never in mind, documents her personal transformation from "male impersonator" to postoperative transsexual woman, which prompts the question, if "boys will be boys," how come so many boys want to be girls?

While the women's movement has been successful in encouraging women to abandon restrictive stereotypes and to question and redefine the very foundation of their identities, men have yet to embark upon a similar mass reeducation, opting instead to—surprise!—suffer in stoic silence. While many gifted and committed thinkers have been working hard on this project of men's liberation for decades, there is still a long way to go before men are able to safely abandon self-sacrifice as a way of life. I hope this book will be a valuable contribution toward this end, and that the fact that I am a woman putting it forth will not keep away the many men who will undoubtedly find themselves in its pages.

I also hope that women readers will reflect deeply on their part in maintaining the male charade. If we want men to be different we must eroticize that difference, and stop saying we want a man who can talk about his feelings, only to marry the strong, silent type who "just so happens" to be a good provider. As mothers we can't freak out and run for the karate school brochures when our sons tell us they want dance lessons, and we can't turn a blind eye to our boys' struggle to hold on to themselves in the face of a million messages telling them to change. Women must look at how we too have abandoned our own tenderness and intuitive knowing, and come to rely more and more upon the empirical and the competitive when navigating the world around us, succeeding in the patriarchal paradigm but failing overall.

Whether we hold tightly to the fantasy of a knight in shining armor swooping down to save, protect, and provide for us, or we believe that by thinking rationally and "bringing home the bacon" we will secure the ultimate happiness for ourselves and our families, we are still looking outside ourselves for the answers. To know peace and have mature relationships in which we no longer look for completion or salvation in the other, men and women alike must face their existential fears and find their true purpose, separate from any societally sanctioned ideas about masculine and feminine.

Because we live in a culture dominated by violence and fear, this level of personal disarmament can seem counterintuitive. We all believe that we need a gun of some kind, even though the guns are killing us. As Jarvis Jay Masters, an inmate on death row, so beautifully illustrates in his piece, the truth is that we can either face our fears of death, abandonment, and ridicule and make a choice to stand calm and whole through the onslaught, or we can pick up our actual and emotional guns and deplete ourselves trying to win an unwinnable war.

Perhaps there is a time and place for both, but for now, if only for the next few hours, I invite you to imagine that there is not, that there is only this choice: to give up the battle, to put down the gun, and finally, finally, to rest.

the gift
michael datcher

I ONCE RECEIVED a pet rock as a gift. It wasn't the kind of pet rock that came in a designer box with a name-tag. It was low end. Literally, a chip off an old block with alley origins.

I've also received the gift of life. When I was an unwanted infant, my adoptive mother handed me a chance at health and love. A lifeline from a child services system waiting to dismantle my potential.

I'm an authority on presents. As my May 17, 1997, wedding approached, I tried to think of the perfect gift for my soon-to-be-wife, Jenoyne Adams. I wanted it to be both supremely original and utilitarian. A hot gift for a supernova sister.

Jenoyne had been working on her novel-in-progress *Resurrecting Mingus* for years. Novels are famously easy to start and infamously difficult to finish—especially when working a full-time job. Jenoyne had been working in high-stress corporate America since she was a high school intern. The time commitment coupled with volatile office politics was not conducive to finishing demanding outside projects. A week before our wedding, I told Jenoyne that I had picked out her gift.

"I'm going to financially support you for a year, so you can stay at home and finish your novel." She was ecstatic.

In 1997, I was three years out of graduate school and living in LA. After leaving my job as a reporter at the *Los Angeles Sentinel*, I had been working for myself as an unpaid poet and a poorly paid freelance journalist writing about politics and culture for various newspapers and magazines. Due to the unstable nature of freelancing, I had always kept my overhead low. Good used cars. Stylish used clothes. Sweaters in lieu of a high-ass gas bill. Top Ramen. Even with my starving artist penny-pinching, I was still struggling to make ends meet. Taking on a wife necessitated confronting one of my biggest fears: that I wouldn't be able to take care of a wife.

When I was considering proposing to Jenoyne, I called my mother, Gladys, to get her opinion.

"Well, I'd love to have her as a daughter-in-law, but I'll tell you, if I was her, I wouldn't have you. You quit a good job at the newspaper. Talking about you freelancing. I don't know why you don't use your master's degree. Seem like you worked hard enough to get it. I wouldn't have you because you aren't in a position to take care of a wife. And I don't care how progressive or modern or whatever you call it y'all supposed to be, but a man's supposed to be able to take care of his wife. It just doesn't seem like you're able to do that."

Not the conversation I was expecting to hear, and not the one I wanted to hear. I was sweating the economics of marriage enough already. Moms had tapped into the truth that I already knew. The financial health of a family was ultimately a reflection on the man. If the family couldn't meet their financial obligations, it looked like the man wasn't handling his business.

A LACK OF MONEY had kept me single up to that point. I had always heard that most divorce proceedings could be traced back to financial woes—and I had the portfolio of a poet. Moms had it wrong. I didn't want to struggle all my life. I was just aware that I was going into business for myself in an extremely competitive profession. I knew I was going to have to pay my dues if I was going to be my own boss. My mother, like most black parents, raised me to get a job at a good business and keep that good job by being a good employee. My white colleagues' parents raised them to start a business and be good bosses.

When I met Jenoyne I was in the early stages of my boss-training program. I explained my Master Plan to literary and economic success. We spoke of dues and career building sacrifices. Although Jenoyne was down with the program, I couldn't shake Moms's fear-inducing opinion— because she had indoctrinated me just enough so that I believed it too. I was barely able to support myself as a single man. As a soon-to-be-married man, I was promising my wife a gift that I wasn't confident I could deliver.

After telling Jenoyne about her gift, I immediately, and very aggressively, began to solicit more freelance assignments. As things stood, I was already working seven days a week to complete the flow of assignments sliding across my desk. I was making a dollar a word, which is typically the max for experienced freelancers, writing for magazines like *VIBE* and *Emerge*. However, some publications paid as little as 30 cents a word. I figured I would somehow double my assignment load by working harder and being fiercely disciplined. By making the absolute most of each of the seven days of the week.

Two months into our marriage my plan was in full swing. I had picked up several more clients and embraced my military-like work schedule, which began every weekday morning at 4:45 a.m. I was pumping out two or three articles a week. However, the problem with deadline-oriented jobs is that you're always working under tremendous pressure. Day in. Day out. The increased workload also ratcheted up my stress levels. I was on edge—and my cool was slipping. Within three months, it became clear that this gift was going to be extremely difficult to sustain.

What I lost in cool, I gained in iconic manhood points. I loved watching Jenoyne write in bed in the afternoon. I loved watching her get an opportunity to pursue her own literary dreams in an unobstructed way. I felt like a Real Man even though I couldn't fully buy into the Real Man mythology. I loved the feeling that came with "taking care of my woman."

Much has been written about the sorry state of black male/female relationships. The pointing finger usually lingers longest on the black man. The word is we want to hit all the ass. We can't stay out of jail. Can't keep a job. Won't commit to a sister but want a wife with lips, hips and personality like a sister—as long as she ain't a sister. Basically, poor marriage material for black women.

Certainly, there are black men who fall under this rubric. I know a few. At the same time, I know many black men who long for the Picket Fence Dream. A wife, nice crib, smart kids, a cool ride. Some *Cosby Show* type shit. They yearn for the Cosby lifestyle because it's so far from their own childhood experience. Like me, they want to fill the holes in the Picket Fence Dream handed down from their single mothers.

Historically, schools that service children of African American single mothers have paltry resources, and generally do a poor job of preparing them for a competitive marketplace. Forty percent of young black men who survive into their twenties are in jail, in prison, or on probation. The remaining struggle in a national workplace where usually white male bosses are searching for comfort level with prospective employees—and black men typically make white men uncomfortable.

As a result of the aforementioned realities, desiring fences is insufficient for obtaining them. Socioeconomic factors loom larger than even the biggest black dick. Most niggas are broke. Shorter than a rainbow with only one color. Even when they want to push for that dream and get married, they're afraid that they won't be able to make enough money to take care of a family. A situation that can be devastating to any male's sense of manhood, and especially devastating to males as disenfranchised as black men. So in place of commitment, they play the field. Measure their manhood by booty call batting average. The home run fence replaces the picket one.

. . .

AFTER THE initial months of Jenoyne writing at home, I felt myself growing increasingly critical. The deadline pressure that had always inspired my best work was starting to break me down. Over the years, I had built a reputation with my clients as a quick-turnaround artist. If a magazine had a crisis and needed a high quality article produced in a few days, they would call me. The short deadline meant an additional boost in my fee. This was money that I didn't feel like I could turn down, so on numerous occasions, I found myself accepting assignments with completely ridiculous parameters. A four-thousand-word article assigned on Friday afternoon and due Monday morning. A two-thousand-word piece assigned Wednesday, due Friday. I never once said no to an assignment.

To further complicate matters, Jenoyne had been raised by her nuts and bolts construction foreman father Virgil Adams. He was a great provider who made extraordinary sacrifices to raise his daughter as a single dad. Just before I was about to propose to Jenoyne, I spoke with Mr. Adams, seeking his blessing on my wedding plans. In that conversation, I gave him my word that I would take care of his daughter with the same type of diligence that he had shown.

My own diligence raised my brow whenever I saw Jenoyne approaching her writing with anything less than intensity. Jenoyne had never been her own boss, working out of her own home. It's quite a transition to leave a lifestyle where someone else tells you when to come to work, what to do at work, how long to stay at work, when to leave work.

Jenoyne was having a hard time disciplining herself. When I would see her sleeping in until 10:30 a.m. or watching TV in the middle of the day or having multiple telephone conversations, I would get hella aggravated. I didn't want to lord my gift over her, so I kept quiet and stayed at my own work. At the time, in the middle of my hectic freelance schedule, I was also trying to finish my book *Raising Fences*.

I was hoping Jenoyne would get a handle on her discipline and start cracking down. At the six-month point, the only crack was in my mental health. I was so stressed that I would work all day, then toss and turn in my sleep thinking about the work I didn't get done.

My critical commentary began to make its way from my subconscious to Jenoyne's nearest earlobe. At first, the criticism was shrouded in questions like, "How's the writing going?" and "What time do you plan to get out of bed today?" However, the questions quickly became a Cochranesque cross-examination. "You said you were going to get up at 10:00 a.m., and now it's 11:00 a.m.—again. How do you explain that?"

I was starting to feel disrespected. Feeling like my gift of sacrifice was not being appreciated. Instead, it was being shat upon. I was working like a runaway slave trying to buy his freedom and Jenoyne was living like the plantation mistress. As a result, I became the overseer. I began to monitor her writing hours, and let her know when she was falling short. I was reincarnated as the supervisor from hell. I had begun to resent Jenoyne's Club Antebellum lifestyle and Jenoyne could feel it. She began to resent my resentment.

"Michael, I place enough pressure on myself. I don't need you adding any more pressure."

"Well, if you'd just get your ass out of bed and get to work, there wouldn't be a problem."

My gift had flipped. I began with such noble intentions but that no longer seemed to matter. Jenoyne and I were getting on each other's nerves. The smallest thing would set each of us off. The cap left off the toothpaste would lead immediately to shouting. The toilet seat left in the "up" position would surely engender tears before nightfall. Our household life was insane when it all should have been so romantic. Two writers, married, working out of their home. On paper, an ideal scenario. In reality, a cold war that was moving toward all-out war with each passing day. I began to question the wisdom of my decision. Maybe I had bit off more responsibility than I could chew. If so, I didn't feel I had any recourse. Since I was a child, my mother had drilled in me that ultimately all a person had was their word. Vows were not entered into lightly. I had to complete the requirements of my gift because I said I would.

I needed help. I felt completely unqualified to rectify the situation. One day, I went to see my friend Kamau Daood, the founder and artistic director of World Stage, a jazz and literary center. He had been married to Baadia for over twenty years. I'd never seen them arguing over a toilet seat.

I picked up Kamau and we drove to a hill overlooking Dockweiler beach. We parked just as the sun was making its descent into the Pacific. I didn't even have to tell Kamau what was going on. He could see it in my face. The first thing he said was, "Marriage is about making the two into one. And making two into one is more than a notion."

Kamau encouraged me to keep working hard and be patient. He revealed some of the struggles that he and Baadia had encountered in their relationship. I was touched by his openness and humility.

Once a week, I would pick up Kamau, or he would pick me up, and we'd sit in the car and talk. Sometimes he would give me very practical advice like, "Just keep the damn toilet seat down, brother." At other times, he would listen as I rambled on about how Jenoyne didn't know a good thing when she had it. Ultimately, he urged me to hold on until my year-long gift was completed.

"See how things look then, Michael."

I'm sure these car seat conversations saved my marriage.

THERE SHOULD BE a college major called "Marriage." A single class wouldn't do the trick. People seek training for such a wide array of less important ventures. Business. Bungee jumping. Computer programming. But people are loath to seek input in their marriages. Especially men—who struggle to ask for driving directions when they're lost. It's as if asking for marital help is tantamount to not being able to handle our marriages. Well, six months of marriage will let you know quite clearly that most of us can't handle our marriages. We'd rather front the role, stay lost and get divorced.

I took Kamau's advice and started counting the remaining days of the 365. Jenoyne and I still argued, but I was able to control myself a little more effectively. I knew that once she finished her book, she could help out more financially and I wouldn't have to work so hard. I soldiered on.

Day 365 finally came—and Jenoyne wasn't finished. She took such a long time to figure out how to get work accomplished early in the year, that she wasn't able to finish the project within the year. I was so disappointed and angry that I could barely stand it. I immediately went to see Kamau.

"You kept your word so you could pull your hole card and make her get a job. But is that what you really wanna do? How many times have you been late with an assignment? Michael, marriage is not about doing the minimum, marriage is about doing whatever is going to make the marriage work. And let me tell you, often that means doing the maximum."

I hated Kamau's good advice, but I couldn't reject it. It took Jenoyne 18 months to finish *Resurrecting Mingus*. Those last six months, she really hit it a groove and worked hard. That's all I really desired. I wanted her to show respect for my gift by aggressively putting her ample literary gifts in action. Furthermore, a magical thing happened during months 12 though 18. I gave the maximum and my gift became noble once again.

In February 2001, Simon & Schuster published *Resurrecting Mingus*. In March 2001, Riverhead published *Raising Fences*. Both books were hailed by critics, which helped them land on best-seller lists around the country. I still leave the toilet seat up sometimes and Jenoyne couldn't keep the

michael datcher

cap on the toothpaste if it was attached with a solid gold chain. Yet, our relationship is much different today.

Many men embrace the idea of the man as household leader. Kamau helped me to understand that if I wanted to lead, I should lead in the area of giving. Lead in listening. Lead in prayer. Lead in saying "I'm sorry." Lead in forgiveness. Leading in seeking marital advice. Lead in giving the maximum.

I don't always reach my leadership goals in our marriage, but I work extremely hard at trying. So hard that my example has inspired Jenoyne to work harder herself. Our mutual diligence has us unearthing elements of each other with the careful caution of world-class archeologists. We have discovered the ancient formula for love. The two have become one.

my girlish boy
martha southgate

WHEN MY SON Nate was two, his favorite item of clothing was a tattered blue baby blanket that he wore on his head every evening while watching TV, playing, having dinner. As soon as we got home, he asked, always in an excited, intent voice, "Where's my blue hair?" And we'd dig it up and put it on and he'd be happy, wearing his long, flowing, simulated hair.

The other thing he loved to do was wear tutus—pink, purple, didn't matter. It got to the point where other kids would save them for him in the dress-up corner—"Don't wear that—that's Nate's." He loved the crisp, sticking-out feel of them. He pulled them on over his little boy jeans, below his little round boy belly and wore them all day while he built with blocks and played with clay and had his lunch. We have quite a few day care pictures of him sparkling, garlanded pink and purple.

He said he was a girl, always, with great intensity, as though any sort of argument was too silly to even be entertained. Wasn't it obvious? That's who he was. We, foolish adults that we were, just couldn't see it.

It's odd to have a son who insists he's a girl. There aren't many cultural exemplars of such a story. There's the French film *Ma Vie en Rose*, where one and all abuse a seven-year-old boy who believes he's a girl. When my husband, Jeff, and I rented that, we sat together on the sofa, Nate snoring in his bedroom—us not talking, tight with nervousness. Was this sad story Nate's future?

Then there was an essay on Salon.com a couple of years ago by a woman whose son was what she termed a "jane-girl." That writer put a more positive spin on the situation, but she too lamented the difficulty of knowing how to behave in the face of her son's behavior. That was it. There wasn't much for us to measure against, or to reassure us.

We're open-minded parents—interracially married, gender-neutral nursery, as many dolls as blocks for our son when he was born and later for our daughter. But when Nate kept insisting with furious vigor that he actually was a girl, we really didn't know what to make of it. Did other kids do this? Was it normal for him to so vigorously assert that he was what his body so clearly denied? As near as we could tell, there was nothing in the way we treated him that would predispose him to such vehemence.

And I'd be lying if I said that I walked beside him in perfect ease the time he picked out the frilliest slip possible and insisted on wearing it home for the walk from day care. Even in the streets of New York, this garnered a few second looks. I wasn't thinking: Oh no, is he gay? But I was thinking that thing that every parent thinks once in a while: Good heavens, is he normal? We weren't worried, exactly— but we were uncomfortable enough that we felt we needed to talk to someone about our confusion. So we visited a child psychologist.

The first psychologist we saw had a tweedy, slightly run-down office and a tweedy, slightly run-down manner. We told her our story and she said, firmly, "You should bring him in. It sounds like Gender Identity Disorder. I could work with him." My husband and I left the office panic-stricken. I got on the Internet as soon as I got home. And fell down a rabbit hole of debate.

The DSM defines Gender Identity Disorder this way:

A. In children, the disturbance is manifested by four (or more) of the following:

1. Repeatedly stated desire to be, or insistence that he or she is, the other sex

2. In boys, preference for cross-dressing or simulating female attire; in girls, insistence on wearing only stereotypical masculine clothing

3. Strong and persistent preferences for cross-sex roles in make-believe play or persistent fantasies of being the other sex

4. Intense desire to participate in the stereotypical games and pastimes of the other sex

5. Strong preferences for playmates of the other sex

B. In children, the disturbance is manifested by any of the following:

In boys, assertion that his penis or testes are disgusting or will disappear or assertion that it would be better not to have a penis, or aversion toward rough-and-tumble play and rejection of male stereotypical toys, games and activities.

In girls, rejection of urinating in a sitting position, assertion that she has or will grow a penis, or assertion that she does not want to grow breasts or menstruate, or marked aversion toward normative feminine clothing.

C. The disturbance is not concurrent with a physical intersex condition.

D. The disturbance causes clinically significant distress or impairment in social, occupational, or other important areas of functioning.

My heart pounded as I read this list—Nate fit most of the criteria. There it was in cold, psychiatric black and white. But as I got my breath back, and reread them, I asked myself the question: Do these criteria make any sense? I am not the only person who has wondered about this—there is a furious debate within the psychiatric community over this issue. There's this from the GIDreform.org website: "[Under these criteria] high-functioning children may be presumed to meet criteria A and B on the basis of cultural nonconformity alone." Or this, from the National Association for Research and Therapy of Homosexuality (NARTH, a group that be-lieves in therapy to shift sexual orientation): "Gender identity problems, including cross-dressing, exclusive cross-gender play, and a lack of same-sex friends should be treated as a symp-tom that something may be very wrong."

Well. This was my kid they were talking about here. He had tons of friends, was intense but happy, and led a fine three-year-old life. What were we supposed to think? Jeff and I stared at each other nervously across the debate. Nate clutched his Barbie. We weren't sure what to do—but we both had a gut feeling that Nate didn't have a disorder. Just a firm belief.

We sought out another therapist. His office was in the West Village. It was beautifully decorated and peaceful. He had a perfect haircut and a perfect manner. I still remember the dried flower arrangement on the wall. And I remember the way he listened to our concerns about what Nate's be-havior might mean for his life and said, "Listen, gender is a fluid concept. If Nate still feels this way when he's eight, maybe I should see him because he'll have some issues to deal with fitting in. But he's only three. I know it's uncom-fortable but I really wouldn't worry at this point." And so, somehow, our minds were eased. Another family might have felt that they couldn't live with a boy like Nate, but some-how we knew that he was OK—just a little different. Not suffering, not anguished, not sick. In the end, we decided that it was the criteria that were flawed, bound by an old, narrow, outmoded vision of masculinity.

.   .   .

WE DIDN'T PUT Nate into treatment and he no longer insists he's a girl. He is eight years old now, a beautiful boy, skin the color of the caramel in a Milky Way, eyes the color of the bar outside. We aren't sure where the girl thing came from, or why he finally let go of his insistence that he actually *was* a girl. Nor are we sure where he got his gentleness of manner, his affection for sparkly stuff, his unwillingness to hew too strictly to "what a boy does." We only know that it's him. He's not like anyone else.

I really don't know what made him change his mind about being a girl, there wasn't one day, one moment of revelation when he stopped. It just trailed off, spurred, perhaps, by the birth of his sister when he was almost four. And in some ways, he hasn't changed. Not long ago, when I went to get my nails done (and I'm not one for a lot of frills—I'm lucky if I make it to the nail shop six times a year, and they always fuss at me and say I should wax my legs), he pleaded with me, "Bring home some fake nails for me, Mommy. Please?" I didn't—not that I would have brought them home for my daughter either. They're tacky and expensive. But the challenge continues. He wants capri pants—we say no. He wants ballet class—we say yes. Most of his friends are girls; he seems baffled by boys' territoriality and aggressiveness, the way they're always building things. When we were on vacation in a community with a lot of other children, I asked him if he'd like to see a fort in the woods that some of the other boys had built. He got a vague look in his brown eyes. "Maybe." But it wasn't long before he was off to play stuffies (that's stuffed animals) with his friend Anna.

What do you do when your son isn't who you expected

martha southgate

him to be? For me, it's been an experience in letting go. Letting go of my notions about what makes a boy, what makes a girl: notions I wasn't even entirely aware I had until I was confronted by my son in full dress-up drag. I would like to say that I was impervious to the stares of people on the street as I walked with my sweet three-year-old son holding tightly to his tawny-skinned, flowing-haired Barbie. But that wouldn't be true. I don't think—I hope—that I never did anything to make him uncomfortable being who he is. But I'm a product of this culture too. So I had to learn to let go of prejudices I didn't even know I had.

I have been forced to see how narrow a path boys, and by extension, men, are allowed to tread in terms of "gender correct" behavior. People just don't look at tomboys as oddly as they do at boys who are not aggressive, who don't like sports, who play with girls. Even now, casual acquaintances inquire about Little League or soccer and I counter with flute lessons, ice-skating and ballet—Nate's three developing passions. "Oh," say people. Maybe they just don't see a point of connection—but I always wonder what they're thinking. I am briefly grateful that we live in New York City, where Nate is less likely to be openly abused for his interests—but even here, he goes against the grain. And there's always that tiny rub as he does.

So which way is Nate's grain? Who is he?

He's a boy who has never liked to talk much—in this, he's like most boys. Ask him a question about anything emotional and you'll be greeted with an emphatic "Don't talk about that! That embarrasses me." He's a boy who loves his younger sister—in first grade, when he wrote a memoir of his life to that point, he dedicated it to her. To see them play together when it's going well—which is a heartening amount of the time—is a beautiful thing, their curly heads bent over a toy, their voices softly interweaving. He's a boy who likes glitter—when we're walking through the Fulton Mall after school, he sometimes asks to go into the wig shop so he can study the falls and weaves and bright neon swatches of hair. He's a boy who loves books—he saved up for weeks and did extra jobs to earn money for his $40 copy of *The Wildlife of Star Wars*. He's a boy with a good imagination—he can spend an hour talking to himself, walking in a circle, telling a long narrative that only he comprehends. And he's a boy who feels things, even if he won't talk about them. On the street, he's all eyes and ears, watchful and intent on the people around us, taking it all in, giving very little of it back.

He's that way about the girl thing too. He's never said anything about it and both Jeff and I have refrained from direct questions about those early years. Neither of us has ever said to him, "Remember when you thought you were a girl? Why'd you want to be?" Maybe someday I'll ask, but it's unlikely I'll get a straight answer. He's not much of a one for those.

Of course, we're not sure he'll be straight at all. That is the deep fear underlying the DSM definition, motivating groups like NARTH—what if your kid is gay? When Nate was two and a half and obsessed with the irredeemably campy hit song "Barbie Girl," Jeff joked that we'd be the only parents at PFLAG meetings with a kindergarten-age child. While that didn't happen, I won't be shocked if he grows up to be gay, though I should add that I believe that labeling him at this age—straight, gay, whatever—is pointless. To my mind, he needs to know gay people, to know he might be gay as easily as he might be straight, and that I'll love him no matter what, but he doesn't need to be fit into a box. He's a child.

Nate's girly side has forced me to examine my own discomfort with extreme behavior. It'll be easy for me to take if he grows up, gets a nice lawyer partner and lives in Montclair. It'll be harder for me if he grows up and decides to be a drag queen. Is that because of the homosexual aspect of it or because of how far outside the norm he'd be if he made that choice? I'm not sure. But I can't say that it would just roll off my back. Certain choices he might make, I'll have to come around to. But that's not just true of his sexual orientation, or his sister's for that matter—it's true of how he's going to live his life, how all children grow up and live their lives. That's part of the deal when you have a child and love him with all your heart. He might break it. He might do things you wouldn't have him do. And loving him in the face of that can take you beyond your boundaries, can make you a better, more generous person than you'd ever imagined.

Before I had children, I knew, theoretically, that they asked a lot of you. But I now see that it is so rarely what you expect to be asked. Much of being a parent, I now see, is relinquishing control. And that's not easy to do. My wild beautiful girlish boy has shown me how hard it can be. As

martha southgate

he's made me look at what I believe about what's normal, what makes a person who they are, I find myself asking: What do parents have to do with it? In many ways, less than we like to think. As I look at pictures of my son in his tutu, I sometimes wonder if we have any influence at all.

this is my story
david coates

AS A CHILD I had most things valued by the outside world and yet paradoxically, I felt trapped. I was ridden with guilt and self-loathing. I spent most of my life believing that through suffering and self-deprecation I would eventually feel deserving of my privilege and prove my manhood. Throughout my life, I went to every extreme to prove I was not what I now struggle to become: myself. This is my story.

AT FIRST I did not know that I was fortunate. As a child my life was simply the way it was, I knew no other. Our house was larger than most, with a swimming pool and a trampoline, both often crowded with neighborhood boys. My daddy was a lawyer, my mom a college professor. I was no more aware of being privileged than I was of the fact that everyone around me had Southern accents. I grew up in the deadening heat and humidity of Baton Rouge, Louisiana, but I never thought of it as uncomfortable. I took my reality for granted. Like the air I breathed, I was unaware of its oppressive aspect.

As I was growing up, Mom was always busy: grading papers, taking care of me and my brother, cleaning the house, cooking, or washing clothes. She packed my lunch and was very active at my small school as a homeroom mother and PTA member. My teachers would often comment on how lucky I was to have a mother who was so interested and involved with her children. Dad was a serious guy whose wrath I feared, although it rarely came. He was a Republican, and cared most about homework and report cards.

My father was a lawyer, and all agreed this was one of the best professions for dads to have. To be white seemed better, and we were all thankful we were not born sissy girls. One of my most vivid memories is of my father telling my mother to "simmer down, honey," when she got emotional or excited. My older brother, Sam, was my hero. Friends always surrounded Sam. In contrast, being more introverted by nature, I often felt like something was wrong with me.

Any sign of sensitivity or weakness would get me teased mercilessly by the older neighborhood boys. We called one another wimp, wuss, pussy, gay, faggot, punk, dumbass, buttplug, coward, and so on. Arbitrarily it was decided I needed toughening up, "doin' you a favor" they would say, as they pounded me in the arms and stomach. Weakness of any kind was not tolerated. The only thing worse than the beatings, however, was being ignored or excluded from the group.

My friend Pete lived next door. Whenever I would confide in him about something that was bothering me, it would often go like this:

DAVID: "Pete, my favorite BB gun broke."
PETE: "What do you have to be sad about, you're rich, your parents will buy you a new one, what's your fucking problem, you big baby."

Pete had it rough, a tiny house, an alcoholic father, often ignored by his mother, yeah, come to think of it, what did I have to be sad about compared to that? My brother would echo this sentiment. He was sure we had the best family in the world and tolerated no dissent. "What do you have to complain about," he would say in a nasty tone. If I persisted inevitably I heard the likes of, "What more do you want, you need Mom to wipe your butt for you too?" Much of the time Sam was a kind older brother, but these are the moments I remember. The message was clear, keep your problems to yourself.

I made good grades, had friends, great parents, was tall and good at sports, and yet I had this gnawing feeling in my stomach, this deep-seated, ineffable fear.

"Oh, we're fine, the kids are fine, I'm fine." Everyone seemed to be doing fine and all smiles. Me, I didn't feel fine. I felt tense and anxious.

I was chewing my nails bloody by age four. Things felt off to me but I couldn't understand why. I was sad more often than not. I had trouble falling asleep at night. Much of my time was spent engrossed in a ritual of counting the syllables of sentences on my fingers with a desperate hope that the total would be some denomination of five. "What about this sentence," for example, has six syllables, close to five but not quite. Hoping each time for a combination of five, I would do this for hours with voices on the television or just with thoughts in my head. I wanted something to add up, I wanted some order, some relief from the anxiety and shame I felt inside. I would look for things to count anywhere: tiles, stars, people, cars, streets, anything. I would solve math problems in my head. I would multiply 2×2×2 into the millions. I would pour water on a slope and follow the various paths that would diverge from the stream completely engrossed in wonder. What do I have to complain about, what is wrong with me, I have everything, 2, 4, 8, 16, 32, 64, 128, 256, 512, 1024, 2048, 4096 . . . 65, 536. . . . 1,048,576, and so on.

What else in the world could I possibly want? By what right did I have to feel withdrawn and empty? I must be "the most ungrateful, spoiled, lazy, unappreciative little whiny bastard" in the world because I possessed much of what the world had to offer, yet felt dissatisfied. I had confirmation from my brother and others that this was the case. I developed an abundance of guilt for my undeserved fortune. Although I enjoyed my possessions, there was always a lingering sense that I was not entitled to them. To compound the situation, my father vehemently maintained that anything outside of bare necessity was an indulgence. I would receive most of what I desired, but his judgment was always present. If something was not practical, connected to education, or necessary, it was an indulgence. This only compounded my feeling that stoicism and self-denial were what defined masculinity.

. . .

HAVING REALIZED that something must be wrong with me, I felt alone in my world and misunderstood. My feelings and emotions seemed to be the source of my shameful woe, therefore they must be overcome. I decided to check out. I developed a persona that was emotionally distant and painlessly rational and pragmatic, using my father as a model. In this world, money mattered. When separated from the heart, what else was there of value? Money became a wondrous solution, my dependable friend. I would count my money incessantly. Purchasing things created a sense of power within me, and created envy in others. I would stand in a tiny room and throw a stack of dollar bills up in the air, elated as they fell over and around me. Money made me feel alive, assured, and safe. I told myself that money was purposeful and what mattered; emotional stuff was just silliness.

Emotions became the enemy of my developing sense of identity and manhood. Inside I felt weak, afraid, and insecure and would do anything to avoid these feelings. I assured myself that I felt none of these unacceptable things by projecting them onto someone else. "Josh is weak, scared, not me..." If someone else was emotional, irrational, or gentle, then it was safely away from me. During this period, I was never completely comfortable. I was competitive, sarcastic, and confrontational. My two best friends in high school were the most obnoxious guys I had ever met. We drank heavily, wrecked cars, stole, destroyed, cursed, and verbally abused everyone including one another. We went out of our way to prove to the world that we were tough and did not care about anything or anyone. Sensitivity was ridiculed in any of its manifestations.

As my persona developed this sharp defensive quality, my body became tense in an attempt to somatically suppress my emotional being. I would suddenly become aware of a severe need to eat as if it had come by surprise. Once aware, I would ignore the hunger pains for hours. Eating was more of a burden than an enjoyment, just another thing I needed to do. I used to fantasize about a pill one could take in the morning that would provide all the daily necessary nutritional needs so I would not have to bother with eating. Eating was an indulgence, too. The severe hunger pains I felt also served to alleviate other tension I held in my body. Not needing to eat assured me I was tough, for to deny a basic need or desire was to be a man. I would suddenly realize I needed badly to urinate when a few minutes before I was completely unaware of my painfully clenched bladder. I often underdressed in cold weather. This state of withholding became the norm for my daily existence.

To suffer was to be a real man. Moreover, there was so much suffering in the world I felt I needed to suffer after so many years of having things so easy. Joy and meaning were passed over in favor of suffering.

MY FRESHMAN YEAR of college in a philosophy course I was exposed to the idea that reality is an individual and cultural construct. I learned there were other ways to experience the world than my own. It was inspiring but since it was not practical, it was my first and last philosophy course.

Holding no visible externally measurable benefit, it was ultimately useless, just another indulgence.

Accounting was dry, impersonal, unsatisfying, dull, stressful, and confusing. Nevertheless, I became an accounting major for its practicality. I believed it to be a good fit for me. The struggle I had been denied to earn my position of privilege and justify my indulgences was found in accounting. No one could doubt my masculinity when I was struggling through something I so despised. This also assured me I was in no way "weak," needy, or emotional, for accounting was far removed from any such nonsense. I was out to prove that I was so indifferent emotionally that I did not even need to be happy, for even that was weakness.

Four years and thirty semester hours of lifeless accounting later, I graduated with an accounting degree and went to work as an accountant for a small high-tech company. That misery only validated my stone persona and encouraged me to soldier on. Payroll taught me that the sales guys were making the money, so I shifted over to an account manager position. My fourth month was a blockbuster, and I received a commission check for $8,000 after taxes and thought I had finally arrived. I took my girlfriend out for a nice meal and purchased some furniture. I sat in my converted loft on my new couch with my feet propped up on my new coffee table, yet there was no food in the house. My stomach ached, yet I did not go to the grocery store. I was shocked and perplexed by my state. I had finally made my own money, I was supporting myself, and I was on my own proving myself in the real world, yet the emptiness remained. And still, I continued. After all, what else was there?

Lured by the technology boom of the dot-com era, I enrolled in a master's program in telecommunications. I hated these classes even more than accounting so I stayed. Graduates of this program were "making bank" and I'd be damned if I couldn't too. I had actually found something more meaningless than accounting! During my final semester I accepted a position with Arthur Andersen (in-house auditor for Enron) as a traveling consultant. My nightmares were horrific; in them I was often chased by some large unknown figure. My back ached and my shoulders were tense. Finally, I reached my breaking point and I snapped. I entered therapy. I had moments of clarity. I withdrew my acceptance of the position. Ironically, Arthur Andersen folded a few years after I did.

What the hell was I doing? It felt like a joke that everyone was in on but no one spoke about. The emperor had no clothes. It was all a façade. I've had money my entire life. I knew it was not the answer, yet I was looking toward money to justify my existence as a man anyway. Therapy provided a space for me to explore these lifelong assumptions in a safe, supportive environment. Why was I following career paths I absolutely detested? Whose life was I living, and for the sake of what? I moved to San Francisco and entered a master's program in psychology. It was what I wanted. There I began the process of rediscovering who I am.

My experience continues to be a rediscovery of my being. I realized that who I thought myself to be was only a series of stories that I had wrongly assumed to be my identity. In putting myself in a supportive environment with fellow travelers and seekers, the ground has been prepared for the reemergence of my emotional being. It is a complete reversal from my childhood. I am no longer creating a persona to cover the shame I feel about being myself. I am now excavating and embracing this self. My struggle now is between the old stories of fear and shame and those newly emerging.

My mind is still constantly working to apply old stories and beliefs to my present experience. When I entered my men's group for the first time, I experienced the men to be emotionally closed and competitive. This was my only experience with men, and therefore the only lens I had through which to view the group. When I was overwhelmed with emotions and tears ran down my face a few weeks later, I expected these men, who were still virtual strangers, to be judgmental and mocking. In my imagination they were all thinking with disgust, "What a crybaby," for this was what I was thinking about myself after years of internalizing the messages I received. To my surprise, as I looked around I saw many others damp-eyed and looking at me with understanding and empathy. I felt loved, supported, and honored by this group of men who are also struggling for their right to be seen and understood in this unforgiving culture. As I risk revealing more of my vulnerability, the intense fear of judgment from others remains but I am experiencing unexpected reactions. Instead of being shamed, I am supported. Instead of shaming and judging others, a shift is occurring and I find my heart is more open and loving.

Like a starving man seeking nourishment in the desert, I was unable to sustain myself in the current cultural myth. Yet I am far from free of its influence. At times, my internal story that I am unable to succeed in the "traditional" system because I am weak and defective rears its ugly head. At times I fear I may not make enough money to support myself as a therapist. However, with each passing day of increased awareness and new experiences, these stories lose some of their powerful grip. I now have a faith in some larger presence beyond my control that contains an intelligence, purpose, and meaning of its own.

I am convinced that the key to finding my way in such a situation lies in learning to allow opposite sides of my nature to coexist side by side, without letting one negate the other. As a boy, I was taught that there is only room for one. You are weak and sensitive, or you are strong and tough. Of course we are both of these things, but given the choice of only one means having to suppress the other. This causes immense suffering. Because my entire persona was built around the denial of my sensitivity, I always had to prove I was tough, that I cared about nothing. I hated all things that were weak and sensitive because they rubbed salt in the wounds of my own being. It was always personal. I became afraid to care about others, the world, anything, for this very concern may have been equated with weakness and sensitivity and that would be intolerable. I betrayed the very parts of myself that made me the most human because I was not allowed to simply be who I was. This is what comes from the choice of one. This mandate is in our culture, religions, traditions, media, and even our language. It is in the air we breathe. Like so many, I chose this betrayal over exile.

Growing up white, male, and privileged compounded my feelings of self-hatred. I believed I had no right to be unhappy. Who of us has not shaken his or her head at a wealthy child's tantrum? Unhappy children of upper-middle-class families are considered spoiled brats or in need of medication. To this day I continue to devalue my emotional experience because I have internalized the belief that I am not entitled to it because of my privilege. Where is the room for the anguish of the privileged in a culture that sells material wealth as happiness?

I AM DISCOVERING that the precious parts of myself that I am uncovering and that give such passionate meaning to my life are identical to the ones I have spent a lifetime attempting to destroy. In my quest for manhood, power, acceptance, and absolution for my privilege, the essence of my humanness was sacrificed. For the first time, as I begin to recover this essence, I feel a radiance of inexpressible hope and reverence for life which is completely transforming my being. Of course I still have many moments in which my masculinity feels threatened by this intimate connection and I completely reject, curse, and damn this experience. Even in composing this story I fear that the reader will judge me in the same invalidating way I have been judged for most of my life, as the "poor privileged white boy." But I am learning to accept that this too is a part of who I am. In opening to these old stories my relationship to them has begun to change. I am able to hold my frightened, stoic, terrified little boy with compassion.

I contribute my story with great honor, joy, fear, and apprehension, knowing that this very conflict is my space of transformation.

loving a one-armed man
tajamika paxton

THERE'S A MAN coming toward me. Together we're in the middle of a city street: people move hurriedly around us, but he and I don't rush. He walks slowly, almost ambling. He's returning home from a war. He went into battle resilient and optimistic that the world would yield for him and if it didn't he would take it down or die trying, extricating from the struggle a sense of power and self-determination. Instead, he's left "head bloody but unbowed" with his jacket neatly folded over the space where his arm once was. He has stories to tell about how the arm was blown off and other battles fought, but no story can match the intensity of living through it, the lesions the living creates on your soul. This one-armed man is an image I get in a dream. He's the symbol of men being torn apart by the impossible demands of one-dimensional manhood. The real man, fully limbed, is my father, Cassius Paxton.

My father is a veteran not of war, but of life lived within the cage of conflicting expectations particular to Black men born in America. Men who are told to be powerful in spite of economic cycles and discrimination that leave them powerless, and ordered to be rugged when the centuries-old healing they so desperately require demands sensitivity. I remember him as easily threatened, his wrath easily ignited. Self-taught and thus well educated, but lacking the resolve to use that education for his own prosperity. Instead, he chose to become an opportunist, a hustler, someone willing to take from others in a world where Black men go to prison for the same crimes that put White men in office. He spent his youth arrogant. He believed being quite handsome and charming would sustain him, perhaps lead him to the good life he saw in men like Nat King Cole and Sam Cooke.

My daddy is 62 and that man he once was is long gone. Now, he wants to tell other men what he's learned so they can avoid roads paved with personal regrets, the lingering numbness of unrealized dreams or ex-wives and children they never see. He's living with the unanswered question of what to do with those years and the sinking thought that he could have done more. My daddy has prostate cancer and cirrhosis. My daddy is dying. Maybe not today or next year but soon, he thinks, and because no one else in my family speaks to him, I feel like I'm the only one watching. I'm witnessing the transformation of his manhood like a scripted Hollywood film where the debonair leading man comes to some conclusive arc that makes the time watching his character worthwhile.

We're growing closer now. An extension of where we were in the picture I keep on my shelf. Cheek to cheek, his strong amateur middleweight boxing hands wrapped around my tiny three-year-old ones. Closer because we're determined to keep our connection despite the past and because of the future. My mother, his ex-wife of 21 years, talks to him when she must. She makes no pretense of truly caring if he changes or not. My father and I acknowledge the pain of the absence of my brothers. One lives locally and is being ravaged by some of the same addictions that plagued my father. High or sober, it's emotionally difficult for him to face my father, to have a conversation like two adults. He resorts to sickening depictions of his masculinity, bragging about his inability to cook and how his wife prepares meals and how other women respond to him when he's in public. My father usually stares at him pitifully. He probably hears his own father's cryptic words, "One day, son, you'll understand," and wishes that my brother would stand still and engage in a realistic conversation about what it's going to take for him not to die dirty in some hallway.

The other brother lives far away with his six children. He thinks having so many children is manly but cries like a baby when he's arrested for not paying his child support. My father sends no money, only admonition. "Son, you made that bed, you lie in it. Don't run from it now. It's not going anywhere." Today his advice is simple, too simple for my psychoanalytic tastes. He says people make two choices: do or don't. It's this simple creed that gave him the resolve to give up narcotics years ago and in 1996, to stop drinking before his habit killed him. So my father is changing and I am alone, listening. Listening to the stories of what life was like for him at 35 and why he sometimes behaved horribly in the name of being a man.

I remember my father as two men, distinct but with the same form. A man-child, he would sit for hours and play Atari Pac-Man with me after school, but a trip to the store that same night could mean a four-day absence. I would walk home wondering if his car was safely back in the driveway, like a friend waiting for me in front of a rickety swing, faithful. When it wasn't there, I suppressed my loss, but it metastasized into a resounding mistrust of all men. I lived, and at times, continue to live, with a sense that I would inevitably be let down, left waiting and alone. When he returned home after those times he offered no explanations and grew sullen when asked. Instead of communicating through the vulnerable places, I learned from my father to get silent and the world will walk away. Not so different from my brothers, I too adapted my father's stoic veneer as protection when I felt emotionally vulnerable.

At a recent birthday lunch, he shared the pain and pressure of the responsibility of parenting when he felt like such a young man, incapable of taking care of himself. He explained and, in his way, apologized for being an inadequate provider; for not having the resilience to consistently raise his children or the patience and understanding to love his wife. When the pressures mounted, he took flight.

I appreciate his candor and experience it as a step toward me. I meet him there, trying to talk to him every day partially because I have so many unanswered questions. Questions like "Why did you get so sad during Christmas?" One Christmas morning we found him in the bathtub obviously high, pupils dilated and stinging from tears. Looking broken and attempting to be coy, he asked what I thought of the gold necklace he had bought and bragged about its cost. He wouldn't respond to our pleading eyes or to my mother's seething resentment. I remember thanking him and wondering what could make a grown man cry at Christmas. To this day I care little for gold.

We don't talk much about the violence. He has taken to believing that he hasn't harmed anyone. It's easier than believing that he's scarred someone beyond repair. I don't pretend to understand this approach but it works for him and after years of tantrums, I've given up the need for blame. Some things must stay in the past so they don't choke the life out of what you're trying to create. But I can't forget. On two occasions, he beat my brothers mercilessly, and I can see clearly the afternoon my mother was cleaning our room and he dragged her out of it by her hair, her leg tearing as the flesh caught ahold of the sharp metal of my brother's bike pedal. Along with horror I was flooded with guilt. Could we have pushed the bike closer to the wall? The sound of her screaming, her open mouth begging, but I can't see his face. I wanted it be someone else, a stranger, not my father. My father who propped me up on the armrest while we rode through the streets of Los Angeles telling me stories of city landmarks and the time he hung out all night with Dinah Washington. My father who played with my hair for hours determined that his baby have an Afro.

I found some aspect of this man everywhere I went to look for love. By the grace of God, he was never violent. He was edgy, intelligent, magnetic and usually unavailable. Armed. He was my roughneck, and I was faithful to his type, always wanting to get beneath the armor, to try to make him be gentle with me. They could all be summed up with one. We met at a club dancing to "O.P.P." He knew all the lyrics and recited them through gold teeth emblazoned with his initials as he guided me to the dance floor. Later, I rejoiced when underneath the sagging pants and the heavy New York accent, I uncovered a man who played lacrosse despite the rough inner city upbringing he feigned; a man who talked for hours about growing up mixed race in Long Island. We talked about many subjects but not each other's needs. We exchanged easy childhood stories, more song lyrics, warm laughs and sweaty, disconnected sex. But we quickly tired of playing games the wounded play, neither willing to truly disarm. And I returned to my pattern of reaching for cool, tough men like my father.

THE FATHER I know now would not strike out against those he loves. In fact he sits in agony as he hears his neighbors beating each other to signal they're alive. In this new man I see a strong desire to be forgiven and loved. His calls are frequent, usually establishing when we'll spend our next moments together. The attention he wants from his family and the advice he needs to share is urgent to him, his sustenance.

Little of his old masculinity is of use to him now, not much of it can help him fight the diseases inside him. Not the white Cadillac, once a symbol of his street status and now delivering him to frequent doctors' appointments every week. Not the women he allowed to distract him from his marriage. Most of them are dead or just gone.

There's a kind one by his side now. She makes it easier to bear but she can't save him. His gold jewelry can't buy him any more time. Not even his once perfect biceps and his right hook. Using our kitchen as a ring, he once showed my brothers and me how to throw and block punches and stay off the ropes. The irony is overwhelming. Even the domi-nator, the dark side of him, is rendered useless. Age doesn't respond to bullying and there's no one else to rule over. He is left cultivating life-affirming skills he never found relevant. He's relying on spiritual fortitude to keep him grounded and hopeful. He's learning more about the cancer-fighting benefits of an organic diet. He listens to his mother.

Twelve years ago when he was injured in a car accident he joked that he had earned a purple heart from the streets of Oakland: he'd been shot, stabbed with a knife and an ice pick and none of those things could take him out. But I know this illness is different. "It's going to be the fight of my life," he says. Indeed. The harrowing facts about the sur-vival rate for Black men are humbling. The doctors tell him to keep a positive attitude and not to succumb to the fa-tigue. He says, "My attitude is positive. And I'm tired." In the next hour, he's buoyant again, doing the calisthenics rec-ommended by the doctor to strengthen his body before the radiation begins.

I admire how he now accepts the range of his feelings, not forcing himself into some stoic display of strength. He plans his life in days, maybe weeks if he's feeling optimistic. He says he just simply doesn't want to go yet; there are more days of sunshine, more long drives, boxing on TV every Sat-urday night, and a longing for creative fulfillment. I talk to him about the summer road trips we'll take together, but it's hard to experience just coming to know someone who could leave so soon.

What we have is a return to tenderness. Much is said about returning to the maternal "womb." I consider what we're engaged in now a return to the paternal womb, that place upon my father's chest where as a little girl I would rest comfortably and listen to his heart beating and think it the most melodious sound, comforting and truly strong. I hug this "one-armed man" frequently, and love him for the way he hugs me back generously, and for the meals he prepares for me with care. I love him for the considerate way he sends me home before it gets too late, and for the way I can cry on the phone with him about a thwarted romance and he'll paint a picture of my tomorrows and all the loves I'll have. It reminds me that this part of him was always there, beneath the fury.

I greedily devour him all for me. My brothers don't want to hear him talk about responsibility; they're sharpening their weaponry. During the three years I refused to speak to him, I did the same, but now I relate to him as a disarmed man, not just because that's what he, in the face of aging and death, has finally become, but because I need my own disarmament.

My life had been lacking true openness, an openness that says I am here, love me or not; and if you don't, I have what it takes to tend my own garden. I hadn't tended my garden. I was coping. In the wake of my internal chaos I had embarked on my own nightmare of working hard to achieve success and unconsciously hoping it would fill the neglected spaces in me, the voids created by unprocessed childhood pains and the slashes made by years of broken relationships. I was looking for a fulfillment that came from high-powered salaries and expense accounts. I adapted the masculinity myth for myself, suppressing yin gentility and overdeveloping yang aggression, convincing myself that aggressive people get farther faster and that the same aggression would repel those who might do me harm. I locked away my sense of play and simple pleasure convinced that only "girls" play and get hurt; tough women don't. I presented this armor proudly to the world until I began to suffocate inside the suit.

I loved the same way. Strong and tough but underneath, easily bruised and braced for inevitable disappointment. I was holding onto resentment for the apologies I hadn't received from my father and for all my failed attempts at disarmament. I relied on my relationships to feel that I was wanted, that what I had to offer was valuable. If a potential lover didn't respond to me, I sat dejected, a flood of insecurity overtaking me. From this desperate place I clung tightly to all lovers. When relationships ended, I was broken, trapped in romantic notions that someone could "steal my heart."

I had been avoiding the truth that I am emotionally responsible for delivering my happiness. In these last months I have come to see more clearly that I am responsible for my inner work, for spending quality time with me, for affirming my radiance, for saying yes to those deepest unspoken desires and living a life unbridled by comparisons or the judgments of others. With this awareness, I now see that no amount of protective covering can shield me. That what I needed and am finding is an inner fortification as essential as breath itself.

And so at 31, I shed my armor. As I do, I see that remarkable scene from *The Wiz*. After the witch has been killed, her former sweatshop slaves peel off their stifling furry costumes and begin to dance. They clap thunderously, gliding in a criss-cross formation stage left and stage right. They sing with rousing gospel harmonies, "Can you feel a brand-new day? Can you feel a brand-new day? Hello, world, it's like a different way of living now. Thank you, world, we always knew that we'd be free somehow."

It is a brand-new day for relating—to my father, to my lovers, to myself. I'm learning to love the men in my life in a place beyond sex and romantic interest, with a genuine closeness that touches the strong and tender beating heart that I once knew. I've decided to love as an act of surrender, not a declaration of war, fighting for my protection and survival. I know now to look for those men disarmed of their own volition, willing to let me touch their soft places and I am willing to let them touch mine, with an understanding of how fragile we all really are. I move closer to a man who can raise his hand in protest to an unjust world and bring it to rest gently on my waist.

I'm one of a collective of people coming home from the same war trying to cross burned bridges with worn-out shoes; we're tired but we have not given up. We're marching forward to a new way of being with and for each other, offering gentleness and attention, exchanging bravado for emotional bravery. Taking responsibility for our individual pasts and sorting through which needs are our own to meet, and which we can expect to be met by others. Willing to offer each other our fidelity not because we're supposed to but because we respect the time it takes to make love in this inundated world. We're creating a space to collectively acknowledge that there has been a war going on and we are committed to the work of rebuilding.

My father and I are doing this work privately, learning how to love each other, to be tender with each other, to put down our guns together. With this newfound freedom, I can finally allow him to make me a promise and believe that he'll keep it, knowing that if he doesn't I can forgive him and he can forgive himself. So much of this has come because we're willing to strain the muscles of trust until they hurt but in the hurting, they expand our mutual compassion and love.

I no longer subscribe to the crippling belief that he, or other men, can't emotionally handle the delicate places in relationships. Perhaps the inner fortification I'm finding is what my father needed long ago to feel safe and truly powerful. He is finding his way to it now. I send grace for his journey and along with it blessings for all of the many men still gasping for air inside their suffocating suits of armor. These men hunger for a new code that will offer them liberation, a code found in books like this one and in nationwide barbershop and boardroom discussions.

I'm getting a glimpse of a new dream, different from the one-armed man trudging down the street. I'm imagining a world without battle-scarred soldiers of life who have to be maimed or die in order to become heroic, a world without men who have to wage war to prove their point. This world is full of men who are heroic because they have the courage to nurture their families with a gentle confident strength, to teach children, their own and others, how to be humane, how to live in harmony with those considered different, how to practice spirituality in a world that overvalues the material. Heroic because they know the task of transformation is difficult but they take action anyway because they know it must be done.

Heroic like my father. He is far from perfect and I am farther but together we're reaching. And I'm like a little West African girl going from village to village beating the drum, hailing the sound of the new arrival.

no means no (and other lies)
bruce stockler

THE LINE for coffee at the Hay Day gourmet market stretches down into the baked goods section. The women are angry because this kind of everyday inconvenience mocks their success at marrying so skillfully. I sit at one of the tables, drinking Sumatra and reading *The New York Times*. It is 9:15 on a Monday morning.

I am the only man in this fishbowl of women who abandoned high-profile careers as lawyers, doctors, bankers, and public-relations executives to stay at home and manage the kids. It is somewhat frightening to see these supermoms channel their hyperaggressive personalities into renovating, decorating, overseeing the household staff and relentless play-date organizing. I keep my head down and drink my coffee.

One of the moms knows me from Asher's after-school program and asks about the family. We moved out of Bronxville and into Scarsdale at the end of August, I explain, right before kindergarten started for Asher.

It is November 1999. The triplets are almost three years old now. They attend nursery school at a local synagogue in the morning and a Montessori school in the afternoon.

"Oh," the woman says. "So you . . . stay at home?"

Yes, I say. I am a stay-at-home dad. For almost a year now.

Mikimoto pearls jangle against bony necks as heads turn my way. The only men visible during the day in Scarsdale are contractors, deliverymen, and Wall Street shysters serving out the house-arrest portion of their sentences. I am an anomaly, like a mermaid or an anarchist.

"I think that's great," the woman says. "I wish my husband spent more time home with the kids. He goes in to the office on the third day of a three-day weekend because he goes crazy being locked up with the kids."

I hear that story a lot, I say, editing out my opinion that it is nonsense. If these women wanted husbands who spent more time home with the kids, they would marry carpenters or painters or chemistry teachers and live upstate in New Paltz or Peekskill or Oneonta, where they would shop at Wal-Mart and buy day-old bread at the outlet store and muddle by with three unrenovated bedrooms and one and a half baths. If any one of these plastic surgeons or investment bankers or personal injury lawyers told his wife he was taking a year off to study metal sculpture and drive the soccer carpool and create balance in his life, he would have more lawyers in his house than O. J. Simpson.

It is 9:45 now. I fold up my newspaper and go home. My coffee break lasts exactly thirty minutes, the amount of time I would spend on the train into the city.

. . .

THE STAY-AT-HOME DAD, a popular trend story in magazines and Sunday newspapers, is a socially awkward reality in
the suburbs, the most reactionary social environment in
America. In cities like Austin or St. Paul or San Francisco,
we would just be another quirky couple. But in a suburb
like ours the other dads look at me with a confusion that
borders on fear, and the moms, while boosterish in their enthusiasm for our alternative lifestyle, are unable to absorb me
into their viciously organized social circles.

Roni suffers the most, since working moms occupy the
lowest rung on the social ladder (the sole exception being
the stay-at-home dad). Moms who work suffer at the hands
of an apartheid apparatus that is all the more oppressive because it is so transparent. Power begins with the Class Moms
and radiates outward in a fiendishly calibrated spiral of social engineering, gossiping, and backstabbing. Hysteria and
paranoid delusions are traded over morning coffee and low-
fat scones. One of the moms in our neighborhood became
obsessed by the fear that her three-year-old son's penis was
smaller than normal, so she lobbied the other moms to let
her examine the competitive field artillery to determine if
she was outgunned. Normally, this kind of behavior would
spell the end for a family's reputation, but this mom was thin
and attractive and friendly enough to pull it off. In this way
the suburbs are like ninth grade.

Roni and I both grew up in row houses in working-class
neighborhoods—Roni in Queens, me in Northwest Philadelphia. She loathes the materialism and high school cliquish-

ness and mindless home-decorating chitchat and would leave in a heartbeat for some small town in Vermont or New Mexico or Upstate New York. Sometimes she scrolls through online real estate listings around the country and calls me over to tell me how much house we could get for $180,000 if only we packed up our stuff and ran away. No more treading water, no more stacks of unpaid medical bills, no more shutoff notices from the cable TV company and cell phone provider.

"Let's buy a Winnebago and drive around the country," Roni says one morning, apropos of nothing, when the kids are screaming around the kitchen, not listening to our demands that they put their shoes on so we can leave the house.

"That was always my dad's big dream," I say.

A cold shiver runs up my spine as I consider the circumlocution of the weirdness gene. I grew up in an unpainted suburban house and my amateur photographer dad took nude pictures of women in an empty upstairs bedroom when he wasn't in the basement yelling at my brother and me to be quiet and stop running around the house. Even though I joke about it, the parallels between Roni and my dad are a bit frightening. They both love hardware stores, power tools, and construction sites. They both love to take pictures and fiddle around in a darkroom. They are both infatuated with bargains and will spend hours to save a few dollars. They both tend to be autocratic and immune to self-analysis, although my father is much more extreme.

The scariest similarity, though, is that both Roni and my dad have the habit of starting projects they never finish, along with the inability to see this character trait. My brother and I grew up in a home with no furniture and unpainted rooms. My dad built a couch and two chairs out of hardwood in the basement when I was a teenager, but he never finished or stained them. The furniture remained in this state of limbo in our living room for years and, after the divorce, moved with my dad into his tumbledown row house, where they remain still happily united—and still unfinished—today, more than thirty years later. Our new house in Scarsdale is filled with temporary, thrift-store furniture because Roni tends to juggle eight or ten decorating projects at a time, unable to finish off any single room. Roni built our first bed from scratch when we lived in the city—and it's beautiful—but never stained or finished it. It has traveled with us to Bronxville and now to Scarsdale, where, ten years later, it is the center of a guest bedroom, still unfinished and unpainted. The bed is a ghost from my past—the ghost of unfinished business—that only I can see.

It took me a long time to understand that part of our connection is that Roni and I both grew up in weird homes. Roni grew up speaking German and Czech and Hungarian and ate fried pork fat and her parents had no friends. Now our kids are growing up in the Mr. Mom and Mrs. Lawyer house. To lean into the weirdness even harder, the kids have different last names: Two are Stocklers and two are Fischers. Long before Roni and I were married, she made me promise that when we had kids, we would split up the last names, because both sides of her family were wiped out in World War II. It was an abstraction, so I said yes. But when people learn the kids have alternating last names they look at us as if we are unbalanced. Even the woman in the hospital administration office looked at me sideways when I filled out the birth certificates. One of my old college buddies, Howard Katz, told me I was going to ruin their lives.

One day in the elementary school parking lot, Liza, one of the friendliest, most down-to-earth of the moms, asks if I want to join her weekly book-reading club. I burst out laughing. "That would be the end for me," I explain. Roni could tolerate my taking up a kinky afternoon sex club or robbing a bank, but sitting around in ladies' living rooms discussing literature would be the marital coup de grâce.

TO FORESTALL criticism from the late-at-work mom, the stay-at-home dad tries to create motivational systems, implementation methodologies, and psychological profiling techniques to organize the children's daily routine. The children have better ideas.

The stay-at-home dad's day begins at 6:30 A.M., when Jared wakes up. Jared is the most physically attuned of the brood and puts himself to bed, even during a favorite cartoon, when tired.

By 7:30 the last child is awake and the getting-dressed game begins. In the rules of this game, the TV is turned on and off, like a morphine drip, to motivate children to dress. The late-at-work mom suggests not paying the cable bill.

Hannah and Jared normally dress without incident. Asher requires repeated warnings and threatened removal of privileges, while Barak extorts adult assistance by filibustering—

lying on his side, sucking his thumb, clutching his yellow blanket. When the stay-at-home dad attempts to put on Barak's clothes, he flops around on the ground like a boneless chicken.

Breakfast begins at 8:05 to 8:10. On any given day the kids may quietly eat a bowl or two of cereal or descend into Balkanized fighting. Some days the stay-at-home dad counts to ten and separates the children. Some days he starts laughing out of nervous excitement and lets entropy work its course. And some days he screams at them to quiet down, which is counterproductive, because screaming only begets more screaming. Asher's lunch is made, backpacks packed, coats laid out, teeth brushed.

The battle over leaving then ensues. This battle pits inertia against momentum. Children instructed to sit on the couch with their shoes develop time-devouring problems elsewhere. Asher is upstairs searching for a library book. Barak sits on the couch with one sock and no shoes. Jared wears one sneaker and dismantles a toy that may or may not belong to Barak but which provokes howls of protest. Hannah actually puts on her shoes and ties them, unassisted.

Inertia demands that the stay-at-home dad forget critical tasks, such as note signing and club paying and conference scheduling. The stay-at-home dad dashes upstairs for the checkbook and returns to find Asher playing the electronic piano, Barak clomping around in Roni's high heels, Jared MIA, Hannah screaming.

The house is locked, backpacks, hats, and gloves double-checked. The Suburban is opened and children given a three-count. The kids fight over air rights for climbing over seats. The detours are legion, like the names of Noah's family running across Genesis.

The stay-at-home dad drives to Asher's elementary school and walks Asher to his first-grade class. The triplets are driven to the Reformed temple in New Rochelle.

The stay-at-home dad works on his freelance writing assignments until 11:15, makes lunch, and dashes back to the temple at 11:45. The triplets have thirty minutes to eat in a lounge that has couches and tables, usually with a few other children and their stay-at-home moms. The stay-at-home dad is cordial to the stay-at-home moms, even as he visualizes his testicles floating in a jar on his wife's desk.

The kids run across the couches in the lounge, even though the purpose of couches for sitting has been explained 37,000 times. Jared shares important information about the teachers and class projects, Hannah explains the emotional ups and downs of the children, and Barak spins elaborate fantasy scenarios about friends, dogs, flying saucers, crabs, and talking marshmallows.

At 1:15 the kids are driven from the synagogue to the local Montessori school, where their habitual lateness is a source of amusement for the warm and generous staff. The stay-at-home dad works on his articles from 1:45 until 2:45, not counting errands and phone calls. The triplets are picked up at 3:00.

Between 3:15 and 5:30 the stay-at-home dad supervises multiple activities, handles minor emergencies, preps dinner, and tries to reduce the state of physical bedlam in the house to a state of clutter. At 6:30 the children are packed in the car and driven to pick up Asher, whose full-day schedule promotes his independence.

At 7:00 P.M. dinner is prepared. The stay-at-home dad is conned into preparing four completely separate meals, in direct violation of the late-at-work mom's one-meal-only food-service philosophy.

After dinner and cleanup and the unpacking of backpacks and inventorying of lost hats and gloves comes the donning of PJs, the starting of laundry, the reading of books, and the watching of TV. This is the bridge to bedtime, a nightly battle for one more show, fifteen more minutes, one more minute, just one, anything for one more minute of blessed and sustaining TV.

The late-at-work wife returns home between 9:00 and 10:00, exhausted and dispirited, horrified by one or more errors of the stay-at-home dad (the garbage! the recycling! the Tupperware!), who is delighted to hear his domestic shortcomings read back to him.

The stay-at-home dad juggles the intersecting trajectories of his family's days—the kids as they fight off the unfair sentence of sleep, and the late-at-work mom, who wants hugs and kisses from the kids but, more than anything, mental decompression time. More chores—adult laundry, straightening up, sweeping, cooking adult dinner, garbage bagged—are layered into the simmering riot of late evening. The stay-at-home dad serves dinner and brings the late-at-work mom a treat as she falls asleep on the couch, struggling to make it through *All My Children*.

At 11:00 P.M. Barak is taken to pee in his sleep, pots and dishes cleaned, the dishwasher loaded, garbage taken outside, kitchen floors vacuumed, lights turned off, house locked. At 11:30 or 12:00 the stay-at-home dad writes for an hour if he is lucky and ambitious. At 12:30 or 1:15 A.M. he retucks the kids in their beds, turns down the heat, double-checks the house, and watches TV.

At 1:30 or 2:00 A.M. the stay-at-home dad climbs into bed, only to wake again at 4:00 or 5:00 to take a child to the potty, fetch someone a drink of water, soothe the victim of a nightmare. Out of the darkness a heavy weight attacks the stay-at-home dad's chest. Is he dreaming of a heart attack? Or is he waking to a major biological event?

Jared kneels on the stay-at-home dad's chest and squeezes his face with his strong hands.

"Daddy?" Jared says. The clock reads 6:18.

"Yes, Jared?" says the stay-at-home dad.

"Can we play a game?" Jared says.

I SNEAK INTO the kids' bedroom after they are asleep and straighten out their covers. Barak is still awake and smiles up at me.

"Grandma's in heaven, right, Daddy?" Barak says. The kids ask about her out of the blue. On the nights I am thinking about my mom, I wonder what this coincidence means.

"That's right," I say. Better to grow up with the comfort, Einstein believed.

Barak smiles and hugs my arm and makes his special little ooey-gooey sounds. I wrap his yellow blanket around him. My mom barely knew the triplets. They were twenty-two months old when she died, and will not remember her.

Mom would be mad at you for yelling at the kids, I say to my-self. She never, ever yelled. Dad yelled. The only thing I ever knew about fatherhood was that I would not yell. I would not be like my dad.

Don't yell at the kids now. You've failed enough. Don't break this one promise.

I look at the picture Asher drew in blue pencil for my mom when she was in the hospital. I peeled it off the hospital wall the night she died, brought it home, and hung it on the wall of my home office. For the first time, I notice there are seven crudely drawn pencil figures—Asher has many talents, but drawing is not among them—and wonder if the seventh figure is supposed to be my mom, standing with the six of us, watching over us, as she promised me the morning before her surgery.

My mother would be so proud of Asher. He is so warm and loving and funny and sensitive. A month or so after she died, we were at a shopping mall play zone for kids. The triplets were bouncing and running and screaming, and I sat off in a corner, staring into space and thinking regretfully about my mom. Out of the blue, Asher snuck up next to me and said, "Are you thinking about Grandma?" He was four years old.

It comforts me to realize that I love my children fiercely because I was so fiercely loved. This was my mother's gift. I don't remember if I ever told her as much, or if she saw in-side me her own enormous strength. But this becomes my myth: My mom will live on, in this randomly ordered uni-verse, through me, as I love my kids above all.

picture perfect
douglas rushkoff

IT WAS BACK around the fourth grade. Before any of us even knew what a homosexual was. Well, some of my classmates probably knew, but I didn't—which is part of what made me so vulnerable to the damning accusation.

I had just endured another one of those difficult mid-year moves from one public school district to another. It was a move up, as far as my parents were concerned, from the marginally upper-middle-class sections of Queens and then Larchmont to the indisputably upper-middle-class zip code of Scarsdale, where the school taxes rivaled the tuition at Andover. The relocation had just about tapped out my dad's income, so we stuck with clothes from Sears for those first couple of years while everyone else at school was already wearing those polos with the alligator on the tit, genuine Pumas or Adidas, and winter coats called "snorkels" with fake fur around the hood.

Me, well, my jeans had generic circles on the back pockets instead of Levi's trademarked double-hump glyph, and I wore PF Flyers that, where I came from, were a heartfelt statement of countercultural rebellion against the omnipresence of Keds. My shirts were of the button-down, reptile-free variety, and my sole winter coat was a Dacron-filled shell of shiny gold polymer. It had a stiff, box-shaped hood with a window-like opening for my face that prompted my first official Scarsdale nickname, "Spaceman."

Somehow, just as word began trickling down from junior high school about the incipient emergence of the first pubic sprouts, the universal taunt for the alien from Larchmont shifted from Spaceman to "faggot." And though I could run as fast and jump as high as almost anyone in the fourth, fifth, and eventually sixth grade, it never changed again.

I didn't really have any attraction to girls at this point—not that I had one for boys, either—so it was hard for me to disprove the underlying premise of the community-composed "Dougie's a Fem" theme song. Did everybody else know something about me that I didn't? After all, they couldn't have reached such a decisive and unanimous verdict by chance. By the time I turned eleven, I concluded on a fairly conscious level that the only way to fend off this onslaught of psychic terrorism was to prove I was a real boy, not a girlie boy, and certainly not a fem—whatever that meant. It was a life strategy that would prove to have diminishing returns.

I started my straight-boy self-education like most American males: with porn. I had no idea where my dad was hiding those *Playboys* he got half-jokingly from his own dad on his 40th birthday, and actually suspected my mom was making him dispose of them as soon as they arrived. My best hope was to cut her off at the pass and take one directly from the mailbox. This would be difficult, because my mom got to the mail first every day except Saturday. There was only a one out of six shot that the magazine would arrive on a Saturday, and even less that I'd be able to snag it without being noticed.

It was the morning that my brother was heading out with my parents for his second day of bar mitzvah portraits—I remember there had been some problem with the first batch—and I had been left alone. I'd have just a two-hour window for the mail to arrive, and it would *have* to contain that month's *Playboy*. So I resorted to another mail-order item my father had purchased a few years before, a cheesy book on how to use witchcraft for power and happiness.

I retrieved the volume from a box in the attic. I found a bizarre spell in there for "wish fulfillment," which involved caressing the leaves of plants with your hands or preferably, your genitals while you concentrate on the object of desire. I considered focusing on a real woman—but a woman is not what I wanted. I wanted the next issue of *Playboy* to be delivered within the hour. Thanks to the spell, I still believe, the magazine came before my parents and brother got back from the photographer.

But I didn't—or hadn't yet—associated pictures of female body parts with erotic excitement, and the magazine's many depictions of primary and secondary sexual anatomy weren't really helping. Sure, seeing breasts was interesting, but it wasn't really titillating, which is where I assumed that word came from. I felt a certain hot naughtiness—more of a flushness, really—whenever I'd pull the magazine from its secret hiding place and attempt masturbation. But I didn't fully understand how the pictures and my excitement were to be connected.

Somewhere between breasts and lens, photos and eyes, frontal lobe and hand, the erotic circuit between Miss July and my penis was not completed. It was far easier to masturbate alone in the bed, thinking about masturbation itself.

It was about a year later that I managed to find an image, or state of mind, that did the trick. I can still see it if I close my eyes: a short-cropped brunette, splayed against a bed of deep green leaves. She looked like a pixie or wood nymph from one of those medieval poems about knights and misty ponds in sudden clearings. Foreign. Other. But sweet. It was from *Oui*—*Playboy*'s Euro-styled sister magazine. And it had etched itself onto the printed circuit board directing my sexual response for decades to come. She was the ultimate woman because she had distinguished me as a man. She gave me my first culturally sanctioned hard-on.

What I didn't realize was that all I had truly accomplished was to train myself to reach an erection by looking at pornographic imagery. It's called classic conditioning. Jerk off looking at pictures of horses for long enough, and you'll get a hard-on looking at them, too. And I contend to this day that most of us who find porn capable of engorging a penis have done the very same thing, in one way or another. Getting aroused by looking at body parts owned exclusively by women is a learned skill, achieved primarily for the purpose of differentiating ourselves from the feminine. That's why lesbian scenes are so popular in straight porn: no penises to confuse the issue at hand.

It's the same reason why, in the fifth grade, I decided that whichever girl with whom I would attempt to "go steady" couldn't be someone I already knew well. The point was not to feel familiar or friendly with the girl, but starkly contrasted. It had nothing to do with her, really. Her purpose was merely to assert and define my masculinity. It was more about my relationships with the other guys, and my place in the prepubescent social schema, than my relationship with the female in question. She had only to prove I was not a fag.

Don't get me wrong: Fear of being a faggot has nothing to do with being afraid of homosexuality. It's got a whole lot more to do with the much simpler fear of being a woman. To the pubescents of my era, homosexuality meant something closer to no pubic hairs than men kissing men. At eleven and twelve, we were at the very crossroads of sexual differentiation. Girls would be going one way, and boys another. We wanted this mysterious division of realms to happen as quickly and painlessly as possible. Yet, at the very same time, society seemed to be collapsing these definitions in our path. My older brother's class was the first one in our junior high school where boys took Home Economics and girls took Shop. Even my dad was taking us to a "unisex" hair salon, instead of the barber. Would that turn me into a unisexual?

At its core, for kids like me, homophobia was the fear of not being a man or, more precisely, the fear of being a woman. And who could blame us? Women have gotten a bum deal for the past couple of thousand years. In this light, who would want to be one of them, if given the choice?

At least that's the way we developing young boys of the

early 1970s understood the failure of the ERA (an aborted
equal rights amendment), the pathos of Mary Richards
cringing before her boss Lou Grant, as well as the professional frustrations and social passivity of our own mothers,
who may have been Ivy League graduates but were still rel-
egated to jobs that appeared to involve mostly the purchase
and preparation of meat, and dressing up to play hostess for
their husbands' business parties. They got face-lifts, took
Valium, got abandoned for younger "trade-ins" and were
left to fight for child support. Plus, they were girls.

That's why it was so very disconcerting for me to stand,
naked, in front of Drew Gershon in the locker room one
winter afternoon in the seventh grade, while he explained
that—from his vantage point, anyway—I was a girl. Of
course Drew had just endured an extended barrage of
gender-based verbal assaults himself. An awkwardly manifesting voice change had rendered his cords incapable of
producing anything below mezzo soprano range for weeks,
which had led to countless mocking impersonations by boys
and girls alike.

"I see you've got a penis, Rushkoff," he said. "A little
one. But in every other way you're a girl. The way you talk,
the way you walk, the way you do everything. Even looking
at your face right now, all I can see is a girl. You know that,
Rushkoff? You're such a fem. I mean it." His contempt for
what he saw as my femininity was almost mixed with sorrow. Still, the laughter from the other boys continued long
after I got my shorts on.

Make no mistake: his ritualistic defamation had nothing
to do with whether I was girlish or not. He had moved to

the next level of sexual self-definition—proving your masculinity not by contrasting yourself with females, but against the measure of other males. Beginning with Drew's verbal barrage, I was subjected to two years of what could only be called sustained sexual abuse by my peers. It went from wedgies, to whale-hooks, to worse. Strange, I remember thinking, I'm the fag, but they're the ones chasing after me to get their hands on my underwear, or even between my buttocks.

It seemed that the more officially masculine they got, the more obsessed these boys were with one another. To be a real boy meant sexually humiliating another boy. But who was I to talk? Everyone was sure that *I* was the fag. The more insight I gained, the less I participated (voluntarily, anyway) in these pecking order rituals, and the more my femininity was confirmed.

BY LATE HIGH SCHOOL and college, things got a bit better. There was no active teasing or abuse, anyway. I had come into my own, and found a few social alternatives unavailable before. More importantly, I realized I had found my "type": short, dark-haired pixies. This felt good. They weren't so hard to find, because they tended to show up a lot in the theater, which is where "fags" like me ended up acting out the same dramas that "normal" boys enacted in locker rooms, the backs of cars, or playing fields. I'd meet one of the beautiful wood nymphs—absolutely unaware, at the time, of their possible connection to that first effective porn image—and fall madly in love. Or what I thought was love.

For me, and anyone trapped in the same vicious cycle, love meant unrequited love. It was the nerd's version of female objectification. I didn't abuse women the way a jock might, as inferior objects; no, I worshipped them as superior objects. Untouchable and unattainable. They'd have no fear of abuse—or of any contact, whatsoever, unless they up and asked outright. Even then, they'd have to convince me it wasn't for charity's sake.

In my scheme, the pursuit became everything. This is where that awful book *The Rules* makes sense—at least so far as it instructs women how to maintain an absurdly pathological relationship with a psychologically immature man. Staying actively apart from women, according to the logic of machismo, confirms male status more than melting into one. For a woman to remain desirous but distant sustains that objectified dynamic between boy and airbrushed photo. This is what generates the boner. We've trained ourselves to respond this way.

Sure, I managed to have and keep a few girlfriends over those years. But I usually broke up with them whenever I was able to detect the objectification game going on beneath the surface. For instance, I ended my first truly promising college relationship when I realized how much I wanted the other guys in the dorm to know my girlfriend was staying overnight. She would have actually tolerated this immaturity, but I could not. I knew that, at least in part, she was serving a need that had no right to be met.

The other choice, of course, was to be like "normal" guys, and revel in the attainment of a sexual partner capable of arousing the loins and jealousies of one's friends. If getting other guys hard was really the object of the game, though, then why not just be gay? I was too self-aware to take this route, yet too self-absorbed to experience a woman as much more than a reflection on myself. Nevertheless, my key relationships with women were still played for the guys in the bleacher seats—to earn social currency with other men. I was so committed to the sexual schema forged in childhood that I sacrificed any real intimacy that may have been available to me. I was forgoing love for the simulacra.

Luckily, or so I thought, my entrance into the adult sexual arena coincided with the greater culture's acceptance of real men who eat quiche. Phil Donahue and Alan Alda were raking in millions as the sex symbols of the kinder, gentler, and post-macho American landscape. Sure, Reagan was President, but his John Wayne-ish cowboy charm was understood as a kind of martyrdom. Stoic gender traditionalism for the sake of the nation.

Turns out we New Age sensitive guys were the martyrs. Women (young women, anyway) didn't really want us, however much they pretended they did. Ironically, they now needed macho guys in order to prove their own femininity. And this was getting harder to do, especially as women became more ostensibly masculine. Business suits and shoulder pads replaced skirts and bikinis. Women had earned real jobs, real stress, and a significant uptick in heart attacks as a result. Mary Richards was replaced by Murphy Brown, and now it was the bawdy, aggressive woman in the corner office, intimidating her simpering male producer.

The sad legacy of early feminism was not to bring men's consciousness upward and beyond our polarized objectification of women. No, it was to bring women down to our level. Now women had earned the right to treat men as selfishly as we had always treated them. Men as merchandise. The same talk-show audiences that berated men for their insensitivity applauded women for theirs. She left her man for one with a bigger prick? Well, go, girl!

As an adult cultural theorist, I began to write and speak out against what I saw as the commodification of human relationships. It's always easier to see one's own faults as they are played out on the grand societal level than it is to make the kinds of hard, personal changes that might actually solve the problem.

I watched with chagrin as the marketplace capitalized on the sexual objectification trend, and strove to exacerbate our worst impulses for economic gain. With women back at work, teens had replaced women as America's target demographic by the late seventies.

Those first Bruce Weber photos of Marky Mark and other muscular teens in their Calvin Klein underwear may not have been any worse than what advertisers have done with emaciated female models since the 1960s. But it gave marketers the permission to objectify boys with the same intensity they had used to drive millions of teenage girls to stick fingers down their throats. Instead of looking at pictures of naked girls, they are now poring through magazines filled with the ripped torsos of young men.

Combine this pressure from the mass media with the availability of stark video porn to replace the glossy photos of Daddy's favorite skin mags, and you've got a recipe for objectification on an order of magnitude unimaginable by those of us raised on *Playboy* and wedgies. Instead of just objectifying females, today's boys objectify the entire sex act, and insist on pulling out before orgasm so that they can watch the "money shot" for themselves.

IT WAS MY RESEARCH into the practices of today's WWF-watching "mooks" and Britney-adoring "midriffs," combined with a few thousand bucks of psychotherapy, that I gained a bit of perspective on my own extended run performing in the Gender Follies.

As an adult, my real audience for these psychodramas was not the boys in the dorm or the kids in the locker room, but my own internalized spectators. The Greek chorus. They had become the arbiters of my sexual identity. And they were a tough crowd, whose sophistication had grown along with my own.

It was no longer about proving my gender or sexual preference. Hell, homosexuality would have been better than any more years wasted chasing after women who were unavailable in one way or another. But, like so many other young men, my attraction to women, and my whole sexual orientation, was developed more as a way of proving my worth and my identity than experiencing any kind of joy or intimacy. Even the goal of marriage and children loomed as more of an abstract idea than a felt goal. It was a plot point in the screenplay of life to which my audience was demanding I conform. And I was failing to meet their expectations.

I began to see women more as static images than as living, changing, dynamic beings. The blonde, green-eyed psychologist from Dallas. The nice but overweight Jewish teacher from Brooklyn. The hot Croatian architect. Each one was processed by my internal Central Casting division, and inserted into my mental script-writing program. The psychologist would be a sympathetic ear. The overweight teacher would never cheat on me. The Croatian architect would challenge me intellectually and sexually for years to come. Two from column A, one from column B. My own, genuine experience of these people was dwarfed by my involuntary tendency to turn them into statistical profiles. The needs of the script, my internal audience and, presumably, the general public, were all that mattered.

Sure, the profiles grew in complexity and sophistication—so much so that they sounded, to my friends, like real considerations for choosing a girlfriend. They were certainly more heartfelt than the kinds of considerations voiced by the neurotic singles of *Seinfeld* or the sexually infantilized women of *Sex and the City*. But I was fooling myself, all the same. Maybe that's why these TV programs became so intolerable to me. I was no better than these characters were at looking past the laundry list of desirable features to the human being with whom I was interacting.

My original motivations for turning my romantic life into a series of test drives—the taunts of my classmates and the fear of never turning into a man—had long passed. But I was still looking for a woman who could define me the

way that first brunette pixie in *Oui* had confirmed my sexual identity as a child. Who would be Douglas's mate?

Looking at potential romantic partners through a lens
like this was doomed to failure. In short, my attraction to a
woman had almost nothing to do with *her*. I wasn't yet capable of experiencing a woman as anything other than a
potential leading lady in the ultimate foreign film screenplay
I was writing in lieu of living a real life.

I had enough going for me to win the affections of quite
a few women with enough intelligence, outward beauty, and
career success to keep everyone happy. And oh, the audience
was pleased. In fact, as long as I imagined what our inter-
twined bodies looked like from the empty chair in the corner of the room, I could be a more masculine, sexual, and
accomplished lover than I ever expected I'd be back in
grade school.

But, eventually, each relationship started to feel flat. It's
no wonder—I wasn't relating to these women as real people, anyway. And I doubt they were using their time with me
for anything more profound than I was using my time with
them. I came to believe that successful relationships were
simply ones in which people fooled themselves better than I
was capable of doing.

My growing self-knowledge made me feel disingenuous. I didn't want to be one of those guys who sought a trophy wife, even though I had managed to upgrade my
obsession to the more palatable goal of an "ideal marriage."
The image I had constructed—of living with a beautiful,
intelligent woman in the hills of Marin County, cooking
healthy whole wheat breakfasts and writing in our separate

studios until late in the night before retiring for an evening of earth-shattering tantric sex—was still just another image.

I suppose I would have continued in this endless cycle of cinematically predetermined but utterly doomed serial monogamy had I not happened to accept an invitation to attend an awful conference about Judaism a year or so ago. For it was there that I met a woman who just didn't fit the script.

Barbara immediately struck me as a person I wanted to know better—if for no other reason than that she hated the stupid conference as much as I did, and wasn't afraid to say so. She turned out to be a person a lot like me. A kid, in some ways. Like one of those girls I liked to play with back when I was ten, before we weren't allowed to like girls that way, anymore. Not without getting called "fem," anyway.

What complicated matters, though, was that I really wanted to kiss her, too.

Barbara's a suburban Jew like me, with a shared distaste for almost everything that passes for Judaism these days. She speaks directly, looks straight into my eyes, and takes no shit. She even looks and acts a lot like me, which is kind of freaky all by itself. But, worse for the incurable screenwriter in the back of my head, I had an immediate sense of connection with her that made objectification impossible. How do you turn someone you're experiencing as so real into a mere image? It's like when you're watching a movie with an actor so recognizable that you can't believe the role they're supposed to be playing.

No, she was too real, and too present to fade into the background while I plastered a stereotype over her. I wasn't going to be able to use her in the same way I had used almost every woman I'd encountered before—the way I used that picture of the pixie in *Oui* thirty years ago—as some vague confirmation of my hetero status.

But I wasn't willing to let her go, either. And that's what forced me to find a way out of the trap in which I'd been stuck for most of my adult life.

To get to be with this woman I had to finally put down the gun and accept that I couldn't shoot my way out of the hostage crisis in which I had imprisoned myself for thirty years. Negotiations had failed, the trail of victims was longer than my conscience would permit, and I was tired of terrorizing myself for an agenda forged during puberty by psychosexual fundamentalists. Besides—I'd found someone I could actually be myself with, and I liked how being me was beginning to feel.

Yes, I think I've found "the one," precisely because she's the one who's forced me to realize there's no such thing. Honestly, I wouldn't want to give her up to find out what "the one" might be, anyway. It's just too good the way it is. Most of the time, anyway. Sometimes it's not, and I'm plagued by the same old nagging objections from the remaining script development people in my head. But that's the price we must pay to live in the real world. Everyone should at least try it. You, too.

What I've come to realize is that being a man means giving up the false security of defining my masculinity against an obsolete and crudely drawn notion of the feminine. Being a man has nothing to do with *not* being a woman, and everything to do with being a person who makes his own choices in real life. When you lose the screenplay you may also lose the approval of the crowd, but you'll be more than compensated with the joy of autonomy.

It may be a little tougher to live life this way, but hell—someone's got to be a real man.

pig farm
jay ruben dayrit

MY SISTER AND I ran down the dirt road that would not be paved for five or six more years, and even then it would quickly revert back to potholes, tall grass encroaching from either side. School had finally let out for summer. We sprinted the quarter mile home, the last house at the end of the island's only sidewalk. Bambi and I, excited about the coming three months of freedom: swimming, climbing, fort building and guava eating. We stumbled through the back door, tossing our tattered notebooks onto the dining room table.

And there they were, two piglets, smeared with mud, grunting, incongruous in my mother's tidy kitchen. Twenty pounds and fully weaned. Ring Middles, so named for the band of white fur around their midsections. They scurried about, sniffing the cupboards, the trash can, their hoofs clicking delicately on the linoleum floor.

The piglets were to be our summer project, my mother announced. She was fond of that word, "project," so focused and productive a word. She often used it to point out that we were not particularly focused and productive children. "You should come up with a constructive project. How 'bout a project? Have I got a project for you!" And suddenly there were pigs in our kitchen. Thanks to our father, who was handy with a hammer and nail, a small pigpen appeared shortly thereafter in the garden behind the trellis of string beans.

The piglets were gifts, in a sense. We should have been thankful for such an opportunity, a means to make money, grateful that summer would not be filled with hours of useless play. We knew not to complain, though our carefree days had just been obliterated by a project that could shit and eat at the same time.

I GREW UP on a farm in a place most people have never heard of: Pohnpei in the Federated States of Micronesia, a small island in an unfamiliar country of islands. Micronesia, even the name implies obscurity. When people ask me where I am from and I tell them Pohnpei, they tend to look puzzled and ask, "Where's that?" Sometimes I must explain it's not the place that was buried by a volcano, where archeologists later found evidence of people frozen in various poses of panic and horror. No. I often say that Pohnpei is a small island above and to the right of Australia, though Pohnpei is about as close to Australia as Iceland is to Maine, but most people are able to visualize Australia on the globe, so at least they have the right hemisphere.

Our farm was not a farm in the sense that my father

plowed fields all day on a John Deere tractor and came home dog-tired, covered in dust. In fact, my father didn't work on the farm at all. He worked for the United States Department of Agriculture in an air-conditioned office with a view of the bay. He spent his days preventing the Japanese from covering the wetlands of Micronesia with golf courses. I vaguely understood that his job was noble and that the Japanese, though very polite, were rich and powerful and prone to overusing fertilizer, the runoff of which encouraged the growth of algae and endangered the barrier reef. I also understood that his job was not as interesting as my mother's.

She worked on the farm. It was, in effect, her classroom. Much in the way that major cities have teaching hospitals, Pohnpei had a teaching farm. My mother headed the Agriculture Department of the Pohnpei Island Central School, the island's biggest high school. She taught agriculture and animal husbandry. All sophomores, boys and girls alike, took her classes.

Technically, the farm belonged to the school, but since our mother was department head, my sister and I regarded it as our very own fifteen-acre playground. We felt free to roam the open fields of corn and sweet potatoes, tapioca and tomatoes. The coconut grove, predating the Japanese occupation, was the perfect place to play war with our friends. A guava orchard shaded the schoolhouse. There were three greenhouses, two for propagating seedlings and one devoted entirely to orchids. We found ourselves enchanted by the strange flowers suspended in the humid air like butterfly specimens. We spent our afternoons swimming in the river that snaked along the farm's eastern boarder, canopied by flame trees and black-pepper vines.

The only place we were prohibited from entering was the piggery, an immense machine of a building in the center of the farm. From the highest branches of the guava trees, I could see over the barbed wire fence into the maze of pens, walkways and buzzing fluorescent lights. Heavy gates swung open and slammed shut, trafficking and containing the enormous pigs. Irrigation pipes snaked along the ceiling and ran down rusted posts into each pen. Gutters carried away manure, depositing it into open septic tanks that seethed with maggots and toads. By the front gate, a chicken-wire shed housed an arsenal of tools: hoes, shovels, scythes and machetes, all well maintained and carefully hung from nails hammered into the two-by-four frame. I would watch my mother hosing down the concrete floor or driving pigs within the corral, slapping their hides with the flat side of a machete blade. Her students moved about with hurried efficiency, communicating over the clamor in shouts and hand signals.

NOW THE PIGS had come home. Each morning and every night, we fed them a runny slop of leftover rice, scraps, and swine ration that my mother brought home from the farm, unappetizing pellets composed of what appeared to be compressed sawdust. The piglets quickly grew accustomed to our routine, squealing happily when they heard us rustling though the beans with their breakfast, their slimy snouts sniffing with anticipation through the wooden slats of their pen. They came to recognize who fed them. My sister's ran to her. Mine to me. She named hers Pirate, a silly childish name, I felt. Mine remained nameless. Why name a chore?

In August, a death was announced on WSZD radio, as are all deaths of prominent Pohnpeians. A constant stream of mourners would arrive at the funeral and dine on a perpetual feast of rice, taro, chicken, pork, goat, dog, Spam and beer, food brought by people wishing to be seen in a favorable light by the family of the deceased. Funerals lasted several days, weeks even, allowing for distant relatives to come in from other islands throughout Micronesia. Before long, the grass would be stamped down to packed dirt, the mournful purpose of the gathering obscured by the heaps of discarded paper plates and beer cans.

The day after the radio announcement, a pickup pulled into our driveway. Four teenaged boys, two of them my mother's students, sat in the flatbed. A fat man climbed out of the cab and greeted my mother in the front yard. They talked quietly with their heads down, looking at nothing in particular, at the ground between them, at the grassy field across the road. Then everybody went around back, the boys carrying thick bamboo poles, rope and a crow bar.

The fat man inspected our pigs, bending over a little and peering through the slats to get a better sense of their size. He nodded, looked at my sister and me and smiled, as if we had done a fine job. Then he took out his wallet and handed my mother the money, snapping out twenties in an ostentatious display of island wealth. The boys pried off the slats and dragged the pigs squealing into the sunlight. After some struggle, the boys managed to lash the pigs to the bamboo poles and carry them back to the truck. The pigs grunted and squirmed, their eyes rolling as the ground passed beneath them.

My sister sobbed, tears slipping easily down her face. Much to my surprise, I felt like crying too, felt the threat of tears in my eyes, but such a display would be shameful in front of this man and my mother's students. Girls may cry over things like this, but boys may not. So I let the relief of no longer having to tend to the pigs, the sudden lifting of a burden, outweigh any sorrow I felt. As the truck pulled away, I watched the boys in the flatbed admire our summer project. Our pigs, having reached a respectable size, would be dead within an hour.

AT THE BEGINNING of each academic year, student groups were assigned a suckling. They were expected to name it, feed and water it, notch its ears to record vaccinations, chart its growth, and at the end of the fourth quarter, slaughter it.

The animal husbandry final exam took place in the guava orchard. Seven porkers, pigs raised specifically for meat, each weighing approximately two hundred pounds, were hung from the trees, their hind feet trussed to the strongest branch. Though disoriented, the porkers remained calm, ribbons of saliva spilling from their mouths. Big pots of water simmered over wood fires, smoke billowing through the trees. The students rushed about, nervously reviewing their notes, sharpening knives on whetstones. My mother made the rounds, observing each group. Were they working well together? Was one student doing all the work while the others did nothing? Were all their tools in place? She took notes on a clipboard, gave no coaching.

Then, on her signal, the team leader stabbed a short knife into the porker's neck. Squeals erupted throughout the orchard. If the incision was clean, the blood streamed neatly into a large bowl placed below the pig's head. If the knife only nicked the carotid artery or missed it altogether, blood would spray in a wide fan, dousing the students, the grass, the trunks of the trees, painting everything a viscous red. When the porkers slipped into cardiac arrest, the strongest members of each team steadied them, bracing their shoulders against the shuddering flanks.

As the pigs died, the screams ceased one by one like the extinguishing of lights throughout a house, until only an unnerving silence remained, save for the crackling of firewood and the soft rumble of boiling water. Then the team leader slit open the belly, releasing the intestines like a pit of snakes into the grass. Sometimes the heart would still beat faintly. Flies swarmed in from the piggery, drawn by the smell of disembowelment.

While some students waved away flies with coconut fronds, the others cut down the carcass and worked quickly, splashing boiling water onto the hide to relax the pores. Then they shaved the hides. The orchard sang with the metallic whisper of machete blades scraping away softened bristles. Then they dissected the pigs into parts outlined in mimeographed handouts, machetes rhythmically rising and falling, hacking through tendon and bone.

For our efforts that summer, my sister and I made a hundred dollars each: the sale price of our pigs minus a summer's worth of swine ration and the original price my mother paid the school for them. We had worked hard and deserved the money, she said. She told my sister that was enough crying and that we ought to be proud of ourselves. Her words did little to console Bambi, who ran off in tears, covering her mouth with her hand. My mother took the money to the local branch of Bank of Hawaii and put it into our college savings accounts.

THE FOLLOWING SUMMER, Bambi and I were finally big enough to help my mother on the farm. She no longer had to hire two of her students as farmhands. The first time I entered the piggery, the smell of shit overwhelmed me. It was a taste more than a smell, a concentrated thickness like a swarm of flies infesting my mouth and nose. I gagged. My eyes watered. My mother's hand was upon me, the collar of my T-shirt gathered in her fist.

"Don't you ever let me see you do that again," she said. "Do you understand me? Pigs stink. Toughen up and get used to it." She let go of my shirt, practically shoving me to the muddy floor. Bewildered by her anger, I stood blinking, shame soaking through me like rain. My sister, who had somehow understood the smell should go unnoticed, had witnessed the whole interchange and now busied herself with distributing sawdust in the pens, distancing herself from me, as if my mother might reprimand her for mere proximity to me. My mother handed me a push broom and told me to make myself useful and sweep manure into the gutters. She couldn't bring herself to look at me, so deep was her disappointment.

As the weeks passed, we stopped going swimming in the afternoons, lost interest in the greenhouse and guava trees. I learned to suppress my distaste for pigs. There was no trick to it. I hauled bags of swine ration over my shoulder, slung buckets of slop and elbowed my way through sounders of hungry boars. I gripped the splintered handle of the push broom and swept the pens aggressively. I stepped in slimy piles of shit and washed it off as if it were mud. My lips no longer curled involuntarily. No longer did I turn away in disgust. The harder I worked, the easier it got. This, if anything, was the trick: working hard.

A SOW DELIVERED on a windy night later that summer, her ghostly moans drifting across the field to our house. I lay in bed and listened to her farrowing. We had been waiting for her to deliver. She was overdue, huge, something out of its element, like a beached whale. She had stopped moving about her pen and could only eat lying down. This was her first gestation.

Early that morning we hurried to the farm, anxious to see the size of her farrow, worried she had not survived. She could barely lift her head as we approached the pen. The newborn piglets had freed themselves from their fetal membranes and were already suckling, eight of them, clean, pink, and perfect as jelly beans.

"Good girl," my mother said, patting the sow's snout. "That's a good girl."

jay ruben dayrit

Bambi found the runt half encased in membrane next to the afterbirth. At first, I thought it was dead until my mother nudged it with the toe of her boot. It tried to grunt but only opened and closed its mouth as if it were hungry. My mother turned it onto its back. Its hind legs were withered and bent inward like the thumbs of an infant.

My mother shook her head. "Too bad." And glancing at the tool shed, she picked up the piglet and handed it to me. "Go bury it."

It was light as a puppy. "But it's not dead."

"It's deformed," she said. "It's better to kill it."

"But how?" Though I was looking at my mother, I sensed the tools in the shed behind me, the scythe and the machetes waiting.

"Use a shovel."

I felt seasick, the ground shifting beneath my feet. I could not move for fear of falling.

"Go on. You can do it."

I turned and walked slowly to the shed. I picked the biggest shovel, guessing it might be the swiftest and most humane. I held the shovel in one hand and cradled the piglet in the palm of the other. I walked into the field where sweet potatoes had been harvested earlier that year, stepping over dirt clods that shot up in precarious angles. With each step, I had to steady myself to keep my legs from buckling. I walked past the center of the field until I reached the farthest corner from the piggery, its tin roof gleaming in the sun behind me.

I placed the piglet on the ground and dug a hole less than a foot deep. I weighed hitting the piglet with the shovel against decapitating it with the edge of the spade but felt incapable of doing either, both equally cruel and horrific. Racked with indecision, I swept the piglet along the ground with the spade, rolling it toward the hole, its damp skin picking up bits of dirt and tiny roots. It let out a grunt when it hit the bottom of the hole. I threw dirt on it as it struggled to right itself. It let out a squeal. I threw more dirt in the hole, just covering the piglet. It wiggled beneath the soil like a worm. I shoveled more dirt but could still hear its cries filtering up through the ground. It would not stop so I raised the shovel above my head and slammed the spade onto the mound repeatedly until the earth stopped moving, until my arms ached, until I realized the cries were not coming from the ground but from me. I leaned into the shovel and sobbed.

My sister appeared behind me. "You okay?"

"No."

She let me cry for a while, allowing the sobs to dissipate. "Go wash your face in the river," she said. "Don't let Mom see you like this."

When I returned to the piggery, Bambi was helping my mother rinse out troughs in the corral. "Did you do it?" my mother asked.

"Yes," I said.

"It would only have suffered."

THE DAY THE DOCTORS began looking for cancer, having ruled out lupus and all three types of hepatitis, brought about a shift in our language. We would utter words like biopsy and pathology, malignant and metastasis, the lexicon of oncology lurching from our mouths like a second language, awkward but necessary. Perhaps it was leukemia that caused my mother's liver to enlarge. Or maybe it was some kind of tumor manifesting itself in mysterious rashes, raging and waning, along the small of her back and across her eyes in the shape of insect wings, as if a dragonfly had alighted on the bridge of her nose and cast its purple shadow there. Sometimes when she thought no one was looking, my mother would run her fingers across these raised bumps with curiosity and bewilderment, the way the seeing touch Braille. What does this mean? Who can make sense of all this?

Though no definitive diagnosis had been made, no prognosis charted, I sat on the edge of the bed and cried, so hunched over in grief I felt my spine might form a complete circle. My father fidgeted quietly with his hands, turning them over in one another. My mother waited for the tears to cease, and when they did not, she asked me, "Why are you crying?" But she knew.

Since boarding school, I could count on both hands the number of times I had seen my parents, summers and Christmases in high school and only twice at college, graduation being one of those times. Despite the generous scholarships, my parents could not afford to bring us home during breaks. Summer school became the norm. The cumulative time of those few and increasingly rare visits added up to less than a year. And now, it seemed the last time I had seen my mother, I was thirteen, saying good-bye to her on the tarmac of the Pohnpei airport off to my freshman year at Mid-Pacific Institute. Eleven years later, I was saying good-bye to her again.

I could not bring myself to say, "Because I am scared." Simple enough, but it proved, even in light of her mortality, an insurmountable task. "Because we haven't had enough time together," was all I could manage to say.

"Your education was more important," my mother said. "It was a sacrifice we knew we had to make."

THE MORNING of my mother's funeral, I awoke to find my father consoling my sister. They lay side by side in my parents' bed, his arm around her as if cradling a child. Shock had engulfed us. We had gone through the motions, signing death certificates, filling out life insurance forms, finding a funeral home, in a white emotionless haze. My sister had finally broken. Her eyes were red with exhaustion. My father motioned me toward them. Though awkwardly conscious of being a full-grown man in my father's arms, I crawled into bed next to them. This was our family now, a nuclear family without its nucleus. Without a center to hold us, we clung to each other as if we might spin away and become lost in our own separate lives: my sister, newly married and settled in Virginia, me in San Francisco, my father alone on Pohnpei.

My father told us of how in the early morning hours of her final days, they would talk about their life together and what might happen after she had gone. The farm would surely fall into disrepair. No other teacher could maintain it as well as she had. Swine production would cease. The fields would be absorbed back into the jungle. But she was more concerned about us. She wanted my father to be more of a father, to offer support and advice whenever we might need it, to visit us often. She wanted my sister to start a family, to raise bold and intelligent children. But she worried about me the most, my father said. She worried that since sending me off to school, she had watched a shy quiet boy grow into a bitter, angry, distant man.

"She said it was like you have barnacles around your heart," my father confessed. "She worried that her passing would close you off completely."

I was startled. How we felt about anything, good or bad, especially bad, had found precious little real estate in the landscape of our interactions as a family. We were practical, hardworking people, with no time for emotions. "Salt of the earth," my father often said with a bit of pride in his voice. And now he had gone against his stoic nature and so poetically laid out their fear before me, the fear that I would be lost to them, to anyone really, forever. Perhaps my mother understood her role in this. I can only guess that regret led her to confide in my father that of the family that would survive her, I worried her the most, the son who stood at the edge of a field and buried more than a piglet, the son who since then would wash his face in denial at every incidence of anger or fear or sorrow, even the sorrow over her death. Was what I imagined to be strength in fact so destructive and isolating as to conjure the image of barnacles? I could feel them adhering to my heart, shielding, suffocating. Still, I lay in my father's arms feeling revealed, and simultaneously, relieved, and on the day that we buried my mother, the first barnacle detached and fell away.

slowly becoming

malidoma somé

THERE IS A CLOSE relationship between grandfathers and grandchildren. The first few years of a boy's life are usually spent, not with his father, but with his grandfather. What the grandfather and grandson share together—that the father cannot—is their close proximity to the cosmos. The grandfather will soon return to where the grandson came from, so therefore the grandson is bearer of news the grandfather wants. The grandfather will do anything to make the grandson communicate the news of the ancestors before the child forgets, as inevitably happens. My grandfather obtained this news through hypnosis, putting me to sleep in order to question me.

It is not only to benefit the grandfather that this relationship with his grandson must exist. The grandfather must also transmit the "news" to the grandson using the protocol secret to grandfathers and grandsons. He must communicate to this new member of the community the hard tasks ahead on the bumpy road of existence.

malidoma somé

For the Dagara, every person is an incarnation, that is, a spirit who has taken on a body. So our true nature is spiritual. This world is where one comes to carry out specific projects. A birth is therefore the arrival of someone, usually an ancestor that somebody already knows, who has important tasks to do here. The ancestors are the real school of the living. They are the keepers of the very wisdom the people need to live by. The life energy of ancestors who have not yet been reborn is expressed in the life of nature, in trees, mountains, rivers and still water. Grandfathers and grandmothers, therefore, are as close to an expression of ancestral energy and wisdom as the tribe can get. Consequently their interest in grandsons and granddaughters is natural. An individual who embodies a certain value would certainly be interested in anyone who came from the place where that value existed most purely. Elders become involved with a new life practically from the moment of conception because that unborn child has just come from the place they are going to.

A few months before birth, when the grandchild is still a fetus, a ritual called a "hearing" is held. The pregnant mother, her brothers, the grandfather, and the officiating priest are the participants. The child's father is not present for the ritual, but merely prepares the space. Afterward, he is informed about what happened. During the ritual, the incoming soul takes the voice of the mother (some say the soul takes the whole body of the mother, which is why the mother falls into trance and does not remember anything afterward) and answers every question the priest asks.

The living must know who is being reborn, where the

soul is from, why it chose to come here, and what gender it has chosen. Sometime, based on the life mission of the incoming soul, the living object to the choice of gender and suggest that the opposite choice will better accommodate the role the unborn child has chosen for him- or herself. Some souls ask that specific things be made ready before their arrival—talismanic power objects, medicine bags, metal objects in the form of rings for the ankle or the wrist. They do not want to forget who they are and what they have come here to do. It is hard not to forget, because life in this world is filled with many alluring distractions. The name of the newborn is based upon the results of these communications. A name is the life program of its bearer.

A child's first few years are crucial. The grandfather must tell the grandson what the child said while still a fetus in his mother's womb. Then, he must gradually help him build a connection with his father, who will help him with the hard challenges up ahead. My father used to complain that his life was calamitous because he never knew his grandfather, who disappeared before he was born. Had he known him, my father said, he would never have lost his first family, never spent his youth working in a gold mine or later embraced the Catholic religion with a fervor grander than the one that linked him to his ancestors. His stepbrothers, who knew their grandfather, did not have the kind of restlessness that plagued my father. The frustration of a grandfatherless male child has no cure.

In the beginning, the intense intimacy between the grandson and the grandfather might create feelings of jealousy in the father. While a grandfather is alive, the grandchildren do not have much of anything to learn from their father—until they reach their preadolescent age. And the father knows that. He knows that a conversation between a grandson and a grandfather is a conversation between brothers of the same knowledge group. To know is to be old. In that, the grandson is as old as the grandfather. Consequently, the father is too young to have a part in this relationship between wise men.

I used to spend much of my days in the company of my grandfather. He was a man worn out by hard work, who at the age of sixty was virtually a child—weak and sick, yet with a mind still as alert as that of a man in the prime of youth. He also possessed incomparable wisdom stored over the course of half a century of sustained healing and medicine works.

Grandfather was thin and tall. Since I had first known him, he always wore the same traditional *boubou*. It had been white when he first got it, but in order to avoid the cost of maintenance, he had changed the white color of the cloth into red, using the juice of some roots that he alone knew the secret of. In use twenty-four hours a day, the boubou was simultaneously his daily outfit, his pajamas, and his blanket. After more than a decade, it had turned into a remnant of himself, blackened by sweat and dirt. Though most of the boubou had fallen off under the weight of filth, it still hung firmly on his shoulders, its general architecture intact. Unlike modern Christianity, which links cleanliness to godliness, Dagara culture holds the opposite to be true. The more intense the involvement with the life of the spirit, the more holy and wise an individual is, the less attention is paid to outward beauty. Grandfather owned a walking stick carved with artistic dexterity, its wood also darkened from long usage. His movements were slow, and I found it easier to be around him than around the other kids, who were older, stronger and more agile than I was. So every day, while everybody was at the farm, I was with Grandfather.

Grandfather knew every story ever told or even heard of in the tribe. And at his age he looked as if storytelling were the only thing he could still do with success. He utilized this talent very well since that was the only way he could gain attention. Each time I sat in his lap, he took it as a request for a story, and he would always begin by asking a question.

"Brother Malidoma, do you know why the bat sits upside down?"

"No. Why?"

"Long, long time ago, and I mean long when I say long because that was when animals used to speak to men and men to animals and both to God."

"Then why don't animals speak to men anymore?"

"They still do, only we have forgotten how to comprehend them!"

"What happened?"

"Never mind. We're talking about bats, and why they all sit upside down."

"Yes. I want to know why they do that."

"Well, see, there was a time when Brother Bat died and no one knew who he was. The town crier took his body to the crocodile, saying, 'The jaws of this damn thing look like they were borrowed from a crocodile. I thought he might be your relative or something.'

malidoma somé

"The crocodile said, 'It's true that this guy's got a mouth like mine, but I ain't got no brother with fur, let alone with wings.'

"So, next the town crier took the dead bat to the head of the birds tribe."

"And who's that?"

"It's Mother Sila, you know, the bird that flies high and shoots herself down like an arrow when she goes to catch her dinner. Mother Sila said, 'This animal looks like it's got good wings and reasonable claws, but I never saw anyone in my family with so few feathers.'

"And so, finally the town crier gave up and threw the bat into a ditch. But when Papa Bat found out about this, he was very angry. He rebelled against God and ordered the whole tribe never to look up to God again. Since then bats never turn their faces upward."

"Grandfather, this is too sad. Tell me another one."

Grandfather never had to be begged. He would tell you a story even without your asking. And the times you asked, he would keep on talking until you "unasked" him.

He also knew how to hypnotize you—to speak you to sleep—when he needed to be left alone to do some important work. He never chased a child away from him; in fact, he always thought children were the most cooperative people on earth. One just needed to know how to use their generous services. A sleeping child is even more obedient than a child awake, and so he would often hypnotize one of us, then awaken us into a state where we would be dispatched to run errands for him. Any child seen silently looking for something, who would not respond when you asked, "What are you looking for?" was a sleeping child on an errand for grandfather. He did not like to request the services of grown-ups because they would grumble and swear the whole time. He always said that the good in a service has little to do with the service itself, but with the kind of heart one brings to the task. For him, an unwilling heart spoiled a service by infecting it with feelings of resentment and anger.

Grandfather knew how to talk to the void, or rather to some unseen audience of spirits. Among the Dagara, the older you get the more you begin to notice spirits and ancestors everywhere. When you hear a person speaking out loud, alone, you don't talk to them because he or she may be discussing an important issue with a spirit or an ancestor. This rule applies more to holy elders than to adults in general. When I was with Grandfather, I felt as if there were more people around than could be accounted for. When he knew I was not following his stories, he used to redirect his speech to these invisible beings. He never seemed bothered by my not listening.

GRANDFATHER'S RESPECT and love for children was universal in the tribe. To the Dagara, children are the most important members of society, the community's most precious treasures. We have a saying that it takes the whole tribe to raise a child. Homes have doorless entrances to allow children to go in and out wherever they want, and it is common for a mother to not see her child for days and nights because he or she is enjoying the care and love of other people.

When the mother really needs to be with her child, she will go from home to home searching for it.

When a child grows into an adolescent, he or she must be initiated into adulthood. A person who doesn't get initiated will remain an adolescent for the rest of their life, and this is a frightening, dangerous, and unnatural situation. After initiation, the elders will pick a partner for the young person, someone who is selected for their ability to team up with you in the fulfillment of your life purpose. If one obediently walks their life path, they will become an elder somewhere in their late forties or early fifties. Graduating to this new status, however, depends on one's good track record.

A male elder is the head of his family. He has the power to bless, and the power to withhold blessing. This ability comes to him from his ancestors, to whom he is very close, and he follows their wisdom in counseling his large family.

Wealth among the Dagara is determined not by how many things you have, but by how many people you have around you. A person's happiness is directly linked to the amount of attention and love coming to him or her from other people. In this, the elder is the most blessed because he is in the most visible position to receive a lot of attention. The child is too, because it "belongs" to the whole community.

Some elders are chosen to sit on the village council. There they participate in decision making that affects the entire village. Women have their council separate from men because of their unique roles and responsibilities. Dagara culture is matrilineal—everybody in the village carries the name of their mother. The family is feminine, the house where the family live is kept by a male. The male is in charge of the family security. The female is in charge of the continuity of life. She rules the kitchen, the granaries where food is stored, and the space where meals are taken. The male is in charge of the medicine shrine and of the family's connection with the ancestors. He brings the things that nourish the family, like food.

FOR A FULL FIFTY YEARS, my grandfather had been the priest, the leader, and the counselor of a family of over fifty souls. Faced with domestic problems of all kinds, he had had to be tough. Judging from his physical appearance—muscles still protruding from tired biceps, square shoulders that looked as if they could still carry weight, big chest that seemed to hide massive lungs—one could see that he had been a robust young man capable of sustaining long hours of demanding physical labor. Grandfather's greatest fame, however, came from his spiritual accomplishments. In the village, everyone knew him as the "upside-down arrow shooter." He was one of the people in the tribe whose name made people shudder, for if he wished to destroy an enemy, he would retire to the quiet of his chambers, place an arrow upside down on his bow, and magically hit his target. The arrow would kill whomever or whatever he named, then re-materialize in his chamber ready for more. The slightest scratch from such a weapon is mortal.

Other tribes did not dare go into conflict with ours because they did not possess the secret of such deadly magic.

Consequently, Grandfather rarely had a chance to demonstrate to the tribe his power in battle. The arrow did have peacetime uses, however. Grandfather used it to protect our family farm from the nocturnal raids of wild beasts. Although he could no longer work the fields, Grandfather could still in this manner contribute to our food supply. He also displayed the upside-down arrow as a persuasive weapon to warn evildoers away from our family, the Birifor.

Grandfather was no longer strong enough to walk the six miles between the house and the farm every day, and as far as I can recall, I never saw him go there. Because the people of my tribe practice slash-and-burn agriculture, their fields are often very far away as people keep moving them around year after year to avoid exhausting the soil. I was born too late to know Grandfather as a more vigorous man. When I was a child, he spent his days sitting in the same place in the central yard of the labyrinthine compound that housed our family group. Sometimes he was pensive, calmly and wisely dispatching legal matters without so much as raising his head or the tone of his voice. He had great knowledge of healing matters as well. Without so much as glancing up from the pots that held the food and medicinal items he dispensed, he could tell young people who had physical problems which roots they should dig up and bring back to him in the evening for their cures.

At night, when everyone else was asleep, Grandfather would watch over the farm and the compound from his room. Through the use of complex and magical security devices, his thoughts were constantly tuned in to the vibration of the farm, and he could always determine whether the fields were being raided by wild animals. The device he used to keep vigil consisted of a clay pot filled with "virgin water," rainfall that had never touched the earth in its fall from the sky. He saw everything that happened throughout the farm by looking into this water. The precision of vision it afforded superseded the simplicity of this device.

Grandfather's magical guardianship had enabled our family to always have enough food to eat. Two thirds of the tribe did not share our surplus and could never put aside enough extra food to avoid the hardship of the hunger season, which ran every year from July to September, when stored food ran out. During this time, a mild famine visited many compounds. Children would stop singing and laughter would vanish from the houses at night. Every morning during that time, a long line of people stood at the door of the Birifor house, waiting for a calabash of grains. Distributing food to all these needy people was another of Grandfather's tasks. So, every morning of those misty days of July and August, after he had given orders to the men and women of the family regarding their daily assignments, Grandfather would drag himself to the door of his room. There, he would take all the time he needed to be seated comfortably. I would wait calmly until he was settled, then I would sit on his bony lap. Aided by a woman whose charge it was to measure up the proper amount of millet to be distributed to each of the needy, Grandfather would dispatch his task until shortly after noontime when the heat became unbearable.

Usually, at that particular time of the day, I would fall asleep on his lap. He would wake me up later with a song that rang more like a cry—Grandfather's voice was terrible. Then he would say, "Brother Malidoma, my legs can't hold you any longer. Please allow them to breathe too." And still half asleep, I would stand up and wait, wondering what had happened.

After the rite of charity, one of the women brought food to Grandfather and me, and we ate together. Grandfather was very frugal. I remember him once explaining to my father that the weight of undigested food closed the body and the mind off from the ability to perceive the surrounding good and bad vibrations. He who ate too much increased his vulnerability. The good taste of food hid the danger it put the body into. Grandfather's philosophy was that food is a necessary evil.

For this reason, the attitude toward food in our family was strange. One ate only when absolutely necessary. Grandfather could tell who was eating too much. For children under six, he encouraged food. For adults, he encouraged frugality. He used to rage at certain adolescents who, in his eyes, had no control of their appetite, saying, "Initiation will be a bitter experience when you come of age. Now is the time you must learn to control the drives of your body. Be alert and firm. Do not let the desire for physical satisfactions temper your warriorship. Remember, our ancestors are spirits, they feed only their minds and that is why they can do things beyond our comprehension."

When Grandfather started speaking, he did not particularly care whether someone was listening or not. Speaking was a liberating exercise for him, an act of mental juggling. He would sometimes speak for hours, as if he had a big spirit audience around him. He would laugh, get angry and storm at invisible opponents, and then become quiet once more. When he had a real audience, as he did every evening at storytelling time, he would teach us all through his tales. He would speak until everyone fell asleep, then would rail at us, saying that sleep was a dangerous practice no different from that of eating too much food. For Grandfather, sleep was tribute we pay to the body far too often. He would often say that the body is merely the clothing of the soul and that it is not good to pay too much attention to it, as if it were really us. "Leave your body alone, and it will align itself to the needs of the spirit you are."

Grandfather's space housed the pharmacy of the entire Birifor clan—an array of roots, daily collected, nightly prepared, to face emergencies of all sorts. These little dwellings contained the prosperity—spiritual, material, and magical— of the Birifor. Some of these roots were good for physical illness, but most of them were good for illness of the soul. These little buildings held the spiritual destiny of every member of the family. There, each one of us existed in the form of a stone, silent, docile, available. The stones represented the birth certificate of every person in the clan. This is where Grandfather went to examine the physical and spiritual energy fields of the people under his care. Through this magical means, Grandfather could check on each of us at his leisure.

He took care of people outside the family too. Strangers used to come now and then to seek medical help, and Grandfather would begin long ceremonial rites that took most of the day. Sometimes the strangers would bring

chickens and, speaking breathlessly in an unintelligible magical language, he would cut their throats and direct the
spurting blood onto some statues, representing different
spirits, carved out of wood or built against the wall. He
never tired of rituals. It took me many years to understand
the reasons behind these visits and how Grandfather was
able to help these strangers.

me and isisara sing oldies
peter j. harris

ME AND ISISARA driving home from a concert at the Hollywood Bowl that featured Tito Puente, Eddie Palmieri and Ruben Blades. Turn on KGFJ-AM, the Black-owned Los Angeles radio station that plays mostly oldies-but-goodies, or "dusties," according to the station's announcers. I've known Isisara since we both lived in Baltimore in the late '70s, and she's one of several girlfriends whose friendships-without-sex ground and extend my manhood.

After the concert, we can barely sit still in the car, wishing that the salsa and musical et cetera buzzing in our heads and bodies would play forever. The DJ answers our prayers through the magic of late-night radio. He starts a powerful medley with "(La La) Means I Love You," by the Delfonics. Before we know it, DJ Genie is granting our wishes with even more house party classics: "Tracks of My Tears," by the Miracles, "Baby I'm for Real," by the Originals, and, summing up sensationally, LaBelle's "Isn't It a Shame."

Driving from one red light to the next, Isisara and I can't

help but sing along loudly to each song. Neither one of us, truth be told, is really hitting too many notes. She's chasing the lead singers of the men's groups right up the scale until her falsetto croaks with enthusiasm. I'm right beside her echoing with mournful exaggeration Patti LaBelle's "unh unh unh unh unh unh" in the middle of "Isn't It a Shame." At first we tried to talk during our mobile karaoke session, conjuring up memories of where we were when such-and-such song came out, what we were doing, and whom we were with. But the beauty of the music and the purity of the recollections finally inspired us into our own version of Marvin and Tammi.

Balancing the moment without one ounce of self-consciousness (just the way me and my boys do it), we link our singing with the jamming we did earlier to the fufu-pounding grooves played by El Rey and Palmieri and Blades. I notice we getting too close to my street where she's parked her car. Oh no! This session will not be ending with us parallel parking. Not long as I'm driving!

I take a right turn down a street into what Richard Pryor would no doubt call a "residential district." I drive around that block twice. The recorded band plays on. I brazenly take unintended turns down other dark side streets. Under the spell of Wilbur Hart of the Delfonics, Smokey the Miracle, and Isisara's passionate testifying, I even start braking for yellow lights hundreds of feet before coming to an intersection, so we can extend our off-key concert and revel in our sing-song friendship.

· · ·

THIS IS DEDICATED with love to the immortal sisters in my life and the woman in me. I honor the laughter between us. The laughter that, from the git go, leavened our togetherness. When we stood at the Crossroads and teetered between stripping off our clothes or stepping into the serious territory of a nourishing friendship, that laughter cooled us out and shored up the common wavelength we felt about ideas, politics, culture.

These are my sisters, yall; not asexual. Aint saying that. We adults and close enough to still feel the sensuality between us. We know how to wring a hug of friendship for all that sincere touch is worth. But these are my sisters, yall; we've cultivated an honest intimacy that has freed us to be each other's sounding boards, honest counsel, and tough-love mirrors when the lovers in our lives drive us crazy.

We love each other, yall. I got their back. They got mine. We do not talk in clichés, snatches of Terry McMillan novels, or across ideological chasms. We got our own diction. I talk about different things with different women. The wealth that one sister has is different from the wealth of another. They look different. They act different. They single. They paired. They make love with men. They make love with women.

They all bad, though.

They in business for themselves. They employed in white-collar jobs. One wear hard hat, Levi's & punch that clock. This one teach children, that one teach adults. She's brown skin and got straight hair. She's redbone and got locks. All can say motherfucker on the downbeat. Quote Mudbone and bell hooks. Will call me with a question, command, or demand. Will not screen their calls when I fire up the fiber optics.

Bone honest!

Will tell me, when necessary, damn brother, maybe you should have thought about this before you did that. Or nod OK OK, I can see why you told that sister to kiss your ass. Will admit they blew it with a lover, if their hindsight really is 20/20. Or will stand ground until it grows vegetables if they believe they did the right thing.

Our thing is not a dick-and-pussy thang, is what I'm saying.

These are my sisters, yall, and we are friends who know that what keeps is love.

Take Nikky, my South Carolina–born pen pal since 1981. Voice like spring afternoons. Dreads like soft white-water. We never even met until 1985, but in those first four years we became friends cause we both loved translating for each other the gospel-voices we'd hear daily while eaves-dropping on the conversations of Black folk. Embellishing their testimony with our own tall tales! We have swapped philosophy and encouragement, turned each other on to magazines and books publishing poetry, consoled each other when the pain of relationships overwhelmed us, and often found cause to cuss out the president, Jesse Helms, or some other rep of official U.S. policy.

Besides that, and deeper than deep, every spring Nikky sends me an envelope full of leaves and seeds and twigs and dirt in the mail.

The first time, she surprised me with a potpourri she'd gathered from the ground in Alabama, where she was working at her alma mater, Talladega College. Then she moved to Atlanta, and I got leaves and flower petals that kept Georgia on my mind. When she relocated to the San Francisco Bay Area, where I was living and where we finally met, we could sift the same foliage without having to pack samples into envelopes. Then I moved to D.C. for four years and she sent me teeny piles of eucalyptus leaves to remind me of the bracing vistas, fresh air and pungent politics of the Bay Area. When she moved to Lexington, Kentucky, to teach English at the university there, I got bluegrass.

Over the years, she's also stuffed her envelopes with poetic notes and letters, sometimes typed, most often written in a camouflaged handwriting that often mystifies me. Even now, I still haven't translated certain words from letters she wrote me in the months after we first met.

I used to bug her to tell me what she'd written, but now I fill in the unbroken code with my own word. I laugh and shake my head that she could become an esteemed Black college graduate with handwriting look like fingerpainting.

Irregardless (oops! I thought her and me were on the phone knee-deep in passionate Black English), after all these years I know that whatever she saying, it's encouraging or loving, or inventive, cause that's her style.

Nikky will tell a cliché to go pick out a switch! We start talking and I get this image of Ashford & Simpson in full, creative stride, ideas strutting and wearing spats. No censorship in the mix whatsoever, two friends intent on turning a phrase that will come back to haunt us.

Like that time she told me, "Boy, you was born six feet under, with your crazy self!" I heard so much blues guitar playing in her voice I promised her I was stealing the line to write a poem. Did, too! It wasn't burglary, neither, cause swapping breast milk is what me and Nikky do for each other.

THEN WHEN I NEED my milk spiked with equal parts sincerity and profanity, I call on JB, Atlanta-born, San Francisco entrepreneur. We can ask each other the hard questions we need, when at home we're looking in the mirrors and reflecting only easy answers. As playful as we get, we can listen so hard to each other sound like rigor mortis set in or the phone line's gone dead. But the follow-up, weighed down with insight or challenge when one or both of us has lapsed into easy-speak, makes it clear there's been a whole lot of listening going to what's been said and to what's lurking between the lines.

JB has been a stockbroker and now manages people's estates and conducts financial seminars. She reads business literature like my aunt reads the Bible, and can do deals while painting her toenails. Naturally, I ask her about money. How to save it. How to make it. How to use it wisely. She got answers and often has her secretary send me an article about some dude who uses his computer, modem, and fax to operate his business successfully out of his own apartment.

When the subject inevitably shifts to relationships, JB will wedge into my logic with monologues of her own. They're full of the lessons she's learned navigating the free enterprise system as a lawyer, MBA, and real estate agent running her own business for five years, and as a single, straight, Black woman dating in the spiritual capital of gay

America. Sometimes, despite her professional success, her interpersonal confidence lapses, and she'll ask me for a "man's point of view." I bring my brown bag full of the benefit-of-the-doubt for the dude who's caused her some grief, and a personal refusal to hang my shingle on the hook of double standards. I know she wants the truth as I see it, but I know JB does not stand for the BS.

After we scrape the mold off our hearts, we might talk about some ball—she's a regular at Golden State Warriors games and will pack up some blankets to brave the winds at Candlestick Park. But we don't talk just the scores—JB brainstorms about how to get access to the players so she can pitch her services as a legal rep. Or we'll let down our guards all the way at a concert by Paul Mooney, who manufacturers comic nitroglycerine from the raw material of Black folk in America. Laughing so hard we make that deep-throat sound like Bobby Blue Bland at full throttle. Afterwards, on the way home or sitting in a club nursing a drink, I hear her asking, "How come I can't have fun like this with the men in my life?"

Not that she's expecting me to answer using a line coated with chocolate from Ghirardelli Square. She's just feeling safe enough to float the moan, knowing I won't take target practice with her vulnerability. Cause after all, she didn't do nothing but cradle my statement that time I owned up to feeling like a failure after the breakup of my second marriage. We both know when to allow for a little wallowing, but never so much we can't sense when it's time to pull each other back to the essential ground of self-worthiness.

There are other sisters with whom I share an adult intimacy.

I might not see Dr. Walker for years, but we stay in touch through her postcards from Martinique or Bahia, Cameroon or Senegal, where she can be found studying African religions and languages, scuba diving to touch the sunken hull of a Spanish galleon, dancing on beat with the exact steps of a national dance, or otherwise living her Zora Neale Hurston–inspired life as a twenty-first-century anthropologist.

Only the miles between L.A. and New York separate me from TV producer JP, who tirelessly tries to ensure that some substantial Black programming winds up on one of America's long-running talk shows. When she takes a break from those battles, she'll call me with a conversation that's both eclectic and weird.

For example: stomach–churning puns and jokes. Sincere offers to give me money if I'm between jobs. Excited sighs about the new long-distance love inspiring her to speak her clearest emotional vocabulary. Then she'll suddenly inter-ject sound effects that melt conversation altogether. Her impression of Curly of the Three Stooges ("Woo woo woo!") always makes me answer with woo woo woos of my own. Next thing I know, she's turning me onto somebody in Lex-ington, Kentucky, or St. Louis, Missouri, who's coordinating a Black Holistic Retreat down on a South Carolina sea is-land. We silly and serious, like that, cause sometimes only friend can give you permission to be free.

. . .

I LEARNED to be cool with these sisters outside my house from being cool with sisters inside my house.

My mother, June Puckett Harris, set the tone for me. At rock bottom she was fair. If I slammed the door, or my oldest brother slammed the door, she'd punish us both by making us open and close the door—and walk in and out the apartment—50 times without slamming it once. We ate food, so we had to wash dishes. We tracked dirt into the house, so we had to get down on our knees and wash floors.

She made me feel smart and worthy. When I started third grade, she transferred me to an elementary school in southwest. On my first day at school, she rode the bus with me from our stop on Trenton Street all the way over to the waterfront and back again. Once. Then I was on my own. She'd shown me all the stops, drawing my attention to landmarks, and convinced me I could do it. From the third grade to the eighth grade, when I returned to a school in southeast, I rode the bus without incident.

Throughout my elementary school years, on one Saturday a year, she used to take me to work with her for a paying gig helping her pack and store outdated files. I didn't get paid until after I'd completed the work to her satisfaction. Ma was what me and my brothers and sisters call "regular," which meant being true to yourself from the inside out. Skin color—and Moms could have passed for white— didn't matter. Only how you acted. She treated everybody with respect until they no longer deserved it. She loved little rituals like playing board games, Friday night meals from Mickey-D's, and blasting symphonic music while we cleaned house on Saturdays. She loved to laugh as long as the joke wasn't at somebody else's expense.

She taught with common sense, like the time during a crisis in my first marriage when she asked me how things were going. I told her it was cool and her smirk X-rayed me so deep I got defensive and protested till tears came to my eyes. She laughed in my face and said, "If this is how you look when you're happy, I shudder to think how you'd look when you're sad!" She was so right I wound up laughing myself.

She had principles up the yin yang, too. When Ma felt my estranged first wife was using our son and daughter as weapons against me, her daughter-in-law received a "Dear John" letter, CC'd to me. Ma told her she wasn't welcome in our family home again until she shared the kids. She never saw my kids again until she was lying on her deathbed at Southeast Community Hospital.

That's where Ma taught me my final lesson about grace under pressure. While lying on her back with an IV in her arm and a tube in her trachea, she dictated her funeral arrangements to me in a husky whisper, making sure I wrote clearly with my shaky hands. When I looked up at her and said, "What the hell am I doing?" she just smiled and said, "Who else?"

I slept in the room that night. I'll never forget the sound of the respirator breathing for her, the beep of the heart monitor. I'll never forget the rasp of her feathery chuckle and the grip of her faith that I could take dictation right.

Ma died in 1984. She was my first girl friend. My first sister. Her vibe still lifts me. Gives me confidence to be regular in my friendships with other women. My normal relationships with my two younger sisters, Carla and Anna, are also part of the foundation of the hook-ups with my girlfriends. I'm three years older than Anna and I got Carla by 11 years. In recent years, I've gotten closer to both of them.

But me and Anna got the neon connection. Rilly, Anna Elizabeth Harris is the ultimate round-the-way girl for me. Black without a whole lot of intellectual tripping. Open minded enough to learn if you come at her without condescension. Open hearted enough to roll with the ups and downs that come with love. Christian without being a missionary, yet down enough every now and then to hit that dance floor, drink a brew, wine, or whiskey, and find Saturday night solace in some classic Delfonics. I can sing oldies with Isisara because I been in the family glee club with Anna for most of my life.

My oldest little sister is also my boy, you know. We not only give each other fives, but crack up redoing them '70s handshakes D.C. folk used to give each other, our thumbs locked, hands raised over our heads, fingers fluttering like butterfly wings. Anna's laugh is like carbonated spring water, a gift that chases depression and intensifies joy. We're twins born 1,000 days apart. Together, we got a profane sense of humor and a fierce sense of intimacy. We can lounge at cookouts, holler at Frankie Beverly and Maze concerts, reminisce with impressions of Ma on a clean-up rampage, and even laugh at ourselves.

During a recent visit to D.C., after we'd spent a day together, me and Anna returned to the apartment where she lives with her husband and children. Soon as we walked in the door, she immediately got to hollering at her 15-year-old son and preteen daughter: "Look at this house yall! Didn't I tell you to . . ." I swear we could have been standing in our old apartment after Ma had just arrived from work demanding to know why we hadn't done the dishes, cleaned up the crumbs on the kitchen counter, and made up our beds. Her kids made the same faces me and Anna used to make—petrified annoyance.

When I thought she'd gone overboard, I did my exaggerated impression of Anna tripping:

"That's right yall! Didn't I tell you this place needed a new coat of paint? How come yall didn't reupholster the cushions in this sofa? And you better had installed some track lighting in the bathroom like I told you!"

The kids relax. Even Anna chuckles. The drama has ended, but I'm on a roll now.

"Unh unh! Didn't I tell yall to build a new wall between the living room and the kitchen? I know I'm supposed to be smelling some new plaster up in here! I bet you still got windows in your bedrooms, don't you; I told you to board them all up before I got back! You don't need no sunlight! Now come on over here and give me a hug!"

Everybody's laughing now. Anna says, "Aww, I aint that bad," owning up at the same time. Recognizing that it is a trip how we can slip back into the grooves that raised us, when we least expect it. Fortunately, that June Harris groove is wide and offers us many rhythms. There was Anna a few minutes later cooling out and hugging her children, accepting that kids will be kids, even though she's committed to helping them become responsible for making their home into a crib where company can come over and always feel at ease.

Anna lets me school her and I let her school me. If I got a crisis, I know I can get her ear. When I got good news, I know she will squeal the loudest. When her son writes a detective story, I'm the first who gets a copy. When her daughter makes the honor roll, the phone rings so Uncle Peter can get the news. If I need to recall a detail from our childhood, Anna is my griot. When she needs reassurance that we can stand tall without our late mother and father, I'm her rock.

Then sometimes, we simply need to celebrate the sacred silliness between us. She surprised me once and mailed me an envelope containing a letter and picture of me in 1973. I'm proudly wearing, insanely wearing a sky-blue polyester double-knit suit (with bell bottoms would make Lenny Kravitz faint with envy). Burgundy bow tie, with white polka dots, match my puffed-sleeve shirt, which is the color of a cold glass of Boone's Farm wine.

Within minutes of opening the envelope, I dial her phone number, staring at that picture as I wait for her to answer. She picks up and we leap immediately into crazy ignant signifying. She derisively reminds me, "You swore you was hip in that suit! The bad thing about it, though, is that I thought you was hip in that suit. I was young, though. What was your excuse? But even the Temptations would have kicked your ass off stage wearing that cheap polyester, and you know they wore some lime green jump suits straight out the Eleganza catalogue their own selves!"

Even if I had a comeback, I was laughing too hard to hit

her with it. But it's cool. She could only come at me with the truth. I'm glad that's the lesson Anna has taught me. It's served me well over the years, whether I'm standing with steel and sincerity behind or between my girlfriends, or sitting behind the wheel seriously singing in deep and friendly harmony with Isisara.

My sister has taught me how to be a brother to the woman in my soul and the women in my life.

from *jarhead*
anthony swofford

DURING OUR SECOND TRIP from the Triangle to the rear-rear, in the middle of October, I become rather sick over the realization that the base we've been ordered to enjoy—showers, private toilets perfect for soothing mastur-bation, two bunks and an air conditioner per room, side-walks, televisions, VCRs, chow hall, pogey-shack—is probably not, as we've been told, an abandoned oil company camp, but actually a military base that had sat vacant for years, waiting for the American protectors to arrive in the event of a regional conflict, protectors who'd be tolerated until they obliterated the threat and returned the region's massive oil reserves to their proper owners. We are soldiers for the vast fortunes of others. I realize this while sitting on a shitter and reading the English-language *Arab Times.* Sec-retary of Defense Dick Cheney is quoted as saying no limits exist for the number of U.S. forces deployable to the Gulf, and heavy mechanized units from eastern Europe have be-gun transport to the desert. Foot and mechanized infantry units, artillery battalions, and planes are integral to a defensive posture, but hundreds and even thousands of tanks mean an offensive operation is imminent. The paper reports on Palestinian–Israeli violence, and if I were apocalyptically inclined, I might well think that the end is nigh.

The intended effect of the barracks is to convince us that despite the hundreds of thousands of acres of desert that surround us, we are civilized men preparing to fight for the freedom of a civilized people. We are being cared for, the story goes. The Saudis are happy to host us in their country, we're told; in fact they're so happy, they've postponed certain drilling activities and removed their workers from the compound so that we may cool our sweat-soaked balls and brains.

So, as much as I should, I don't enjoy the rear. One STA team is still in the Triangle, and I ask Sergeant Dunn if I can arrange a ride to join them, because I'm tired of the air-conditioning and the $2 candy bars the Egyptians hawk in their pogey-shack. Dunn tells me no, that I have orders to enjoy myself, and he wonders aloud what my problem is:

"What the fuck problem do you have with air-conditioning?"

"I just don't like this place," I tell him. "It's spooky. Pre-ordained. In the desert at least it doesn't look like they were waiting for us with a prefab red-carpet barracks."

"Stop thinking so hard. Jerk off and take a shower and sleep in the AC. Fucking relax, man. Who knows the next time you're gonna get a hot shower and a rack."

For most jarheads, such propaganda works. Any grunt in his right mind will do anything for a hot shower and a rack. The grunt is an addict; the rear-rear is his fix. You've been in the desert for six weeks. The colonel lied about the hot showers your platoon would receive after the MOPP-suit football game. You heard rumors that field units would receive ten pounds of ice per platoon per day. You've seen no ice. One day, because someone stole a case off a mail truck, you drank a warm soda. In the rear you may drink ten or twenty or thirty cold sodas in a day. And the word is that they're showing war movies in the rear-rear, *Platoon, Apocalypse Now, The Boys from Company B, Full Metal Jacket, Sands of Iwo Jima*. And the pleasure of the violent films is like the pleasure of cocaine or a good rough fuck.

I don't leave my small room for five days. I eat MREs and canned tuna and whatever else I scrounge from my platoon mates' care packages. Troy Collier is my roommate, and his mother has sent him ten pounds of caramel, and I eat half of it. My platoon mates urge me to *please shut up* about the place being rigged, about the Saudis wanting us to die for their oil. Everyone in STA but me enjoys the rear. Ten phones have been installed, and what the fuck is my problem, why don't I get on the phone to my girlfriend even if she is cheating on me, or my mom, who will love me no matter what. Make the best of the situation. Stop bringing everyone down with your negativity. Watch a couple of war movies and get pumped. Prepare yourself for killing.

One night I'm alone in the barracks, cleaning my M16, while the rest of the platoon watches movies at the Fox Company barracks. They're hoping for a replay of last night's showing. A Fox Company grunt's wife had sent him a video with his last care package. A homemade porn film had been spliced into a Vietnam flick. The barracks full of unsuspecting marines cheered a screen full of jungle carnage as the on-screen marines charged a VC bunker, then in midcinematic combat frenzy the barracks went silent when the screen turned from overwhelming firepower to the sleek power of sex. After a few seconds, the room erupted. The marines were elated that the amateur smut had made it past the censors, it was another coup! But the excitement only lasted until the marine whose wife had sent him the movie noticed something about the hooded woman, and what he noticed could have been a mole on her ass or the way she moaned or how she threw her head back as she came, but that coming woman was his wife, and the man was his neighbor, and he began to scream, "That's my wife! That's my wife fucking the neighbor, a goddamn squid!" At first the jarheads laughed, because they thought he was joking, but when he continued to scream and then began weeping, they knew that it really was his wife, and someone had the decency to turn the video off. But tonight they want a replay, because why not, the damage is done and when is the next time you'll be able to witness infidelity? And fuck that poor jarhead anyway. He's down at sick call on suicide watch, and as soon as the docs okay him, he'll be on an emergency-leave flight to the States, he'll be the fuck out of the desert.

I remove my firing pin from the bolt carrier and place it in my mouth like a toothpick, and with my tongue I dance the tip of the pin across my teeth. The sound is like a soft tapping against a fragile pane of glass.

The term *suicide watch* always makes me think of my older sister. I didn't know what suicide was until she tried to kill herself a few times. I was between the ages of twelve and fourteen at the time of her first attempts, and after a few sessions of family counseling and her extended stay in an institution (the place was called Serendipity, so it took me some time to realize that it was an institution), she was back living at home and the family situation, as the counselors say, was progressing normally. But, of course, my sister was not normal, and she'd spend the next many years trying to kill herself, and still now occasionally finds herself in the corner, with pills usually—so statistically we are supposed to understand she is not serious about ending her life but is only in the throes of a cry for help because she is a woman and she is in the corner trying pills, yet again—and then she stays at an institution with a dreamy, druggy name, such as Serendipity.

I liked visiting my sister in her institutions. Often they were in the foothills of the Sierra Nevada, slow-rolling foothills thick with trees and the various bent forks of snow-fed rivers. My mother and I would drive up the Sacramento Valley and exit the smoggy freeway for a slow and winding country route, where thick shadows cooled the asphalt and most sharp turns in the road yielded a stunning and steep view of one of the chilly rivers. By the time we arrived at the hospital, I'd have forgotten our destination.

We'd wait first in one waiting room and then in a more interior waiting room and finally an even more interior visiting room, and soon my sister would appear, in what I considered a robe, though the hospital I'm sure had a more appropriate name for the garment, and the three of us would visit. My brother would not visit because he was stationed somewhere with the army, and my parents didn't allow my younger sister to visit, fearing that the institution would frighten her, and my father didn't visit because he and my sister didn't get along, and often she blamed him for her mental condition, though as much as he was sometimes unfair to her, we all now know that it was the chemicals in my sister's brain and not her sometimes harsh father that caused her to open the bottle and swallow one hundred or however many pills. Incidentally, my father was never a bastard to me, and there are different theories as to why this is. I am a spitting image of my father, and I think that he wasn't a bastard to me because it would have been like being a bastard to himself, and he'd had enough of people being bastards to him while growing up.

The visits with my sister saddened me, but nonetheless they were comforting. My mother and I would offer my sister encouraging words and we'd all hold hands and cry, and also smile and occasionally laugh. We'd give my sister the family update so that she wouldn't feel so isolated, even though she was isolated. Sometimes her brain had recently been fried, as in electroshock therapy, though I believe they call it some other, better name these days, a name that sounds not unlike *serendipity*. If brain work had recently occurred, we'd barely talk, because my sister was incapable of responding other than with an occasional grunt or a flutter of her eyelids. We'd sit there, the three of us, holding hands and crying, and nearby usually another patient or two was busy visiting with family members.

Watching the other visitors react to the sickness in front of them, the related sickness, fascinated me. It is difficult for most people to face related sickness. I know this because through the many years of visiting my sick sister in institutions, I witnessed people related to sickness react poorly to the sick person and the sickness. I watched fathers berate daughters for hurting their mothers and brothers berate brothers for driving their parents mad, when everyone should've known the poor crazy person in lockdown couldn't help himself or herself. No matter the group counseling or the pills or the months or years of confinement, the crazy person nearly always returns to the island of their grief or madness. If you are on the outside, no matter how sick you might consider yourself, you are on the outside and cannot claim the lunacy or the malaise.

Throughout the years of visiting my sister in mental institutions, I also watched my mother react to my sister. My mother's reaction was a many-years-long sigh. As much as my mother loved her daughter, it was difficult for her to understand this related sickness, hard for her to comprehend that while she'd raised the daughter she loved, she was at the same time raising a sickness inside of the daughter, breastfeeding the sickness, driving the sickness to ballet lessons and clarinet lessons and softball practice, throwing birthday parties for the sickness, purchasing back-to-school clothes and new grade-appropriate dictionaries for the sickness.

The sigh is my mother's default setting for dealing with grief. While in Saudi Arabia, about to go to war, in the few letters my mother writes to me, I recognize the sigh blowing through her perfect script, and I feel as if I'm again in a visiting room with my mother, but this time I'm the patient, and the institution is not named Serendipity, the institution is named War.

I reassemble my weapon. I've been in the Marine Corps for less than two years, and I've probably performed this one act, assembling the M16, more than ten thousand times. I break it down again. I wonder if mothers worry because their marine sons live with high-powered rifles always within arm's reach.

Sometimes marines kill themselves when they've received bad news from home, from the woman they love, a wife or a girlfriend. This bad news often involves the genitals of the involved parties—in graphic detail the woman describes the other man's skills in bed, and particular acts the marine would never perform, such as with the mouth or the ass or even with innocent toys or easily acquired cooking oils. Even if not specified, these acts are always imagined by the marine.

Kristina, the woman I'm currently supposed to love, the woman who is supposed to love me, is having sex with someone else, a guy who works at a hotel with her, one of the clerks. Even though she has not described their sex in her letters, I know the sex is occurring because she has called him a good friend and a great listener. Also, a coworker and friend of hers, Katherine, who writes me honest letters, has referred to Kristina's "new friend." But I have a sense of humor. I recall Drill Instructor Sergeant Seats saying, "If I ever find out one of you goes and kills yourself over pussy, I'll chase you down into hell and kill your ignorant ass a second time."

When, a few weeks into this deployment, Kristina told me she'd found a job at a hotel, I imagined that soon she'd be sleeping with one of the clerks—during their breaks they'd use vacant rooms, the same vacant rooms that all of the other employees use, not even changing sheets between fornicators. My platoon mates talked me out of this scenario, insisting that I'd probably seen something similar on TV or in a movie, but that the likelihood of such a crime being perpetrated in real life was slim. I did not believe my mates, nor could they have believed themselves, but I appreciated their good-hearted attempts at soothing me.

I close my eyes and reassemble my weapon in seven seconds. I stand. I toss my rifle from hand to hand, marking a sharp cadence with the slap of my palms against the hard plastic hand guards.

Kristina's absurd insistence that we stay together in the midst of her infidelity is a result of her desire to be connected to the military, specifically the Marine Corps, and now, while I'm in a combat zone, receiving combat pay, she considers herself connected to combat. (During and after my various infidelities I never insisted we remain boyfriend and girlfriend, but somehow we would always be classified as such.) Combat must seem sexy to Kristina. I treat her military fetish with disdain because I know that the power of the fetish will not usurp the power of her simple desire to feel flesh, even the flesh of the lonely hotel clerk. I know that she takes pleasure in telling people that her boyfriend is a combat marine. I imagine her smiling as she tells the poor hotel clerk that the man whose girlfriend he's fucking is a marine. And I'm sure the hotel clerk likes telling his friends that the new girl he's stiffing is a dumb jarhead's girlfriend. Everyone loves to get over on the jarhead. Especially other jarheads.

I know that while I was in boot camp, Kristina slept with a marine recruiter. Some people might insist that this replacement lover signified her love for me, that by fornicating with the marine recruiter she included me in her infidelity, bringing herself closer to me because she could not touch me during the tortuous thirteen weeks of boot camp. In this version she'd shown me respect by choosing a marine rather than a civilian, and the recruiter was doing me a favor because while he fucked Kristina, he prepared her for the rough-and-tumble life of loving a jarhead.

But Kristina's various infidelities are not the reasons I'm standing in the middle of my small barracks room, placing the muzzle of my M16 in my mouth and tasting the cold rifle metal and the smoky residue of gunpowder. The reasons are hard to name. The history of my family and the species? The reports that the enemy to the north are elite fighters who learned how to throw grenades when I was barely off the tit? To move closer toward my sister? Cowardice? Fatigue? Boredom? Curiosity? It's not the suicide's job to *know,* only to *do.*

I have ammunition everywhere: hanging from my body, stored in metal boxes and wooden crates under my rack, packed thirty deep into magazines. It is hard to know why I've selected the M16 over the sniper rifle, the weapon with the larger caliber. The round the sniper fires is much more advanced than the basic M16 projectile, precision versus ball. But the weapon I've locked and loaded is my M16. Though less powerful than the .308 round the sniper rifle fires, the 5.56mm M16 round has a lot of bounce and turn, and one hears countless stories concerning an M16 round entering a guy's neck and exiting through the tip of his left big toe, or going in the toe and exiting through the left eye socket. In the event of a proper head shot, the result is what we call pink mist. I've spent many hours of my life imagining what my bullets will do to the enemy.

The medulla oblongata shot is the most coveted shot, the epic shot. Entry through the mouth or the eyeball is also acceptable. The marine does not shoot to injure but only to kill. Sometimes my imagined enemy has been a Russian, sometimes a Chinese, sometimes an Arab, depending on world events and what version of those events I'm receiving or currently involved in.

I bend at the waist and place the buttstock of my rifle against the deck. My thumb rests on the trigger. I bite into the steel muzzle and feel my teeth reversing into my gums. With my tongue running between the slits of the flash suppressor, I imagine the trip my bullet will take, its movement through cerebrum, cerebellum, corpus callosum, pineal body, medulla oblongata. I think of a bullet traveling around my head and exiting through an eye socket or never exiting but rather spinning and spinning and ripping my brain to shreds until the momentum of ballistics is overpowered by fleshly resistance. Stop. Dead.

When you have the muzzle of a high-powered rifle in your mouth, there are many things to consider other than your despair.

Troy walks into our room and sees me. He stops. My trigger selector is on burst, so that rather than one bullet rounding my skull, there will be three, and this must have been the reason I chose the M16 over the sniper rifle. Burst.

Troy says, "What the fuck?"

And I might be only a half a second or many seconds, or even many years, from pulling the trigger, because who knows how many tries one is allowed until one gets it right, but Troy slaps me hard across the back of my head, and the muzzle plays around in my mouth, and I chip a tooth.

I look at him and say, "I was fucking around, I knew you were walking in the door."

He unloads my weapon, calls me various names, and throws my rifle on the rack with his.

He says, "They played it! That poor jarhead. Half the battalion plus assorted tanker assholes have watched his wife getting fucked, really getting fucked, by the neighbor. But I'd watch it again tomorrow. And *you* want to kill yourself? I need to go for a run. You coming?"

I put my boots on and we fill our two-quart canteens and strap them to our backs. Our side of the barracks, what looks like an extended double-wide trailer, is filling up with our platoon mates, and the story of the video is on all of their tongues. Kuehn asks us why the hell we're going for a run, and Fowler calls us suck-asses. Troy insults them both with numerous imaginative profanities involving farm animals and their mothers, and the two of us head into the hot night. We stretch outside of the barracks, and the whir of the hundreds of window-unit air conditioners sounds like one large motor idling at the start line, a motor without a body and without a driver, just pure power and fuel.

We run the perimeter of the base. It's absurd to be in the desert and at the same time confined. Marine MPs in Humvees are stationed every few hundred yards. I wonder if they know what they're looking for. If we scream, they might shoot us.

Troy says, "I really don't know what you were doing back there. If this is over Kristina, you need to pull yourself together. She ain't suicide-pretty."

"It's not about her. It's about the desert."

"The desert my ass! Motherfucker, I picked out and bought for you your first hooker in the PI. Don't try to jack me off! I don't give a fuck what it is, just don't pull the god-damn trigger!"

Troy had indeed bought me my first prostitute in the Philippines, and he considered that a blood bond. A year before our West-Pac he was stationed in the PI, and he knew the islands and the bars as though he'd been born in Manila rather than Greenville, Michigan. But on barracks duty in the PI he got busted from corporal to private for failing the marijuana portion of a piss test. He'd blown a choice assignment and been sent to the Fleet Marine Force, so he was particularly belligerent and disrespectful and thus great for morale. He was a terrible crying drunk, constantly moaning about a girl at home named Lisa who'd refused his advances since grade school.

Even before we both passed the STA indoc, Troy and I often drank together in Okinawa, and after taking in a few porn films and a $2 plate of *yakisoba,* we'd end up in my barracks, yelling profanities and asking for free beer. On Okinawa, it was easy to bum free beer. The Michelob semitruck pulled onto base every Wednesday at noon and sold cases of bottles for $5. There weren't enough refrigerators on the entire base to hold the beer all of those jarheads bought. After drinking a case of $5 Michelob, yelling at people for no apparent reason was rather common. It wasn't just drunkenness, it was stupidity and youth and forgetfulness. You must forget who you were before the Marine Corps. You must also forget the person you might be in the future, after leaving the Marine Corps, because when war comes, you might die and then all of your fantasies and predictions for the future will have become lies.

We run in silence. Troy is smaller and faster than me, but I can outdistance him. He tries to tire me out quickly, and I attempt to finish him off slowly. We run and run and the hours pass, and even though we're going in circles, I'm running away from whatever I left back in the barracks. I'm swirling around the thing until it becomes part of the swirl, and the swirl becomes part of me, and I'm still a part of that small sickness, and that sickness is still a small part of me, but it no longer has me bent over at the waist, chewing on the muzzle of my rifle. Maybe someday in the future I will revisit the sickness, but for now I'm done with it.

Troy snaps his fingers as he runs, a trick his high school track coach taught him to keep on pace. Our boots slap the sand with the sound of a theater curtain falling. And we are actors running around the stage. We are delivering our lines as we run. We are proving to the great theater director of All Time that we are ready for war or whatever. We can run all night, and we will run all night, through the sand, in circles around our fake encampment. The wagons are circling. We are the wagons. We have no reason to challenge one another this way, to prove anything to one another, there is nothing to prove, there is no challenge. We are the same body. We are nearly the same brain. We are running ourselves into the earth, literally; we run a path around the fence, like wild animals circling prey they don't yet know how to eat.

My shoulders hurt and my stomach aches and we have been running so long that even my fingertips hurt, but we continue. My crotch is raw, and Troy's is too, because he says to me, "I wish I had rubbed some petrol jelly in my crotch," and I affirm this desire. But we will not stop. The sun rises. Reveille plays over the same speakers that call the Egyptians to prayer. We continue to run.

Perhaps I wouldn't have pulled the trigger. My despair is less despair than boredom and loneliness. Maybe Troy's good timing saved me. I think about my sister, this very minute living in an institution in California, and I consider myself a poor impostor, an actor speaking the wrong lines. I don't know what I want, but obviously I don't want badly enough to be dead. I think about Hemingway. What a shot. What despair. What courage. Some insist that the suicide is both a coward and a cheat, but I think the suicide is rather courageous. To look at one's life and decide that it's not worth living, then to go through with the horrible act. Millions of people live lives that aren't worth living. Many fewer people end their worthless lives. To look down the barrel of the gun or over the lip of the pill bottle and say, "That is what I want, that is the world that needs me, better than breath, better than banging my bones through the remainder of these sorry days"—there is the courageous man and woman, the suicide. But I don't own the courage to kill myself. I must return to the thing I know best, possibly the only thing I truly know: being a jarhead.

confessions of a
pull-proof trigger
kenji jasper

FAIRFAX VILLAGE was supposed to be a nice place to live, neat little rows of spanking new town homes and condos on the edge of southeast Washington, D.C. The leaves and lawns were of the richest greens imaginable. The playground equipment was always freshly painted and accident-free. The sidewalks were free of trash, glass, or a single crack in the concrete. All of the neighbors knew my name and the mayor, our beloved Marion Barry, Jr., pre-crack-smoking-demise, lived right up the street on Suitland Road.

It was heaven on earth for Melvin, Jr., and Angela, my parents, who had grown up in meaner streets on the other side of the city. They had both been of the few to ever leave the confines of the old neighborhood, many having fallen victim to drugs, crime, early pregnancies and worst of all, complacency. They moved to "The Village" just after their wedding, and remained there for 14 years in three different residences, before they separated. Because the Village was then free of all the things they'd left behind, making it the perfect place to raise their first and only child together.

And it was, at least for a little while.

In the early years it didn't seem any different than living in the suburbs that stretched toward forever beyond the city line. My best friend Butchie and I ran and rode the green and gleaming turf, playing in the sunshine until the sun took its nap below the horizon. The red berry tree just beyond our house became the spaceship we chartered for missions, shaking berries loose when we needed to drop bombs on treacherous alien enemies.

We bought five-cent candy from the Asian-owned deli at the top of the hill (where they always followed us in the store and never wiped the dust off the merchandise), and climbed carports and garages to attain better views of our chosen domain, which went on forever, into Hillcrest and back down toward Anacostia. And as long as our chores were done and our homework finished, we were free to roam wherever we wished.

But the older we grew, the more dark clouds thickened in the distance, clouds that threatened to end the sunny days they sang about at the beginning of our daily dose of Sesame Street. Different, and less savory individuals found their way through the gates of our paradise. And that was when all of the rules began to change.

I was barely eight years old when a kid named Keith stopped me while I was cruising down the street on my brand new bright red Western Flyer bicycle. Keith was much older than me, maybe 12 or 13. And though we were almost exactly the same size his two taller and bulkier friends tipped the scales in his favor as they towered over me. I had sense enough not to give in. Offering them a free spin on my bike meant that one of them would speed off down W Street while the others ran interference. And I would never see it or its custom-fitted BMX handle grips again.

I told them "no" and headed down the hill at top speed, certain that I could outrun any potential danger and be home just in time for dinner. But I wasn't fast enough to evade the piece of loose asphalt Keith hit me in the back of the head with as I made my escape. The high wood fence that surrounded our basement apartment couldn't clot the blood that flowed freely from the top of my skull. But I had kept my bike intact. And that was all that had immediately mattered.

I wasn't scared of Keith. I was just pretty sure that I couldn't beat him. And when I saw the warm red water in the bathroom sink, and the wound my mother was dressing in the mirror, I wasn't in the mood to try. Then my father came home. And from the look on his face at the sight of me, I knew that I'd better not take my shoes off.

"You know where this boy lives," Pop asked me, his bearded face looking down at me from almost six feet in the air. I nodded, knowing exactly what would happen next, though it had never happened before. My father was taking me back to the scene of the crime, not for vengeance or retribution, but to make sure that Keith never hurled another chunk of rock at me again.

Night had fallen by the time Pop and I headed back up

the hill. His eyes scanned the sidewalks and courtyards carefully, hoping that we spotted the kid before he had a chance to run. But there wasn't a soul or sound anywhere. Then we heard the echo of voices, coming from the other side of the playground. I led the way and Pop followed close behind me.

The playground was deserted as we crossed its surface. The moonlight from above was the only thing that kept us from bumping into the equipment, its beams reflecting off the shiny metal on the jungle gyms and sliding boards. As we got closer I could identify Keith's loud voice amongst several others. They were just beyond the row of apartment buildings that separated the Village's western and eastern halves. We followed the sounds until they became louder and more distinct. And then we finally found him, standing on the lawn in front of his building, saying good-bye to the two towers he'd had as backup when he'd made a move on my bike. I gave my dad a nod that these were the culprits. The two towers scurried away before Pop could stop them.

"Are you Keith?" my father asked.

"Yes sir," he replied in a voice so affected that you could have mistaken him for Hugh Grant.

"Kenji says you hit him in the head with a rock over his bike," Pop replied sternly, his eyes scanning Keith's with pinpoint scrutiny.

"No sir," he replied without the slightest ruffling of a feather. "But I saw the boys that did it, and I went after them but they got away." Pop turned to catch the disbelief on my face and then turned back to him with a smirk of disgust. "Is your mother home, Keith? I'd like to talk to her."

"No, sir. She's at work. But I'll have her come down to the house to talk to you as soon as she gets home." Keith gave me this little look of victory, as if my father had actually bought his story.

"You do that," my pop replied. I showed a slight grin at my father's sarcasm, feeling proud that I had someone with me to back me up. A moment of silence hung between the three of us. And then Pop motioned for me to follow him back toward the house. I felt Keith's eyes at my back until we were beyond his field of vision. And that was it. I let out a sigh.

"I thought you were gonna make me fight him," I said. Pop smiled and shook his head.

"Fighting is always a last resort, son. First you have to try and talk to people, try and work out whatever problem it is you and the other person have between you. But if someone attacks you, you have to defend yourself. That boy back there is a chump. He hit you in the back of the head, when you weren't looking. And then he wouldn't even own up to it. But you won't have to worry about him much longer."

I was silent as I walked down the moonlit hill behind him, his words a Star Trek phaser on its lowest setting. He didn't want me to bust the boy's lip or knock his teeth out. He didn't want me, at eight, to show Keith just how much of a man I was by standing up to him. My father's words and actions were contrary to everything I'd heard in the streets, the pure bravado that spewed from the mouths of many others.

In contrast, my best friend Butchie went into everything with fists flying. It was learned behavior. His father, Butch

Sr., a tall and slender man with permed hair and a '78 Corvette with a custom paint job, gave his boy lessons diametrically opposed to what his best friend was being told. And before I knew it, Butchie no longer played in the sunshine. He'd become a creature of the night, rolling with packs of boys who considered themselves above parental rules and curfews.

Not long after the incident with Keith, Butchie and I stopped seeing each other as often. Things began to change amongst all of us boys pretending to be men. The gun replaced the fist. Shots and sirens shattered the nocturnal serenity of where I lived. My parents got divorced and I lived my life between the Village and a few different homes in other neighborhoods. Keith ended up in a reform school. Butchie ended up a teenage father, and later, a prisoner at the Lorton State Penitentiary in Virginia.

In a Hollywood sense the Keith story always seemed anticlimactic to me. I, the supposed underdog, was supposed to guzzle down a cup of courage and topple the neighborhood bully before he could continue his reign of tyranny. But I didn't live in Hollywood. In the real world the bad guy defeated himself, got picked up by the cops too many times for shoplifting and ended up doing a stretch in the school no one enrolled in by choice.

And my father had seen it coming. Pop knew that a beef between Keith and I would've done me more harm than good. If I lost I could've been hurt. If I won I had to worry about payback, about getting jumped some Saturday morning on the way back from my Cub Scout meeting. So the best thing was to let it all go. But I was too young to fully learn that lesson.

CONFLICT CAME my way again in 1991, when I was a sophomore at Benjamin Banneker High School, the city's school of distinction for the academically gifted. By then things had moved far beyond bricks and bikes. There were more guns and drugs on the street than books in libraries. Turf wars had erupted in various drug territories and the casualty count went up every 24 hours.

If you didn't have a piece it was best to move with as many people as possible. Catching a stray bullet or getting hit in the face by a group of strangers, *just because*, was not an uncommon phenomenon. So if your boy had a problem then your whole crew did. And that crew took action to alleviate all traces of the specific problem. Steel-toed boots sold in record numbers as potential threats covered their heads and faces from the rain of blows coming down on them in a stomping motion. Every neighborhood, street, and even apartment building made its own flag, and enlisted a small army to defend it.

My brigade was a group of four or five kids from Hillcrest, the hill-and-dale-filled haven of upper-middle-classdom right across the road from the Village. The kids over there went to the better schools, wore the better clothes, and had the kind of family lives most of my Village peers dreamed about. They hadn't grown up in the middle of any danger zones. They were not a part of all the "at-risk" youth the local politicians always talked about saving. And neither was I.

Nonetheless, we looked and behaved as if we were, packing into my mother's Chevy Corsica, or Bobo's Mom's Audi, or whatever car we could get our hands on, every weekend, and headed out into the D.C. night, to wave our flag, at any and all costs. And we saw a lot in the first two years of high school. Shots were fired into the basement windows of a party we attended. Rival factions turned a rented ballroom at the D.C. Navy Yard into a brawl of cinematic proportions.

Three soldiers from the Village ended up outlined in chalk. And plenty more went to prison. The high school nightlife was a huge pressure-cooker that exploded for one crew at a time, when they least expected it. So it didn't surprise us when our turn came.

"I'M GONNA KILL THAT MUTHAFUCKA!" my man Marcus had yelled, his voice echoing amongst the greenery in front of his house on Bangor Street. We'd been tight since the fourth grade, a lifetime in tenth-grader terms. "I can't believe that muthafucka did that shit to my girl!"

I had been the last to arrive at the scene, fresh from the V5 bus stop at the top of the hill. But all that I had missed was quickly explained. Marcus had gotten a call from his girlfriend Josephine, who had told him that a guy Billy (named changed to protect the guilty) had made advances toward her. And when she declined his harassment escalated: groping her, shoving her, pinning her to the bed, everything but rape itself. The girl was crying uncontrollably all through the phone call, a hellish ordeal for any man who truly loved his woman. So every moment since had been filled with inner torment for my dear friend. He couldn't sleep, and was lifting excessive amounts of weights on the machine in his basement just to keep him from heading to the local arsenal and doing something rash. He needed to avenge her. And he needed us to help him.

Billy lived on the outskirts of our own neighborhood. He was one of our own, and a target more than within our grasp. So it would be easy to catch him on his own street, where he would never expect an ambush. I mentioned a party that a friend of mine, Marquis, was throwing in our area code that weekend. And everyone agreed that it was the perfect place to strike. But there was only one small problem, for me: Billy just happened to go to school with me, and Paul, another neighborhood boy of ours.

Though he was three years ahead of us, we couldn't take the risk of him recognizing us during the assault. If we took part, we could be payback punching bags the following Monday, the only recognizable faces he'd see while walking the halls battered and bruised from the proposed beatdown we were to deliver. So Paul and I were both forced to abstain from opening cans of whip-ass. Instead, our job was simply to make sure that Billy showed up, and that he had absolutely no idea of what would be waiting for him when he got there. That was too easy. It was Tuesday. And the party was on Friday.

All through the week we ran our mouths about how "crankin'" Marquis's party was going to be. We spoke to people and in places where we knew Billy would take no-tice. Our trap was heavy with the proper bait. And Paul and I were pretty certain that it would all go down perfectly. Then I got another phone call.

"That nigga found out about it!" Bobo's cousin Mike screamed, his deep voice bellowing above the other six on the double three-way calling enhanced phone line. Mike, having never liked me in the first place, was certain that I was the culprit. And the others seemed just as skeptical. I was known for not being able to keep a secret. And Paul was as solid as a rock. But I hadn't said a word, which meant that someone else was playing a game with us.

I told them that we had to stop pointing fingers and fig-ure out what happened. That was when Marcus explained that Billy was now amassing his own army for the party. Stealth had gone out of the window and we were facing the most important fight of our lives, against an unseen number of foes. Now I was going to have to fight, for real. And I was starting to get scared.

I'd been in a few fights before, mostly with Bobo when he'd said one wisecrack too many, or when I wanted to test out my green-belt-level tae kwon do skills, or when Claude Craig had said something about my mother in grade seven. But all of that had been nothing but adrenaline and testos-terone. This battle was for a reason. And on this battlefield, anything, from knives and bottles to fire-breathing firearms, could have come into play.

We couldn't back down. We could not be the crew peo-ple talked about at Monday's lunch at every high school across the city, wearing shades and pulled-down hats to try

and hide our still-swollen and pathetic faces. Our reputation, our flag, all that mattered, was on the line. And I, Kenji
Nathaniel Jasper, had to be there for my people.

The night in question came and I stood in front of my
closet, trying to figure out which of my five rayon party
shirts I would don for the occasion. I wanted to look good,
especially if it was going to be my funeral. I practiced shad-
owboxing and rehearsed all the kicks and punches I could
remember from my classes in the sixth grade. Then, just as I
reached for the green long-sleeve with the paisley pattern,
the phone rang. It was Marcus. The party had been can-
celed. A tree had crashed into the side of Marquis's house.

I remembered the two of us laughing for a brief moment, the irony of the whole thing being too funny not to.
Then we said we were going to get together to come up
with a Plan B. We were going to find another way to make
Billy pay. And the next time we'd have the element of surprise on our side again. The next time we'd be on the offensive once more. But it never happened.

It turned out one of Josephine's friends, and Billy's cousin,
had been the one to tip him off about the initial attack. Marcus's anger became less and less important and his woman
quickly seemed to forget about the incident. And before we
knew it the whole thing had gone limp. And we went back to
stepping away, or hitting the deck, playing the background in
a city full of other crews and their various conflicts.

BUT THERE WERE plenty more incidents in the years that
followed. My homegirl Cheryl's ex-boyfriend almost left

on a gurney when he had words with Bobo and ten other dudes from the neighborhood at my sixteenth birthday party. Four freshmen and a countless number of sophomores squared off in a senseless brawl at a back-to-school party for Morehouse, Clark and Spelman students during my first year of college. Shots were fired just a few feet away from me as I followed rappers Naughty by Nature for a magazine article. The group and I ended up running at top speed out of the back of the club, followed by a stampede of frightened clubbers and the gunmen.

There's so much aggression in this world, and all of the death and injury that stem from it. Its always been there, but now there seems to be more of it than ever. Not only has it been a part of all that I've read and viewed on big and small screens, but it's also been prevalent in so many of the environments that have shaped my life, and in the many scenes I've borne witness to in my 27 years on Planet Earth. But no matter how hard I've wished and tried, I've never managed to be an active part of those forces.

I wasn't home when the call to fight arrived. Or we had more people than they did. Or I ran, or I'd simply been confused with someone else. Or I prayed. Or there was some kind of a sit-down. No matter which reason, the fact of the matter is that I haven't landed a legitimate punch in 14 years. I've only fired a gun once, on a range. And though I know my way in the streets, I am not of them.

I've often fallen victim to the definition of black manhood brought about by hip-hop and Blaxploitation flicks. I've dreamt of being like the men spoken of in their lyrics, ready to challenge any personal affront with physical prowess, prepared to level the opposition with one swift, indifferent strike, throwing caution to the wind in favor of the all-important ego. But men like those only live long lives through MC lyrics.

The truth of the matter is that I've survived because those things are not a part of who I am, because I was, to quote a Black Mama cliché, "raised better than that." My friends and I, most of whom were also fortunate to not grow up as the "children of the ghetto" our own culture had glamorized, learned and know that it is true *love* (as a principle) and not *like* that might be worth dying over. It is principle and not posturing that should, if ever, bring one man to blows with another.

And as a result we have all clenched our fists less and less frequently. We withdrew our wannabe-thuggish looks and stares for straight faces standing against the ills of our community. We became men, relearning what my father had taught me at age eight. Manhood had nothing to do with who can beat whom while a crowd looks on. Manhood is about taking responsibility for one's action, and resolving conflicts in the best way possible, from paying bills, to paying dues, to being there for your children's first steps and to protect them from all dangers until they are ready to protect themselves.

I am a man now, and I know these things. I also know the blessings that have been bestowed on me to have never broken a bone, or to have never been shot, stabbed or stomped out on a basement floor by multiple attackers. Yet there's a part of me that still wishes that I had been. There are still feelings of shame when I'm amongst men who've lived more turbulent lives, who have literally fought to survive in ways I never had to. That makes me feel as if I don't have the required "right stuff" to be a "real nigga" that so many of my brethren view as a title of merit and prestige.

I feel guilty for the little bits of privilege I've had, for having parents who did a good job in contrast to multitudes of those who did not. When I am among them I wonder if they question me, if they see me as some kind of a fake because we wear the same clothes and know the same streets and yet I have not had to drive a blade into a neck or abdomen. I didn't have to fight off those three kids who were right on my lady and me in that Boston subway station.

And that makes me inferior, lesser than them in the eyes of so many of my peers. Because I have not lived by the sword, nor the gun, nor the fist. I have only watched and reacted, moving out of the way rather than engage, hoping to keep my own skin intact for a little while longer.

Years ago I received a spiritual reading from the Ausar Auset society at their temple in Atlanta, Georgia. A woman wrapped in white ran her hand over a fanned-out deck of cards and told me my future. A strange wave of energy rushed over me as she scrutinized my destiny to determine who I was, and what I was here to do. Then she told me that my life was governed by Tehuti, a deity who served as the scribe and force of wisdom for human existence. She told me that Tehuti are not warriors, nor are they victims. They are those who watch and wait, who analyze and document. They are the ones who remain long after the battlefields are paved over with asphalt and strip malls. And then they tell their tale.

not a man

caitríona reed

"YOU DON'T KNOW what you're talking about, do you? You're making all this up! You've never been a man. You've never even really been with men!" I was sleeping over at my girlfriend's house. We were commiserating over our mutual frustration with our respective would-be boyfriends, advising each other, strategizing—laughing a lot. She was right. My perspectives had never truly been those of a man. I was born a boy child, but like many other transsexuals, I had known that something was terribly wrong from the beginning. I had tried for years to conform to what I saw in the mirror, to be a man, even though I had never really felt like one. Now I am a tall middle-aged blonde with a Marlene Dietrich voice. I sometimes tell people that I spent the first part of my life as a "full-time male-impersonator."

In my role as a male impersonator, I was afraid a lot. I was fearful of being exposed as a fraud, fearful that I lacked important pieces of information, fearful that I was in the wrong place. When I spoke, I scarcely recognized myself. I was awkward, shy, disconnected. My earliest childhood memories are haunted by the vague recollection of always wanting to be otherwise and elsewhere. The desire was so acute, and at the same time so vague, that when I allow myself to move back into it now, I am horrified by how frozen in confusion and shame I must have been. At the time, it did not seem to have anything to do with sex, or gender, or identity. I simply inhabited an ongoing discomfort that I took to be standard issue.

I started life as a quiet boy, a "sensitive little chap." It was England, in the 1950s. I was six years old. I lived alone, or so it felt. I divided my time between my grandfather's enormous house by the river and my parents' house, supervised by a governess who had been my mother's before me. At night, I would stuff a cushion into my pajamas and imagine that I was pregnant. I do not remember how I understood this act. It was both exhilarating and confusing, and I was instinctively secretive about it.

In kindergarten, a boy named Roger threw a brick in my face. He took exception to my playing with the girls on the swings, rather than with the boys in the sandpit. Until he brought it to my attention with the brick, I had no idea that this was even an issue. At the time, I did not understand that there was any absolute difference between boys and girls, and I do not remember having any clear sense that I was either. I was simply myself. I learned that boys could be rough and unkind. They did their own thing, which I never seemed to understand or feel I was a part of. I was safe with girls. We liked to do the same things. I used to sit in the tree by the stream with my friend Rosemary and eat raw green beans from my grandfather's kitchen garden.

When I was eight I went to an all-male boarding school. Everyone was fluent in a language I could not understand. It involved toys and games and sports that I had no inkling of. I had no role models. What could they have been? I would not have recognized them, even if they had existed. At boarding school the desire to be otherwise and elsewhere was as strong as ever, though I still had no clue what it might look like, or where it might be.

Decades later, I am lying in my friend's bed. I am amazed and delighted that she accepts me, without hesitation, as the woman she recognizes me to have always been. My driver's license reads "F." My sex has been reconstructed with a surgeon's knife. We laugh at the absurdity of our brilliant lives. I am learning to trust myself, and to see my life as a journey that has its own integrity and beauty. She is a psychotherapist! I am a Buddhist teacher! For years our training and work have been to encourage others to see themselves more clearly, and to accept themselves for who they are. Late into the night, we lie in a room in Los Angeles, talking about men and women, love, truth, poetry, politics, and religion. We laugh and cry like fools, and wonder that either of us is ever taken seriously—considering our never-ending hilarity, and our playful, merciless irreverence. We marvel at the struggle that has led us to accept our own lives so fully; and we wonder too how on earth it was that I ever mistook myself for a man!

I spent nine years in boarding school. At puberty, I swam with the others into the testosterone ocean where we discovered *Playboy* magazine, girls as sex objects, and each other. *Playboy* was exciting, but it was also confusing. I wanted both to possess and to become the women in the photographs. I was beginning to recognize myself as something other than male. My years at a single-sex boarding school had made girls remote and scary. As for the boys, I still did not feel that I was one of them, though I took to mutual masturbation readily enough.

By the time I was a teenager, I sought refuge in rebellion, outsider literature, music, art, marijuana, and psychedelics. I identified with liberation struggles, Che Guevara, Mao, and Malcolm X. I listened to jazz when everyone else was listening to the Beatles. I fell in love with boys, and I fell in love with girls, though it usually came to nothing. It was England of the 1960s, a golden age!

In the summer of 1967, when I was seventeen, I was on my way to a jazz club in London to hear Ornette Coleman with a friend from school. We were early, and so we decided to go into a nearby strip bar. Women were taking turns dancing to the Rolling Stones, Bob Dylan, and Aretha Franklin. Gray men sat in rows in front of the little stage, their raincoats on their laps. The men belonged to a world that had nothing to do with me, but the women were instantly familiar. They each danced for two songs, affecting ennui as they stripped, timing themselves so that they stood naked for a single short moment before the curtain came down and another dancer took their place. I watched them with amazement. They seemed to embody something that I had just forgotten, an instant before, and was now beginning to remember again. I felt the same combination of desire, and of wanting to be, or to become, or to be seen as already being, one of them. I recognized myself—physically, energetically, sexually—unashamedly erotic, playful, self-aware, embodied. I imagined that my affinity with them was completely obvious to everyone in the club. Later, as I walked along the street with my friend, I came out to him, awkwardly, partially, sure that he already knew. But I did not yet understand what "transsexual" meant. I did not have the words. We ended in clumsy silence, and then changed the subject. We arrived at the jazz club and nothing more was said.

Soon afterwards, I was expelled from school. Two years later, I dropped out of university. I became a Buddhist and started practicing yoga and meditation. I went to live in a commune in the French Alps. I had no plans for the future. I retuned to England and managed a bookstore. I married an Iranian, became a Muslim. Then I took up my Buddhist practice again. I was a photographer. I was divorced. I went to Asia for a year where I immersed myself in meditation. I came to the U.S., was married again. I started teaching yoga and meditation. It was a haphazard and restless journey.

I had been cross-dressing ever since those childhood days when I had stuffed a pillow into my pajamas. I no longer kept it secret. I confided in friends and lovers, and went to parties as a Dietrich wannabe. I wanted to normalize myself. I wanted to dispel the shame. I also wanted to go further. I came to North America, ostensibly to attend a long meditation retreat; but my real reason, even though I barely recognized it, was to change my body, to change my sex. I knew that such things were possible and I could now begin to imagine them for myself.

I looked for professionals who might help. Some were uncomfortable with the subject of gender identity. I found others who seemed to genuinely care, who prescribed estrogen, and encouraged me to make my own decisions, even if it meant changing my sex. However, I was shocked by their underlying assumption that one must be, in some absolute way, either masculine or feminine and comply with all the unwritten rules that society projects onto men and women. I had hoped for allies. I had imagined that, of all people, psychotherapists and physicians working in the field of "gender dysphoria" would understand gender as a spectrum of possible identities and expressions, but they seemed to subscribe to the common view of gender as a caricature. Anatomy, gender identity, sexual orientation, and outward appearance had to conform to each other—as in movies where strong, impassive, clever, butch, heterosexual males rescue helpless femme females, whose lives are meaningless without them. Androgyny and ambiguity were not options. Since I had already spent a lifetime of questioning, these conservative professionals to whom I had gone for help made me very uncomfortable. They reinforced the message that unless I conformed to one stereotype or the other, unless I found ways to fit into someone else's view of who I should be, my desires would remain hidden, and I would remain invisible. I accepted the estrogen and went on my way.

By now, I was cross-dressing less and less. The dissatisfaction of putting on a costume was stronger than the momentary thrill of the masquerade. I began to express myself in an increasingly androgynous way, while the new hormones began their work of transforming my body.

"THIS ISN'T WORKING! I can't stand it. You're killing the person inside you. Something has to change!"

My partner, Michele, had told me that from the time we had first started going out together she felt that I was different from other men. She said that she had never dated anyone who communicated, and loved her, in the way I did; or who was present to the relationship in the way I was. She said that it was like dating a woman.

Last year my Iranian ex-wife told me the same thing. "Caitríona, you know the reason we broke up is that I always knew you were a woman."

"Thanks, Saf. I wish you had mentioned it at the time. It might have helped me clear things up a little sooner!"

Two decades later, Michele is saying, "You have to change. You have to start living as a woman." She is a warrior. She has trained in the martial arts for more than twenty-five years. With or without her sword she has learned to cut through the ideas either of us might have that we are separate from each other, or from the myriad elements of our lives. She also understands what it is to have a foot in two worlds. Her mother was Japanese; her father is European-American. Together, we have learned to embrace complexity, and to take whatever risks are necessary for the truth (however we might understand it) and to trust, even to enjoy, the dance.

We had been facilitating meditation retreats and workshops for several years. We ran our own retreat center in Southern California. We taught meditation, deep ecology, and socially engaged Buddhism. We encouraged our students to embrace the fullness of their life, rather than just trying to escape from it. We were wary of unexamined transcendentalism, latent in so much contemporary spiritual teaching. It seemed to encourage complacency; and a tendency to not ask difficult questions, to comply, to accept simplistic answers, and to avoid feeling the horror of what was happening in our society and to the planet. We created an environment where it was possible for students to embrace difficult feelings for both personal and global issues. My insistence on authenticity and truth telling was about to backfire and force me out of my closet.

I did not come willingly. Part of me had hoped that if I was *really spiritual*, it would all go away. Perhaps if I meditated more, my desires, even my body, would disappear altogether! Perhaps I was caught in some fetishistic fantasy that was driving me to become the object of my desire; that I was locked into some infantile misidentification that now manifested as a longing to become my own mother, lover, daughter. I tried to think my way out of it. I came out to people I met. I told them that I was transgendered, or that I was a woman. I described myself in all sorts of different ways. I looked for clues in their responses, in the hope that they might tell me something new. I occupied myself with projects. I moved on with my life, but I was always pulled back to my central preoccupation. I was irritable, easily distracted. I wanted to have breasts and a vagina. I wanted to

caitríona reed

be *seen* as a woman. I wanted to engage in the world with the sensuality I had denied myself, and live without always feeling awkward and out of place. I did not know with any absolute certainty that by living as a woman I would become whole. But I hoped it was so. It was clear that nothing else was working. I was a meditation teacher! I encourage people to find their own authenticity. There was no way I could sustain the contradiction. There was a precipice right outside the closet door. My own proclivities as a spiritual teacher were pushing me very insistently towards it.

"You're stifling both of us," she said. "If you don't start living as a woman I'm going to leave this relationship." It was a rare moment of singular clarity. In that instant, we both understood that there was no going back. It was not important whether we stayed together as lovers. It was not important whether we continued teaching together. It was hard to imagine that I had any viable future. I felt that I was about to commit a kind of suicide. The possibility that I might never again be taken seriously as a human being, let alone as a spiritual teacher, seemed very real. I was finally dying to the strenuous pretense of impersonating a man both of us knew I could never be. I *had to trust* that somehow I was opening to a richer truth.

I jumped!

THE CHINESE PHILOSOPHER Chuang Tzu once dreamed that he was a butterfly. On waking, he wondered whether he was a man who had dreamed that he was a butterfly, or a butterfly dreaming he was a man. I wonder if I am a woman who is dreaming she was once a man, or a man who dreamed he was a woman. In truth, I never fully knew what it is to be a man, any more than I now know what it is to be a woman.

Men and women are admired for different things at different times and in different cultures. Women bear children, men bear arms. But life is long. Not all women bear children, and not all men bear arms. Only a tiny percentage of people, at the very far ends of the bell curve, fall into the stereotypical pattern of masculine men who get into fights, and race cars, and who never talk about their feelings; or women who are content to be a domesticated Barbie doll. Personally, I prefer men with qualities that are often considered feminine—patience, sensuality, and a willingness to confide; and I favor women with qualities usually admired in men—assertiveness, physical courage, and the ability to change a flat tire.

Masculine and feminine are not absolute opposites, abstract points at either end of a continuum. We find our way towards wholeness by balancing different attributes and qualities within ourselves that are never completely masculine or feminine. Masculinity and femininity are like points on the compass. We move between them in an ocean of limitless possible manifestation, among attributes that are interchangeable and overlapping. None of our experience is absolutely gendered. In medieval Europe, the alchemists used the image of the androgyne, who is both man and woman, as an archetypal depiction of wholeness. Today, we can meet men with vaginas and women with penises. If I say that I am more in touch with qualities stereotypically associated with femininity than I was when I masqueraded as a man, I must also say that I am more in touch with qualities associated with masculinity as well. I am more in touch. Period. I am whole, and wholeness includes all the dimensions of possible human expression. The invitation for all of us is to be both, and neither, and all. The one we think of as "other" is always inside us.

There are societies that do not polarize men and women. The Navajo have at least forty-nine different gender designations. In the Americas, Siberia, Africa, Asia, even in Europe, into the early part of the twentieth century, there are accounts of gender identities that do not conform to the rigid binary we have come to insist upon. Variant gender identity and expression is often held as sacred; and "two spirit" people were frequently the healers, shamans, and teachers.

Yet, the idea that there is a fundamental difference between men and women pervades our culture. It is still an insult to call a woman mannish, or a man effeminate. When we meet someone for the first time we automatically look for the clues that will determine their gender. If there is any uncertainty, it makes most of us uncomfortable. "Is it a boy or a girl?" is the first thing we ask about a newborn child. Physicians still surgically alter the genitalia of ambiguously sexed infants. Until a few years ago young children were given electric shock treatment if they behaved in a manner deemed inappropriate to their sex, and violence is perpetrated daily against ambiguously gendered and otherwise queer folk. Difference is held as absolute, and transgression is seen as a threat to the status quo. Generations of men have been silenced and shamed by trying to become John Wayne, just as women have been oppressed trying to become Betty Crocker, or Aunt Jemima.

Most constructs of social difference are inherently violent because their purpose is to maintain the status quo, and the status quo is all about keeping power in the hands of an elite. Categories of difference lead to categories of superiority and inferiority. It was once the officially held view that Native Americans were less than human—and therefore had no human or legal rights. In the not so distant past, pseudo-scientific research claimed that people of African or Jewish descent were fundamentally different, and inferior, to people of European descent. Since the time of the Roman Empire, colonizing powers have described the lands and people they colonized as feminine, different, and thus inferior. Today, the safety, well-being, and values of white middle-class North Americans takes automatic priority over the lives of others around the world, and within this country, whose toil supports the lifestyle of the privileged few.

I have come to see, more than ever before, how collectively we deny our bodies while we despoil the world—lest the pain of it overwhelm us. If we were to let ourselves feel the full force of our collective grief, and shame, and rage, we might be crushed, or we might see ourselves as someone entirely other than the person we imagined ourselves to be. We might be forced to make dramatic changes in our lives, or else feel the impotence of not being able to change. So we modify our desires and fears lest they consume us. Yet our denial of them consumes us anyway. What we hide, or hide from, usually returns to haunt us—whether as the conflagration of war, or as a little "white" lie. Everybody suffers in the end. The psychic, emotional, and physical violence of homophobia, racism, cultural chauvinism, and economic oppression wounds us all. We pay lip service to the idea of individuality, yet we are afraid of the "other" who embodies difference. Unwilling to accept complexity and difference, we settle for oversimplifications—personally, politically and spiritually—that perpetuate division, dehumanize people, and create real suffering in real lives.

Surely, I did not have to change my sex in order to understand that identity is fluid, and that injustice and oppression is rife. This just happens to have been my journey. Apparently, I took a risk in order to establish some sort of inner integrity and ended up looking into the face of our collective demons. I never imagined that my experience as a transsexual woman would radicalize me in the way that it has. I now live dumbfounded that we have invented a world of constructed identities—of gender, sexuality, class, race, culture, and religion. My own body, and the ambiguity I represent, reminds me of it every day. Especially during the time of my transition, fear, lust, confusion, ridicule, and anger were mirrored back to me on a regular basis, as were warmth, trust, sympathy, and even love. I became a touchstone to which people could respond in their own self-revealing way.

THE TERM "Dharma Door" is used in Buddhism to describe anything that awakens us to the truth. A Dharma Door is something that leads us into the fullness of our life.

There are said to be ten thousand Dharma Doors. Perhaps there are as many doors as there are people to pass through them. Even a closet door, something that hides our deepest secret shame, may turn out to be a Dharma Door.

The "truth," even the most personal "truth," is not determined by whether one is a man or a woman any more than it is determined solely by race, culture of origin, faith, or economic or personal circumstances. The body, and the body of the world, is sacred, and given to us in sacred trust. Life always reveals itself in the end, and we can always depend on that revelation, beyond the categories by which we seek to define them. What we all seek, and what defines us most intimately, is the desire for love and connection with others, the ability to trust and listen to each other, and the freedom to do meaningful work. Our identities, however strongly they define us, are the context—always fluid, always dependent on perceptions and circumstances.

Maybe, once upon a time, I was just a regular guy.

But memory fades and it is hard to imagine what that was like.

men holding hands
meri nana-ama danquah

AT SEVENTEEN, I already knew the pleasures of sex but I hadn't yet come to fully understand the power of touch. It was senior year. We were fresh, we were fine, and soon we'd be free, legally admissible to adulthood, that much-anticipated paradise of privilege. By "we," I mean my friends and I, that gang of girls to which I belonged back then. We were known as "The Hallway Crew" because we spent more time loitering by the school lockers than we did in class, preparing for our futures.

It seems amazing to me now, given all the hours we spent obsessing about men, how little we really knew about them. From time to time we did actually talk to them, but not nearly as much as we talked about them. When we went to watch them play sports, we concentrated not on their moves, but on their parts, those thick arms and muscled thighs, those firm butts. We oohed and aahed and imagined ourselves holding those perfectly sculpted bodies. We believed, I suppose, that by filling our open embraces, those young men would somehow also be filling our empty hearts. Little did we know that nothing could be further from the truth.

I remember those days so well, getting dressed in front of the mirror for a Friday night in the city, my clothing so tight and inappropriately inviting I could barely exhale for fear of coming undone, the Pointer Sisters on the stereo declaring their desires: a man with a slow hand, a lover with an easy touch. And me singing along forcefully, as if I really knew anything about either. On one of those nights, the crew and I, fake IDs in hand, decided to go to Genesis, the newest, hottest club around. It was a theme club, devoted solely to R&B or Rock & Roll on some nights, and House Music or Over-Thirty-Only or Ladies-Get-In-Free on other nights. That one time we went, it just so happened to be Gay night.

Back then, my friends and I liked manly men, the shoot-'em-up-bang-bang types, the tall-dark-and-handsome broth-ers, the strong-but-silent ones; you know, all those cliched descriptions that somehow slide themselves into a hetero-sexual woman's vocabulary as she paints her picture of Mr. Right. When we walked into Genesis, the room was full of them: tall and short men, black and white men in dinner jackets and in blue jeans, men in leather and pastel-colored *Miami Vice*–style linen suits. There were women too, but not very many. In fact, we had already plopped ourselves at the bar and ordered drinks before any of us in my group real-ized that it was a same-gender coupling scene.

"Oh my god," one of the girls I was with screeched. "They're all gay."

"What?" asked the rest of us in unison. Before she could

repeat herself, we saw what she was about to say. Right in front of us strolled two men holding hands and gazing deeply into each other's eyes. It was arresting. I couldn't stop staring at them, at the shy, bashful way they smiled at each other, the way they slowly laced their fingers together only to unlace them and gently caress each other's palms. Their tenderness took me by surprise. They were clearly in love, oblivious to everything and everyone around them.

I was not as interested in the other guys at the club, the ones who were on the shiny wood floor with their mates dancing suggestively, or following a flirtation that would later lead them into some back room where they would tongue and grope and moan their way into ecstasy. What they were doing was nothing less than what my friends and I would have also been doing had we been provided with either an opportunity or an accomplice. I was used to that kind of passion, that kind of lust, raw and urgent and ravenous.

"Let's get out of here," my friends suggested, "and go where there are some straight guys." They gulped down the last drops of their drinks and got up to leave. I couldn't move. My eyes were still fixed on the two men. "Stop staring and come on," they insisted, while leading me to the club's exit. My girlfriends assumed the reason I was so taken by the couple was that I had never seen two men together. Not so. I was extremely comfortable with the concept, as well as the sight, of men partnered with other men. It was as much a part of my world as a so-called traditional marriage, one with a Mr. and a Mrs. I had an uncle who was in a committed relationship with a man, and theirs would ultimately end up being one of the most compassionate and stable unions I would ever witness in my life.

What held my attention was not the sexuality of the two men at the club; it was, rather, the lack thereof. It made me realize that I had never been touched like that. I had never held hands with a man for nothing more than the sake of holding hands, of being close. I wouldn't have even known how to approach a man for that purpose, how to request such a simple gesture. In my young adult reality, when you were touched by a man, it was one of two things—a sexual overture, or an act of violence. Men were to be feared or they were to be fucked. And that's all. To expect more was to court disappointment.

It seemed as though with each other, men were often easily able to achieve, and display, a certain type of sensitivity that they were not able to with women. Sure, the men at the club were probably not the best examples of this theory because they were gay, but I believed that it also applied to men who weren't gay—the frat rats, the boxer buddies, the Saturday-morning hoop-shooters, and the Monday-night cigar-smoking poker players—all the guys who usually went out of their way to avoid touching with one another for fear that they might be seen as gay. (And what could possibly be worse than that?)

I had noticed that even those men shared a deep emotional connection, an intimacy that was commonly referred to as "male bonding." At times that intimacy was manifested physically, too. The way, for instance, they lightly tapped each other's asses on the courts and on the fields, the way they leaned on each other in the ring between rounds, bare shoulder to bare shoulder, their sweaty chests meeting somewhere in the slick middle; or the way they sometimes embraced, their arms tightly and fully wrapped around, their noses resting on the fleshy bridge between neck and shoulder.

In those rare moments when it was, for whatever reason, permissible for a man to place his hands on another man as an outward show of affection, I saw a vulnerability that completely challenged my preconceived notions of masculinity.

And what were my preconceived notions of masculinity? Those images and ideas that were written in books and song lyrics, shown in movies and on television, of what men—real men—were supposed to do and be: breadwinners, white-collar businessmen, lawyers, doctors, and accountants, blue-collar contractors, plumbers, and mechanics; strong, stoic, aggressive, dry-eyed and unemotional. What else, at seventeen, did I know but that? Sure, I could probably blame it on my upbringing, come up with some Freudian explanation like "such ignorance would be expected from a girl with an absent father and no male siblings in the home." But what of the other girls, my friends who were raised with their nuclear families intact, with a daddy and a big brother or two? What excuse could they offer for their knight-in-shining-armor expectations that mirrored my own?

That night at Genesis something momentarily shifted in me. Suddenly, surrounded by scores of men—gay men, some of whom were visibly effeminate, some of whom were frighteningly macho, and the remaining majority of whom were ordinary, everyday people—I found myself wondering how it all fit into the larger picture of masculinity. At least, the larger picture that I had been envisioning. I wondered if masculinity was as much a show, a well-constructed myth, as femininity. I thought about how my girlfriends and I dolled ourselves up in silly, ill-fitting girlie-girl clothes, how we polished our nails, blushed our cheeks, lined our eyes, and colored our lips; I thought about how we wasted our money on magazines with enticing names like *Allure* and *Glamour* and *Cosmopolitan,* magazines which were supposed to teach us how to be more feminine, how to be the sort of women that men would want. None of it was real.

When my friends and I were together, when we were dressed down and not made up, we were no princesses or damsels in distress; we were simply ourselves. We didn't smile and giggle coquettishly like we had learned that ladies were supposed to; we laughed, deep-bellied and loud. We cussed if we wanted to, and when we grew tired of talking about men, we turned to topics of greater substance, topics that required us to use our intelligence, to show that we were actually capable of originality.

Was that true of men as well? Were they only free to be themselves, their real selves, when they were together, when they were shielded from the quixotic wishes of women? I didn't have the answers, but those questions inspired me to consider the possibility that my search for a flesh-and-blood man who could fit perfectly into my fantasies was, perhaps, a wasted effort.

That was a huge idea, maybe too huge; it was definitely

one whose implications I was not prepared to accept because if not the dreamy Don Juan, then who? The tragically thin president of the AV Club? The bespectacled pedant who, though Harvard-bound, was neither hot nor cool? Not a chance because I truly believed that I would find him, the man that I was looking for. If not through destiny, then surely as a result of my determination. So no amount of time or energy devoted to that cause would be done in vain.

Adulthood altered my priorities and, in the process, the nature of my encounters with the opposite sex. By the time I reached my thirties, my life was filled with men. They were no longer these curious creatures that I watched, and wanted, from afar. They were my colleagues, my friends. Over the years, some of them had even slowly come to occupy the "best friend" and "confidant" positions that had once belonged solely to women. Not unlike my sister-friends, these men laughed with me and kept my secrets. These male friends of mine—gay and straight alike—knew me as well as, or better than, any woman had ever known me. The friendships were platonic, but they were not devoid of touch. There was hand-holding, light lip-to-cheek kissing, and there were hugs, lots and lots of hugs. How I relied on those embraces, on the ability to be held without the prospect of sex, the awkward anticipation of it on the part of either individual.

There were moments, in their presence, when I completely lost myself, when I forgot that they were men, that I was a woman. With the handicaps and hindrances of gender gone, we were just people who understood each other, people who loved each other, who had each other's best interests at heart. Ironically, it was this same fluency, this kinship that was warm and pliant and enduring, that I attempted to duplicate with my boyfriends. Except it never worked, because the men with whom I had these relationships never bore any of the likable and essentially kindhearted traits as the men with whom I had friendships.

Any ability that I had with my friends to see past the smoke and mirrors that separate men and women did not apply when it came to me and potential lovers. Where romance was concerned, my faith was still firmly placed in some intractable vision of men. It seemed as if I chose my male friends expressly for who they were, for their humor or their compassion or their creativity, whatever characteristic that was uniquely their own, that touched my heart and moved us confidently into each other's lives. Yet I chose my lovers not for who they were, but for who I wanted them to be—the hard-muscled miracle that I was waiting for, the one who would come and sweep me off my feet.

It shouldn't be much of a surprise that I found myself involved with creeps—emotionally crippled misogynists and smooth-talking philanderers—who, while giving me that which I wanted, the seductive pretense of masculinity, always left me with much to be desired. There were no comfortable exchanges, no inside jokes or knowing glances. What existed were silences that drew us deeper into our distance from one another, no matter how lip-locked and horizontal we were. We played our parts, acquiesced to those paralyzing roles—me as the coy, obedient, batting-eyelash lady, the prey; him as the dynamic, self-assured pacesetter, the hunter. It was a terrible masquerade, a dance that swung me back and forth between the cultivation of fear and the surrender of flesh.

To be sure, it was a mindless pattern, one that I drew from habit or memory; but I didn't recognize it as such. Not at first, anyway. I thought I was just unlucky in love, kissing the proverbial frogs until I found the one with the crown. I still believed. Why? Mostly because I wanted to believe. But also because I was encouraged to keep believing, to keep hoping that despite every ill-fated liaison, despite all the heartache that I had experienced, there was a man out there waiting for me, a man on bended knee, with a glass slipper and a diamond ring, who would make it all worthwhile. "Hold out," so many had advised, "for the one." "Hang in there for Mr. Right." It was such a familiar refrain, so overplayed. I had heard it, sung it, and seen it so many times, why wouldn't I want to believe?

WHEN I LEFT for a month-long sojourn in Ghana, I was ready for a new reality. A native, I had emigrated to the United States during elementary school. It was my first time there in over two and a half decades so, by all reasonable definitions, I was a stranger. It was, I knew, a trip that would change my life, if for no other reason than that, the fact that I would be courting my past, returning to the customs and lifestyle that had shaped my early consciousness. I expected whatever new insights I would gain to center around language, food, clothing, music, family—all the immediate representations of culture and home. It never occurred to me that I might also gain a greater understanding of relationships and the impact that society has on the way in which we imagine and arrive at them.

While in Ghana, I stayed in Accra, the capital city, and spent as much time as I could with relatives, matching the faces that I was seeing as if for the first time with the names that I had read in volumes of letters and the voices that I had heard through so many static-filled phone calls. When I wasn't at the home of an uncle or an aunt, I was at the beach, or the busy downtown market, at a restaurant, or a side-of-the-road chop bar, taking in the landscape, studying the movements and the routines of the people who came and went, the people who could just as easily have been me, had I not left and been brought up elsewhere.

There were a few nights when a good family friend, with whom I had been fairly close while he lived in the United States, took me around to some of his haunts. One night, early in my stay, we went to a neighborhood jazz joint where they served kebabs, grilled tilapia with banku, and tall bottles of the nationally brewed beers, Star and Club. The place, which was packed, had indoor seating, but nearly everyone was outdoors. There were a few couples in the area reserved for dancing, but most of the patrons were standing around in groups, loitering in the various corners and at the entrance nearest to the parking lot, a small rectangle of red earth that was full of Peugeots and Mercedes-Benzes.

As soon as my friend, whom I'll call David—a slender, late-forties financial analyst—and I were shown to our table, he was spotted by a friend, who took it upon himself to join us. In a matter of minutes, we were joined by yet another

friend and pretty soon, our table was full and there were a
few other friends standing around us—all men. After the
obligatory introductions—which were always courteous
and accompanied by polite handshakes—my presence became meaningless to them. I wasn't sure if it was because I
was a stranger, or because I, a woman, had no place in their
discourse. Whatever the reason, I was happy to observe, to
eat, drink and listen as they talked politics and economics,
punctuating crucial points with raised voices and animated
hand motions.

I'm not sure how much time had passed before I noticed
that the two men standing behind David were holding
hands. They had, for some time, been engaged in their own
side conversation, but would periodically jump into the
main discussion when things seemed to be heating up. I
searched the faces of the men at the table to see if they, too,
had noticed. As I looked around, I saw that many of the men
there, at the establishment, were also holding hands. At that
point, I didn't know what to think.

On our way back to his car, David and I were walking
behind two men who were holding hands. Actually, they
weren't holding hands; their pinky fingers were hooked
around each other and they were slightly swinging their
arms back and forth, back and forth, as they walked together
through the parking lot.

"I think it is really cool," I said to David, "that people
here are so out and open about homosexuality."

"What?" he asked, stopping cold in his tracks. "Homosexuality? We don't have any of that stuff going on down
here. Not out and in the open anyway."

"Then what do you call that?" I pointed to the men in front of us.

"I don't understand. What are you talking about?" David asked. He looked at the men, again, and then returned his gaze to me. It was obvious that nothing seemed out of the ordinary to him.

"They're holding hands."

"So what? It doesn't make them homosexuals," he laughed. "They're friends. In places all over the world, men hold hands, and it has nothing to do with sex. It's quite common, you know."

He was right. Riding around Accra the next day, I saw more men holding hands. I found it all rather unsettling, and was both shocked and embarrassed by my level of discomfort. Had I been in America, I thought, I would surely not have responded that way. I would not have even given it a second thought or glance. But in America such activity was restricted to specific locations. There were places where you know there is a greater likelihood of witnessing it: the Castro, Dupont Circle, West Hollywood, the Village. These men in Accra were presumably heterosexual; they were black men; big men with well-defined everything from head to toe. And they were holding hands. Holding hands! I just couldn't seem to bring myself to think of it as anything other than bizarre.

That was the first week. After the second week, I got over it. I started adapting, reminding myself that I was not in America; I was in Ghana, where the gestures of intimacy were different, assigned by the societal mandates and mores of that land. Those differences were not brought to light solely by the way the men interacted with each other. They were evident in the way the men interacted with the women as well. If all of that hand-holding and emotional bonding made the men more sensitive, it didn't show when they were dealing with women. The only time during my stay that I saw men publicly touching women was when they were dancing. Not once during that trip did I spy a couple stealing a kiss, standing with an arm around the other's waist, holding hands.

What I saw were women preparing meals, hand-washing clothes outside in the scorching heat, and selling meat, fish, and vegetables in kiosks and at outdoor markets. I saw a line, that was clear and pronounced, a line that placed men on one side and women on the other, a line that was as real and recognized as the prime meridian that ran directly through the country. As is usually the case with segregation, separate was not at all equal. One gender held power, with free access to all its privileges and rights; the other did not. It was as simple as that.

One evening, shortly before my departure, I stopped by the Shangri-La for a drink. David had taken me there on one of his guided tours. It was a fancy hotel for moneyed tourists which though occasionally frequented by the local bourgeoisie was, for the most part, a place for foreigners. With the exception of a few masks, bows and arrows, and patches of mudcloth sewn into this and that, the bar there was nothing special. It was your average Western watering hole with uncomfortable stools and a jukebox in the corner.

I ran into one of the guys I had met with David at the jazz spot. He was alone, and he waved me over to join him at the other end of the bar. I was impressed that he even re-membered me, seeing as how the night we'd met he had barely spoken two words to me beyond the "hello." He bought me a beer and we made small talk for a few minutes about the few weeks I'd spent in Ghana. Then he told me he wanted to take me out to dinner, to spend some time with me before I returned to the States. At first I thought it was a joke, the way he'd slid his hand along the bar until it was touching mine, the way he'd cleared his throat and de-livered the words, not as a question, but as a request, a de-mand. I soon got that he was serious. Not knowing what else to say or do, I pointed to the gold ring on the third fin-ger of his left hand.

"Aren't you married?" I asked, as if that was even the point, the part that was offensive. He pulled the band off, held it up with the fingers of his right hand for a second, as if to inspect it, then he put it back on.

"Ah, this," he said, staring at the ring. "It's for my wife. She is the one who is married, not me." I was too stunned to conjure a witty comeback, or even an insult. He seemed to find the situation amusing; he smiled and shook his head.

"What can you do?" he shrugged. "Men will be men." Still speechless, I gave his words some thought.

"You're right," I managed, with a smile. "Men will be men." I thanked him for the drink, and left.

LATER THAT NIGHT, when I took the time to think through it all, I knew that he was right. Men will be men. It was such a simple truth, one that I had been unwilling to accept until that very moment. But just then, it made perfect sense to me. All those years I had spent thinking that there was some mystery to masculinity, some secret code that I had to learn to crack. Being there in Ghana, so far away from the cues to which I had been conditioned to respond, being able to watch the men and the women there as they went about their lives, as they flirted and flaunted and flexed and fought, made me appreciate that it was all a performance. Like a peacock fanning its tail feathers, we attempt to lure others to us by exhibiting the assets and behaviors to which we think they will be attracted: the tight pants, the thousand-dollar suit, the plum lipstick, the patented pick-up line. More often than not, we learn to accept those traits that others—magazines, movies, sappy song lyrics, romance novels—have defined as appealing, empowering, deserving. And so the games begin!

That's not masculinity. It may be insecurity, it may be arrogance, it may even be stupidity. But it's not masculinity, as defined by the heart of an individual, the truth of who they really are. Men will always be men if they hide behind that mask, that term, that generic, nameless, faceless word. They will always revert to type.

I was correct to wonder, at seventeen, whether men were better able to be themselves when they were not around women or, more specifically, when they were not in the company of those whose expectations set the stage for a farce, a fantasy. I could tell by the way they talked, by the way they touched when there was no judgment, when they were not required to be the object of anyone's predetermined desires. There was freedom, there was laughter, there was a person, a real individual, someone with whom you could possibly even fall in love, someone who could possibly even be the one.

sanctuary
jarvis jay masters

WHEN I FIRST ENTERED the gates of San Quentin in the winter of 1981, I walked across the upper yard holding a box called a "fish-kit" filled with my prison-issued belongings. I saw the faces of hundreds who had already made the prison their home. I watched them stare at me with piercing eyes, their faces rugged and their beards of different shades—all dressed in prison blue jeans and worn, torn coats—some leaning against the chain fences, cigarettes hanging from their lips, others with dark glasses covering their eyes.

I will never forget when the steel cell door slammed shut behind me. I stood in the darkness trying to fix my eyes and readjust the thoughts that were telling me that this was not home—that this tiny space would not, could not be where I would spend more than a decade of my life. My mind kept saying, "No! Hell no!" I thought again of the many prisoners I had seen moments ago standing on the yard, so old and accustomed to their fates.

I dropped my fish-kit. I spread my arms and found that the palms of my hands touched the walls with ease. I pushed against them with all my might, until I realized how silly it was to think that these thick concrete walls would somehow budge. I groped for the light switch. It was on the back wall, only a few feet above the steel-plated bunk bed. The bed was bolted into the wall like a shelf. It was only two and a half feet wide by six feet long, and only several feet above the gray concrete floor.

My eyes had adjusted to the darkness by the time I turned the lights on. But until now I hadn't seen the swarms of cockroaches clustered about, especially around the combined toilet and sink on the back wall. When the light came on, the roaches scattered, dashing into tiny holes and cracks behind the sink and in the walls, leaving only the very fat and young ones still running scared. I was beyond shock to see so many of these nasty creatures. And although they didn't come near me, I began to feel roaches climbing all over my body. I even imagined them mounting an attack on me when I was asleep.

This was home. For hours I couldn't bear the thought. The roaches, the filth plastered on the walls, the dirt balls collecting on the floor, and the awful smell of urine left in the toilet for God knows how long sickened me nearly to the point of passing out.

To find home in San Quentin, I had to summon an unbelievable will to survive. My first step was to flush the toilet. To my surprise I found all I needed to clean my cell in the fish-kit—a towel, face cloth, and a box of state detergent. There were also a bar of state soap, a toothbrush and comb, a small can of powdered toothpaste, a small plastic cup, and two twenty-year-old *National Geographic* magazines, one of them from the month and year of my birth.

It seemed that time was now on my side. I started cleaning vigorously. I began with one wall, then went on to the next, scrubbing them from top to bottom as hard as I could to remove the markings and filth. I didn't stop until I had washed them down to the floor and they were spotless. If I had to sleep in here, this was the least I could do. The cell bars, sink and toilet, and floor got the same treatment. I was especially worried about the toilet. I had heard that prisoners were compelled to wash their faces in their toilets whenever tear gas was shot into the units to break up mass disruptions and the water was turned off. I imagined leaning into this toilet, and I cleaned it to the highest military standards.

I spent hours, sometimes on my hands and knees, washing down every inch of my cell—even the ceiling. When I had finished, I was convinced that I could eat a piece of candy that had dropped onto the floor. The roaches had all drowned or been killed. I blocked off all their hiding places by plugging up the holes and cracks in the walls with wet toilet paper.

After the first days had passed, I decided to decorate my walls with photographs from the *National Geographic* magazines. The landscapes of Malaysia and other parts of the world had enormous beauty, and I gladly pasted photos of them everywhere. These small representations of life helped me to imagine the world beyond prison walls.

Over the years, I collected books and even acquired a

television and radio—windows to the outside world. And I pasted many thousands of photographs on the wall. The one that has made my prison home most like a sanctuary to me is a small photograph of a Buddhist saint that a very dear friend sent to me. It has been in the center of my wall for a number of years.

I now begin every day with the practice of meditation, seated on the cold morning floor, cushioned only by my neatly folded blanket. Welcoming the morning light, I realize, like seeing through clouds, that home is wherever the heart can be found.

pablo's wish

I knew something wasn't right when I left my cell that morning to go to the yard. It was nothing more than a feeling, a convict's instinct, perhaps, as I observed the strange maneuvering of some other prisoners also making their way down to the lower yard for three hours of exercise time.

I had been in San Quentin less than two years, but by then I had seen more than enough to realize as I passed through the lower yard gate that a hit was going to come down. Someone was going to be stabbed.

It was no business of mine. I went about the yard, taking in some air before getting into my daily routine of playing a few games of dominoes and then jogging several laps around the yard.

While jogging, I spotted an old familiar face and smiled

in a misery loves company kind of way. I hadn't seen Pablo since the early spring of 1972. In those days we had both been juvenile delinquents who always showed up in the same corridors of Juvenile Hall. We liked it there, we'd once joked.

"Damn, Pablo! Is that you? Where have you been, dude?" I asked, elated to see my old road dog and friend squatting down against the south block wall, puffing on a cigarette. I could tell that he had just arrived at San Quentin and didn't know his way around the exercise yard. He seemed nervous.

"Hey, Jarvis!" said Pablo, with obvious surprise. "How you been doing? Shit, man, I haven't seen you in ages. I thought you were dead. How long has it been—ten, fifteen years?"

"Yeah, it's been about that long." I smiled. "Man, I been here almost two years now. But what about you? Where have *you* been? The last time I seen you, we were both in juvenile detention for stealing a pack of cigarettes. You remember that?"

"Yeah, I remember," Pablo said, grinning. "We crawled out of the dormitory that one night and got caught trying to steal a pack of Camels out of the counselor's shirt when we thought he was sleeping." Pablo laughed. "Man, since then, I've been all through this rat hole system. I did a little county camp time after I seen you. Then I did a few years in the California Youth Authority. I hit the big time after that—man, straight to the penitentiary. This is my fourth time in the joint. Plus, I did five years for the Feds in Lompoc!"

"How much time do you have now?"

Pablo was silent. The cigarette in his mouth began to puff like a hot chimney. His face twitched with fear. Then with his eyes fixed on the prison yard, he answered, "Well, Jarvis, I estimate two hours, tops."

"Damn, Pablo. What's going on?" I asked. I had only to look at his eyes to see that I had been right about the hit, and that Pablo was the marked man.

Pablo lit another cigarette. "Man, it's a long story," he said, exhaling. "All I can tell you is that I really fucked up this time. I've gotten into somethin' I can't get out of, and I know they'll be comin' for my head before I leave this yard. So it's best that you don't know."

"What can I do to help?"

"Man, there isn't really nothin' you can do. Just reach into my coat pocket," he said, trying to hide even from me the weapon slipped up his sleeve. "There's an envelope with an address and a photograph of my little girl Alice inside. She's my heart. If anything happens to me today, Jay, do me this favor and write to her. Tell her that I love her. Tell her something sweet for me."

"Ah, man! You know I'll do that for you. But what can I do now? Pablo—talk to me. Check: I'm willing to stand here and go down with you."

"No!" said Pablo. "Jay, this is *not* your fight. We'll both die, man, if you hang around much longer. This is some real serious shit I'm caught in, and if it goes down, I want to be by myself. Don't worry about me—I'm goin' down with a fight. And they know it."

I didn't know what to say. Pablo held out his hand and

began laughing as we shook. "Man," he said, "I sure wish we could've ran into each other without all this other shit happenin'. We must have a million things we could talk about, huh? But now isn't the time. I'm serious, Jarvis. You have to get away from me before it's too late." My friend stared at me with certainty.

It was hard to walk away from Pablo, the last thing I wanted to do. But I left him, with the smell of violence in the air.

I walked as far as I could, trying to contain myself until I got to the opposite side of the yard. I didn't want to see what would happen.

Almost an hour passed. Then all the nerves in my body quivered at the sound of a prison alarm shrieking like an out-of-control bullhorn on the lower yard. I heard rapid gunshots. Pow! Pow!...Pow! Pow! Pow! Pow! Pow!... Pow! Pow! The shots came from a gun tower not far from where I had talked with Pablo. A guardsman's rifle was pointing down at the spot where I had stood. I knew instantly that Pablo was dead. My mind froze.

It was days later, after the prison came off a major lockdown that kept all of us confined to our cells for investigation, when I found out what had happened. Pablo had been stabbed eighteen times, and shot once in the thigh by one of the tower gunmen. He was pronounced dead in the prison hospital.

A friend who had witnessed the stabbing told me, "He was crazy. He never stopped fighting. They told him to stop, but he kept going. It was like he was chasing death, and wasn't going to stop, no way, until he caught it—until he rode it on out of here."

A week later, I lay on my bunk, trying to find words for Alice. I wanted to write a beautiful letter saying what I thought her father had wanted to express.

Until that night, I had never opened the envelope I had taken from Pablo's pocket, because I didn't want to come face to face with her. What right did I have when I should be dead with him?

I finally brought it out of hiding and looked at the photograph. I could see in the dim light of my cell that Alice was a lovely girl with a strong resemblance to her father. I stared at the picture for some time, trying to compose a letter in my mind. Then I turned it over. The writing was barely legible:

> Dear Alice,
>   Your Dad loves you. When you get this, my troubled life will have probably ended. But certainly not my love. Alice, with this photo, please know how I've always held on to you, and have kept you always in my heart. I love you. So take care, my darling, and please forgive me for all my wrongs. I wasn't a real father to you.
>   Love, Pablo

Pablo had already said it all.

a reason to live

"Man, I wonder why that dude Alex keeps trying to kill himself," Tex said to me as we stood along the fence one hot summer day out on the exercise yard. "In Texas, where I come from, boy, black folks thank the Lawd, I mean daily, that white folks ain't lynching there no more. And here we are, man, in the eighties, standing right in the middle of San Quentin, staring at this young black man that's out trying to lynch himself. I tell ya, that boy needs his damn ass whipped!"

"Is that him over there," I asked, "with the basketball?"

"Yep, that's him," said Tex. "That boy is one sad case if I ever seen one. All he need, man, is one of those royal ass whippings, that's all!"

"Naw," I replied, "I don't think that's going to solve anything. He just needs to sit down with one of us who's been here a few years and get schooled on how to cope with all this prison madness."

"Man, don't you know I spent four long aching hours talking to this dude the last time he tried committing suicide? We sat right there in that corner, man, rapping about what was going on. Shuh! It didn't do no good, though, because in two weeks, not even two weeks, that nut went and tried it again. That pisses me off."

"Well, hey, you probably didn't get at him right. You probably did all this gabbing, thinking he was listening when he wasn't. You know how young dudes are. They only hear what they want to."

"Nah, man," said Tex, "it wasn't nothin' like that. I really approached him with good intentions. I went all out trying to give this young brother the benefit of my experience."

"Is that right?" I asked.

"Ah, man! When I found out for the first time that a youngster in this building had tried to take himself out by the back door, it really hurted me. I rose straight out of my bunk, smoked half a pack of cigarettes, and decided right then that I was going to try to convince him that suicide wasn't cool."

"When you first got wind of it, did you know who he was?" I asked.

"The only thing I got off the grapevine that night was that a young con had tried to hang himself in our cell block but was cutted down in time by the guards. It wasn't until the following morning that I found out it was Alex."

"So how long after this did you have an opportunity to get with him?"

"He spent a few days in the prison psych ward before they brought his tail back to the cell block. I think it was about a week after his first attempt that we sat down in the yard."

"Did he ever tell you why he tried to take himself out?" I asked.

"Oh, yeah," Tex said. "We kicked that at length. This dude is only eighteen years old. But trip out: he told me it was because his girlfriend stood him up two weeks in a row."

"What?" I shouted. "Is that all? Tex, you must be jiving. You really don't mean to tell me this fool tried to kill himself just because his girlfriend stood him up? Is he nuts or just straight-out stupid?"

"Man, I don't have the slightest idea. All I know is what he said. And he told me that she stopped writing him, too."

"How much time did this fool say he had left?"

"Jarvis, man, you ain't going to believe it. This guy only have, get this, eleven more months left. Man, he is only doing *wino* time."

"It must be his cell that is really getting to him, huh?"

"Hell, no. That boy got boo-coo people to write and mo' appliances than I ever had and I been in S.Q. almost eight years," Tex said with envy. "That dude has a lot mo' people than me who really cares for him on the outside. They already sent him a color TV and a radio."

"So what's his problem?"

"Hey, man, your guess is better than mine. All I know is, I sat there talking to this dude for hours, sharing all my experiences and trying to give him, you know, the strength to live."

"Did he listen?"

"Oh, yeah, he listened, but what got rocks in my jaws is that afterwards he turns around—and I mean right around—and tries to hang himself again."

"Maybe, Tex, he just wants attention."

"Well, if that's what he's after," said Tex, "he damn sho' ain't going to find it in San Quentin. Hell! This here don't look nothin' like no Betty Ford's center."

"Tell me this," I said, "did he come real close to dying both times or did it seem he wasn't for real?"

"Man, he was most definitely serious," Tex said. "From word off the grapevine, the boy really wants to die, man!"

"Is that right?" I said, lighting a cigarette. We stood in silence, staring at Alex across the exercise yard. In any other place, he would have looked like a typical high school teenager.

"Hey, Tex," I said, after a while. "Check it out: I'm going to call this Alex dude over here and try to reach his senses on this, because, man, if I don't and he ends up killing himself, I'm going to feel terrible that I never tried."

"Jay, it ain't going to do no good. Man, you know just as well as I do this dude is going to do whatever he wants, so why try?"

"You may be right, but at least I'll be able to say, like you, that I tried."

"But why repeat everything I already said? Anything you tell him is going to go in one ear and out the other."

"No, Tex, I don't think so. I'm going to approach it differently. And we really don't have nothing to lose."

"What do you mean?"

"You'll see. Just hang out with me while I talk to him, OK?"

"Yeah, but I bet you anything," said Tex, "he's going to smile and nod, acting like he did when I was trying to pour some sense into his empty head. But man, this boy is high on a serious death wish."

"Well, let's just find out."

I called Alex over.

"How you be?" I asked.

"I'm doing pretty good." He stared at me curiously, leaning his shoulder on the fence.

"Hey, check. My name is Jarvis. Tex here has told me

that you are the youngster making all the headlines around this joint—trying to do a hari-kari on us—so I thought I better hurry up and introduce myself before you fool around again and get it right, you dig?"

"Uh-huh," Alex nodded. "I hear where you're comin' from."

"Now, Bro," I said, "I don't mean to half-step you with a lot of shuffle 'n' jive—this is the real deal, the real McCoy, you dig?"

"Yeah, yeah. I hear you," Alex muttered, looking bored.

"I'm told that you only been in the prison system a short while. Is that right?"

"No, that ain't right." Alex pulled away from the fence. "I been in for 'bout six months."

"Yeah, OK!" I grinned. "That is just what I mean. For me, six months is short—in fact, so short that if you were a wino, you'd still have alcohol on your breath. Bro, let me tell you somethin'. Unlike Tex here, I personally don't care what you do. And you can wipe the bored expression off your face, dude. You can kill your damn self tonight and I'll snore right through it, you dig? I don't give a mad fuck! And most cons in this joint have the same attitude. We wouldn't give a rat's ass about what you do, you dig?

"Now, aside from that, I think you were really fortunate that Tex spent his entire yard time a few weeks back trying to give you all the benefits of his experience. Because he knows why it is important for you to stay alive."

"Hey, Bro," said Alex, trying to explain. "I understood what Tex was saying that day—I'm just having problems with my wom—"

"Whoa! I need to cut you off right there." I shook my head angrily. "We don't need to get into all the whys, man. Trip: I'm not here, like Tex, to persuade you not to kill your damn self—no way! In fact, I was just tellin' him I kind of wished your cell was next to mine whenever you try that foolishness again."

"Huh?" Alex was puzzled.

"He is serious!" said Tex. "Dead serious!"

"You goddamn right!" I said. "Why wouldn't I be? The way I see it, I would get all your food—your breakfast, your lunch, and that hot dinner—because, hell, everybody knows it doesn't make a lot of sense to eat on the eve of killing yourself. At the morgue, before they embalm your young stupid ass they just going to cut your stomach open and take it all out and dump it, anyway. So if I was in the next cell, you wouldn't have no qualms about sliding me over all your grub, huh?"

"Man," Alex took a second and swallowed. "I don't know too much about all that."

"That's what they do to all the stiffs. But moving along, don't you have a brand new color TV and radio in your cell?"

"Uh-huh . . . that my folks got for me."

"Well, hey, Alex, I don't mean to sound rude, but instead of giving the prison first grabs at 'em—you know they're theirs after you kill yourself—why not let me have 'em? That would be cool."

"No way, man. I am keeping my TV and radio."

"How's that? You thinking about having someone put 'em in your coffin?" I retorted.

"No," said Alex. "I'm keeping my things, though."

"You don't understand, Alex," I said. "I don't want 'em right now. No, man, I'm talking 'bout before you clamp that rope around your neck the next time—right before you kick the box under your feet and get to dangling 'round on your air vent, jerkin' and kickin' your feet against the back wall of your cell, all that saliva dribbling out your mouth and those big, fat snot bubbles blowing from your nose.

"Man!" I began laughing. "I bet that'd be real fun to watch—just seeing your feet vibrating, you turning purple in the face, then watching you hang deader than a doorknob on your vent…Man, man, man! What I want, though, is that color TV you got. So, Bro, how 'bout it?"

"Man, you are crazy," Alex stuttered, his eyes open wide, as he backpedaled away. "Uh-uh, I'm keeping my TV. You crazy, dude!"

"Aw, man!" I said. "What is it wit' you? Why are you calling me crazy? I never said that suicide was crazy. I mean, whatever is right for you is all right with me, too. I just want first cracks at your TV. What's wrong wit' that?"

"No, man. No way!" Alex stared, terrified. "You dudes is crazy. Man, you can't have my TV." He shook, looking for an out.

"Wait a minute," I said. "Where are you going? I haven't finished talkin' to you, Bro!"

"Man, I'm gettin' on," said Alex. "You's nuts. I swear you dudes is crazy."

"Before you go 'bout your business," I said, "check it: how 'bout them tennies you have on? You should at least let me have *them*."

"No way!" Alex stared down at his shoes. "I just got these Nikes last week. You can't have these for all the world."

"Those aren't Nikes. Let me see," I said, stepping toward him. "Wow, they *are* Nikes!" I snatched Alex by his coat and quickly pinned him to the fence. "Listen, you young chump." My eyes stared inches from the frightened kid's face. "You don't know nothin' 'bout this world. Trying to kill yourself—you don't know shit—and you know what? Since I still got big plans for being on this here planet, dude, you going to give me those damn shoes.

"Say, Tex," I said, turning. "Take off this chump's shoes. He's a dead man anyway, so fuck him and feed him fish. Man get his damn shoes off."

"Man . . . are you serious?" asked Tex, stunned.

"Hell, yeah!" I shouted. "This chump don't need no shoes where he wants to go." Tex crouched down to remove Alex's shoes.

"No, please don't," Alex begged. "Please don't take my shoes."

"Chump, shut up!" I threatened, wondering if Alex would find the will to fight.

"Man, let me go!" Alex burst out, shoving and gritting his teeth like a threatened wild animal until I gave way, letting him break loose. "Man, you dudes is fuckin' crazy!" he yelled, storming across the yard, his shoes unlaced.

"Ah, man, come on back here. I still have some mo' rap—"

"Hell, naw!" he screamed, staring over his shoulder.

"Well," I said, "just hurry up and take care of that business, so I can watch me some color TV. It's mine when you kill yourself. So don't take too long."

"You know what? Fuck you!" Alex shouted bravely from the middle of the exercise yard. "Your ass will die before mine's—and guess who is going to get your TV? *I* am! So you hurry up wit' your own damn business, you crazy nut."

"Oh, yeah? We just have to see about that."

I turned to Tex. "What do you think?"

"You wanna know what I think?" said Tex, flabbergasted. "I think you're crazier than all outdoors—tellin' that young'un about danglin' on his vent and saliva dribblin' out his mouth and that snot bubble in his nose. Ugh! Damn, where 'bout did you get all that crazy stuff?"

"Man, I don't know. I needed to reach that dude."

"Were you serious, though? Is that what happens when someone hangs themself?"

"I don't know. I never seen anyone hang himself. All I wanted to do is give this boy a reason to live. So do you think he'll try it again?"

"Hell no, he ain't goin' to try no shit like that again. Didn't you see his eyes? Man, he was scared shitless."

"Is that right?" I chuckled.

"I'm tellin' you, the boy was so scared of killing himself that I wouldn't doubt it if he outlives us both. This boy wants to live—if for nothin' else, to see your butt die before his."

"You know something, Tex?" I said as we looked out across the exercise yard. "That was the best damn 'Fuck you' I ever heard."

the end of men

michael moore

EARLIER THIS YEAR, my wife and I attended the baptism of our new nephew, Anthony. Our teenage daughter had been asked to be his godmother, a job that would require her to be there for little Anthony should he need to be burped, or raised Catholic, or both.

The baptism ceremony, we discovered, has changed a lot in the Catholic Church. Instead of just "hurry up and pour a little water on his forehead before we lose his soul to Satan," the Church now makes it a joyful event during Sunday Mass.

About halfway through the service, Father Andy asked the entire extended family to gather round the big baptismal font while little Anthony Proffer was submerged in the holy water and then wrapped in a pure white garment. The priest then held Anthony up for all the congregation to see, and everyone in the church applauded enthusiastically.

No one was applauding louder than me.

For this was the first time in thirteen years a BOY had been born into our family.

Thirteen babies in thirteen years in our family. That's eleven girls and two boys.

Now, I think most of us would agree that having a girl is, well, a little less work. Not that we love boys any less; and with a strong health insurance plan that covers broken arms, teeth, and collar bones, with additional coverage for fingers caught in car doors and personal injury claims from neighbors who allege our dear sweet little boy torched their Celica "just to see how fast Toyota paint burns," they're no more difficult to raise than girls.

I have lived my entire life in households where men were decidedly in the minority. I have no brothers, but two wonderful sisters. Between them and our mother, they made sure I did all the "woman's work" in the house, while my dad was granted occasional leave to watch a Sunday golf tournament. I tried to even things out a bit, claiming I deserved more of a say because I was the oldest, but that only galvanized my sisters' childhood feminist majority. To this day, as testimony to their assertive behavior, those who meet us when we're together are convinced that my sisters are older than I am, and that I'm the baby of the family.

I now live with my wife and my daughter. Outnumbered again. Whatever frightening male habits were not exorcised by my sisters and mother, these two have been merciless in finishing off. The latest was breaking me of spitting toothpaste all over the bathroom mirror while brushing my teeth. That one only took nineteen years.

They tell me the list is now down to a single page, with only three or four appalling behaviors left to annihilate (balancing my Big Gulp in the open space on the steering wheel while driving; leaving permanent ink stains on the arm of the chair I fall asleep in; snoring—though I fear this one may ultimately only be corrected by a pillow being "accidentally" slipped over my face and mysteriously held there, tightly, for a good three to five minutes).

Truth be told, I am a better person for having lived my life surrounded by strong, intelligent, and loving women. It just would have been nice to play catch. Once.

My parents have no grandsons. My sisters and I have only daughters. My wife's parents had four daughters and only two boys. They, in turn, produced eight more girls and only two additional boys. My wife's two brothers and I have only girls. Our family hasn't seen a game of tackle football or mumblety-peg since high school. This sacrifice appears to have gone unnoticed by nearly everyone involved.

I offer this little glimpse into the gender makeup of my family to point out a much larger discovery I've made. Pondering this lopsided ratio, I began asking around to find out if other people were experiencing the same thing—more girl babies being born than boy babies. Much to my surprise, I was not alone.

Lately, when I'm asked to speak at a university or community group, I leave the prepared agenda for a moment to ask how many in the room are seeing more girls being born in their families than boys. Scores of hands always shoot up.

Countless people began sharing their secret with me—that the ranks of boys are dwindling. In some families, it seems, they're altogether extinct. I always reassure them that there's no need to feel any shame in their inability to produce male offspring.

Then it hit me ... *something* is up.

And sure enough, something is. The Census Bureau confirms that the number of male babies being born has been *declining every year in the United States since 1990!* Plus, women are living longer and longer: 80 years, on average, versus only 74.2 for men. When I was a kid, the country seemed pretty much 50–50 male-female, with women maybe holding a slight lead. Then the ratio went to 51–49, with women in the majority. Soon it'll be 52–48.

So I have come to one ugly but irrefutable conclusion:

Guys! *Nature is trying to kill us off!*

Why is Mother Nature doing this? Are we not the carriers of the seed of life? What have we men done to deserve this?

As it turns out, plenty.

In the early years of Man, we served a critical and necessary function in the growth of the species. We hunted and gathered the food, protected the women and children from larger animals conspiring to eat them, and helped the number of *Homo sapiens* multiply rapidly through a lot of random, unrestricted sex. It's been downhill for us ever since.

In the past few centuries, things seem to have taken a fatal turn for our gender. As is our wont, we commenced work on a series of projects that stunk everything up and made a mess of our world. Women? They deserve none of the blame. They continued to bring life into this world; we continued to destroy it whenever we could. How many women have come up with the idea of exterminating a whole race of people? None that I've met at the gym. How many women have spilled oil in the oceans, dumped toxins in our food supply, or insisted that the new SUV designs had to be bigger, bigger, BIGGER? Hmmm. Let me see. . . .

Of the 816 species that have gone extinct since Columbus got lost and landed here (another man who wouldn't ask for directions)—most of which are necessary links in our fragile ecosystem—how many do you think were eradicated by women? Once again, I think we all know the answer.

If you were Nature, how would you respond to such a brutal assault? And what would you do if you noticed that it was one particular gender of humans that was going out of its way to destroy you? Well, Mother Nature has a habit of cutting to the chase. She'd defend herself *by any means necessary,* that's what she'd do. She'd pull out every stop to save her life, to survive at all costs, even if it meant eliminating one half of the very thing that was supposed to keep her most advanced species going.

Yes, Nature had graciously granted our species the highest form of intelligence and entrusted us with her future—but suddenly it looked like one of the genders had decided to throw the kegger of all keggers on Mother Earth's watch. Now, hung over and cranky, Mother is pissed at whoever slipped the mickey in her drink.

The culprit has a receding hairline, a potbelly, and never screws the cap back onto anything.

Yup, guys, we've been fingered; there's no way to hide

michael moore

from Nature's wrath. We can't pin any of this on the women: it wasn't a woman who dropped napalm bombs, or who invented plastic, or who said, "Dammit, what we need is a beer can with a pop-top!" Unfortunately, every bit of plunder and pillage, every attack on the environment, everything that has brought horror and destruction to all that was once pure and good has come from hands that, well, when they aren't busy bringing pleasure to oneself, are working overtime to wipe out this beautiful, wonderful home we were given free of charge—no security deposit required, no background check needed.

No wonder Nature is getting rid of us.

If we men had any sense, we'd try to get Nature to forgive us by cleaning up our act. You know, do the obvious stuff: quit desecrating the Arctic wilderness, pick up after ourselves, stop throwing Whopper remains out the car window.

Nature would probably put up with a lot of our guff if we still served some important purpose. For eons we had two things women didn't have that made us a *necessity:* (1) we provided the sperm to keep the species going, and (2) we were able to reach and get whatever they needed off the top shelf.

Unfortunately for us, some traitor guy invented *in vitro* fertilization, which means that now females only need the sperm from *a few of us* in order to have babies. In fact someone (probably a woman) in Arizona has announced that science has found a means of human reproduction that doesn't even require sperm to fertilize an egg—now they

HOW TO TRICK NATURE
INTO MAKING MORE MEN

■ A company in Virginia has developed a method
  that allows you to choose the gender of your baby.
  The Genetic and IVF (In Vitro Fertilization)
  Institute, an infertility clinic in Fairfax, Virginia,
  uses a process that separates the male chromosome
  from the female chromosome sperm, allowing
  parents to determine the sex of their baby before it
  is conceived. Be EXTRA nice to your wife before
  going to this clinic, because ultimately it's her right
  to decide what is placed inside her body. And give
  these people in Virginia more federal funds!

■ Keep Your Sperm Strong. Quit violating yourself
  on a daily basis. It weakens the sperm and lessens
  their numbers.

■ Before sex, think *manly* thoughts. Go over the
  instant replay one more time in your head. *You*
  would never have let that ball roll between *your*
  legs in game six of the '86 World Series. Hear the
  crowd at Shea fall silent as you scoop up the ball
  and step on first. Mookie Wilson out! You did it!
  You da MAN!

■ Conceive your children earlier in life. A recent
  epidemiological study concluded that older
  parents are more likely to have girls than boys.

OTHER THINGS ALREADY RENDERED USELESS BY NATURE

- Typewriters
- The Washington Senators
- Bosco
- Walking
- Skorts
- The busy signal
- Bank tellers
- A college degree
- Malt-O-Meal
- Hair on a man's back
- Ayds weight-loss candies
- The Supreme Court

can do it with DNA. No longer do women have to crawl out from underneath some slobbering man with his face buried in the pillow simply because they wish to have babies. All they need now is a test tube.

The other invention that did the male population in was the stepladder. *The portable, easy-to-carry aluminum stepladder,* to be precise. Who was the bastard that came up with that bright idea? Now what possible excuse can we have for sticking around?

Nature has a way of getting rid of its weakest links, those that no longer serve a useful purpose, the dead weight. That, my friends, is *us.* Reproductive science and three little aluminum steps rising above the earth's surface have made us guys about as useful as an eight-track tape.

Well, look at the bright side: We've had one helluva run! Thousands of years of total domination over the social order—and still going strong! Think about it—there has not been a *single day* when we weren't in charge, when we weren't calling the shots and running the world! Not even the Yankees can claim such an unbroken reign of unchallenged power. I mean, here we are, *the minority,* and yet we men have ruled over the female majority since time immemorial. In other countries we call that apartheid; in America we call it normal. Since the birth of this country, for more than 225 years, we have seen to it that not a single woman has held either the number one or number two offices in the land. For the better part of that time we've made sure that damn few of them have held any office at all. In fact, for the first 130 years of presidential elections, it was illegal for women even to *vote.*

Then in 1920, just to show women we're good sports, we gave them the right to vote. And guess what? *We remained in power!*

Go figure. Suddenly, women had more votes; they could have thrown our collective male ass into the political trash heap. But what did they do? They voted for *us*! How cool is that? Have you ever heard of any group of oppressed people that suddenly, by their sheer numbers, takes charge—and then votes in overwhelming numbers to keep their oppressors in power? The blacks of South Africa, once free, did not continue apartheid by voting for whites. I know no Jews in America who voted for George Wallace or David Duke or Pat Buchanan (Florida debacle included).

No, the usual thing a sane society does is give the boot to the boot that's been on its neck for umpteen years.

Yet more than eighty years after they gained the right to vote—and despite the growth of a massive women's movement—here's where we stand:

■ Not a single woman has been on the ballot of the major parties for President or Vice President in twenty of the twenty-one national elections since 1920.

■ Currently there are only five women governors in fifty states.

■ Women hold only 13 percent of the seats in Congress.

■ 496 of the top 500 companies in America are run by men.

■ Just four of the top twenty-one universities in the United States are run by women.

■ 40 percent of all women who are divorced between the ages of twenty-five and thirty-four end up in poverty, compared with only 8 percent of married women who live below the poverty line.

■ Women's earnings average 76 cents for every $1 earned by men—resulting in a lifetime loss of over $650,133.

■ To make the same annual salary as her male counterpart, a woman would have to work the entire year PLUS an additional four months.

Sooner or later, women are going to figure out how to seize power—and when that happens, let's pray for mercy. After all, they *are* the stronger gender. Contrary to popular myth, it is men who are the weaker sex. Consider the evidence:

■ We don't live as long as women.

■ Our brains are less well formed and shrink at a faster rate than women's as we age.

michael moore

■ Proportionately, we are more likely than women to suffer from catastrophic illnesses such as heart disease, strokes, ulcers, and liver failure.

■ Men are more likely to carry sexually transmitted diseases (which they pass on to their unsuspecting wives and girlfriends).

■ Men's major body systems—our circulatory, respiratory, digestive, and excretory functions—are all likely to break down long before women's (though I guess the breakdown of the excretory system was no surprise, considering the case of air freshener you've got under the bathroom sink).

■ Only our reproductive system—the ability to produce sperm—lasts longer than a woman's ability to produce eggs, but our delivery system peters out years before a woman discovers the benefits of enjoying a warm bath and a good novel.

■ Men are unable to give birth, to keep the species going.

■ Men lose their hair.

■ Men lose their minds (we're four times more likely to attempt suicide than women).

■ Men are three times more likely to die in an accident than women.

■ Men are just not as smart as women: girls generally score higher than boys on the elementary school tests—and face it, we don't get any smarter with age.

Perhaps there's no logical explanation for this disparity. Maybe, as the nuns taught us, it's just all part of God's plan.

michael moore

MIKE'S FANTASY LIST OF
WOMEN PRESIDENTS

- President Cynthia McKinney (the best person in Congress today)
- President Hillary Clinton (only if I could get invited for sleepovers)
- President Oprah (the fireside chats with Dr. Phil would save us all)
- President Katrina vanden Heuvel (editor of *The Nation,* a perfect candidate for president of the nation!)
- President Sherry Lansing (she runs Paramount Pictures; she put me in a picture; 'nuff said)
- President Karen Duffy (correspondent for *TV Nation;* would run circles around any foreign leader who dared to challenge her)
- President Caroline Kennedy (just because it would be right)
- President Bella Abzug (even dead she'd do better than Junior)
- President Leigh Taylor-Young (the first naked woman I ever saw, in the movie *The Big Bounce,* also starring Ryan O'Neal. You see, there were like six of us guys, all sixteen years old, and we had snuck into the South Dort Drive-In, and ... oh, never mind)

HOW TO SURVIVE YOUR BED
BEING SET ON FIRE

- Get on the floor and crawl. Stay low.
- If you can, put a wet washcloth or towel over your face.
- Head in the direction where you believe the door is. Always feel the door before opening it. If it's hot, DON'T open it. Find another way out.
- If she's locked all the doors, break a window and climb out.
- Always keep a fire extinguisher handy. Place it by the gun under your pillow if necessary. A fresh bucket of water nearby is also recommended.
- If you've been abusing your wife, it's probably best to wear only fire-retardant pajamas to bed. They might just save your life.
- Call the local fire department and get your name placed on the special "bastard" list—the roster of local men who believe they stand the best chance of being eliminated by a "loved one." The fire department will then know exactly where you live and where your bedroom is.

But if that's the case, why did God make women so much better? The nuns must have had the inside dope on this—after all, they were all women themselves. They knew God's secret, and they certainly weren't going to share it with the likes of me.

It is my belief—and this is purely from my personal observation of the woman I live with—that when God was creating the world, he spent the better part of Day Six creating what women would look like. I mean, you can't help but notice the skillful craft of an artisan at the top of His field. The shapes, the curves, the symmetry, all constitute extraordinary art. Their skin is soft and smooth and perfect; their hair is rich and thick and vibrant. I am not speaking from a prurient perspective here—these are simply the conclusions of the art critic in me. Women—I think we all agree—are stunningly beautiful.

So what happened to God when it came to us? It's like he used up all his best tricks inventing women. By the time he got to us, he was obviously ready to get it over with, move on to something more important, like that seventh day of rest.

So men ended up like Chevys, rushed off the assembly line and guaranteed to break down after limited use. That's why we try to stay in our Naugahyde recliners as long as we can—the exertion required to pick up after ourselves can lead to an early coronary. Our bodies were built to lift, carry, haul, and throw, but for a limited time only. And, I have to say it, what's with this extra *thing* we were given? Well, let me put this as delicately as possible: In God's rush to finish up, it looks like he just grabbed a stray part he had lying around in the shop and stuck it on us—'cause it sure as hell don't look right. If you took an item like this and glued it on to a lamppost or a tree, you'd say, "Naww, I don't think so." But nobody questions its presence on a guy. Like a creature from *Alien* reupholstered by Frank Perdue, the male organ is testimony to the fact that every now and again, as with the floods in Bangladesh or the teeth of the British, God just fails to get it right.

Saddled with the odds against us, some men have simply gone insane and taken to fighting back any way they can. If Nature is going to favor women, they figure, then they must take matters into their own hands. Their attitude: If we can't beat 'em, let's beat 'em.

These days, the tendency of men to injure, maim, or murder women is seen by most as "politically incorrect," and laws have been strengthened to protect women from us. But as we know, laws are only made to exact punishment *after* a crime has been committed. Few laws have stopped those men who are intent on wreaking their vengeance on women. Women know all too well that 911 is only there to notify the police that they'd better bring a body bag and some strong cleanser to mop up the mess, because by the time they get there that restraining order the court issued to keep him away will be stuffed in her mouth and rigor mortis will be setting in nicely, thank you.

Men gifted with more subtlety often resort to means other than outright murder to even the score between men and women. For instance, the tobacco companies (all run by men) have been extremely successful in convincing women to smoke—at a time when the number of *male* smokers is

declining. Thanks to all this new female smoking, lung cancer has now surpassed breast cancer as the leading cancer
killer of women. Total number of women eliminated each
year by smoking: 165,000!

Denial of treatment is another trick men employ in par-
ing down the female population. If you need an organ
transplant to stay alive, you're 86 percent more likely to get
it if you are a man. Men suffering from heart disease are 115
percent more likely to undergo a heart bypass than women
with the same condition. And if you're a woman, you're
more likely to pay higher insurance premiums than men for
this shoddy care.

Of course, when all else fails, you can also go back to
murder. It usually works. A woman is five times more likely
to be killed by a husband or boyfriend than a man is likely
to be murdered by his wife or girlfriend.

Keep that up, and we might just make it after all.

how men can avoid extinction

As bad as the future looks for us, there is some hope that we,
as men, can delay our demise—if we learn to adopt some
very important new behaviors. There are many things we
can learn from women and how they function sanely. Here
are a few:

**1. Remember That Your Car Is Not a Weapon of Mass De-
struction.** Stop getting pissed off at that car that just cut you

off. Why do you really care? You're going to get home in the same amount of time anyway. So some jerk cost you four seconds on the road. Big deal! Get a grip. Women couldn't care less about stuff like this, and they live longer for it. When they see an asshole on the road, they just shake their heads and laugh—and it works! Guys, we have *got* to relax. We're damaging our hearts with every minute of uptight, tense, and angry behavior. Quit walking around like you've got a pineapple up your ass. Nothing matters THAT much. (Except a real pineapple. *That* would matter something awful.)

2. Lighten Up on the Food and Drink. We need to think more about what we put in our mouths. If you and I would eat less and drink less, we'd live a lot longer. When's the last time you saw a woman pig out like it was her last meal? Sure, we've all seen women pound back the liquor, but how many females have you seen just drop their pants and start peeing on the curb? Why do you think so many of us men get colon and stomach cancer and liver disease? Because we can't say no to Jack (Daniel's) or Jim (Beam) or a pound and a half of half-cooked beef topped with fried onion rings, year-old jalapeños, and Tabasco sauce. There's a reason you've never seen a woman take a newspaper into a bathroom. Get a clue!

3. Step Aside, You'll Live Longer. Listen, why don't we retire and let women run the world? Okay, so you don't want women having power, because you're a conservative redneck. But what would you say if I told you that letting them worry about building that nuclear plant in Bahrain, or declaring war against China, or finding a solution to the continuing abuse of the infield fly rule, would give us men eight more years of life? Let's step aside and shut up! Is it that big a cheap thrill just to be "the boss" and have to deal with hundreds of employees and all their crap? Who needs it? Let's back off, take a break, and let the women have this crazy unmanageable world for the next ten thousand years. Think of all the reading you'll catch up on.

4. Wash Your Hands Across America. It's time to wise up: our personal habits are so revolting it's a wonder women are willing even to breathe the same air we do. If we men could only get our act together and change a few simple things, we'd immediately score more empathy and companionship. For starters, we should keep our hands where they belong. They weren't intended to be used in nostrils, anuses, ears, or navels. They were not designed to tear out articles from the newspaper before she has a chance to read it, or to pick a loose piece of kielbasa skin from between your teeth, or to sandpaper that patch of dandruff on your head. Stop checking (and adjusting) your crotch in public—nothing has disappeared since your last inventory, roughly a minute ago. Keep your legs together, so you don't take up three seats on buses and trains. Wear underwear—preferably underwear that's been washed *this year,* in a *washing machine,* with actual *laundry soap.*

5. Learn How a Toilet Seat Works. All right, boys, I thought for sure we'd be over this by now, but the foul evidence in airports and train stations and fast-food emporia all over this great land tells me this: despite the constant carping of TV comics everywhere, *we just haven't gotten the message.* So here's a quick refresher course:

■ First, lift the movable oval cover into an upright position. Then lift the movable oval seat beneath it into an upright position. They will both automatically lock into place. That's so you can use both hands. It's just like steering a car. You wouldn't want the car to go off the road, would you? Fine, and the women in your house feel the same way about your piss all over the wallpaper.

■ Aim, hold, release, return to pants.

■ Take one hand and gently return oval seat and its top to their lowered positions. No audible sound of the seat hitting the ceramic bowl should be heard.

■ Grasp the little silver handle at left and FLUSH. (This is not optional, even in a public restroom.) If the first flush doesn't take, you may not leave the scene: stay there till you're looking at a clean bowl.

■ Wash hands. Dry them on the towels provided, not the shirt you're wearing. Throw the paper towel into the trash receptacle—or, if the towel is made of cloth, place it back on towel rack (usually a metal or plastic rod protruding from the wall near the sink). If you're in your own home, put the cloth towel into the laundry at least once a week. Wash. Return to bathroom.

6. Bathe Daily. Throwing some water in your face to wake up in the morning does not constitute bathing. Neither does being doused with a Heineken at a party the night before. Step into the tub. Turn handle halfway between HOT and COLD. Lift stem on faucet to create shower effect. Take bar of soap and washcloth and scrub all areas of the body. Do NOT place the bar of soap in body cavities to "get them extra clean." Someone else has to use that bar of soap on her face. Rinse. When finished, leave shower area and dry off, creating as little a water trail as possible.

7. Tone It Down. Lower your voice. Try listening. Here's how it works: When someone else is talking, pay close attention to what they are saying. Maintain eye contact. Do not interrupt. When he or she is finished, pause and reflect on what was said. Try saying nothing at all. Notice how what you have heard is stimulating thoughts, concepts, feelings, and ideas in your head. This may lead to something brilliant. You will then be able to take those ideas, claim them as yours, and become famous!

8. Get Your Hearing Checked. If the above doesn't work, there may be something physically wrong with you. May is National Better Health and Speech Month; many hospitals and community groups offer free screening for hearing loss. Check your local newspaper for announcements of free hearing tests in your area. In addition, most hospitals offer periodic free hearing tests throughout the year. You can also find on-line quizzes to help you determine if you should seek a professional hearing evaluation. One such test can be found at: health.aol.thriveonline.oxygen.com/medical/wgames/gen/health.hearing.html.

9. Know that Women Are onto Us. Cut out the sensitive-man crap. They know the drill. Don't try convincing anyone you're a "feminist." You don't qualify: you play for the other team. It's like a Klansman chanting, "KEEP HOPE ALIVE!" You are a specimen of the gender that will always make more money, that will always have the door swing open wide and far to wherever you want to go in life.

This does not mean you can't help make things better. The best way to help women is to work on your fellow men. That's where the real struggle is—getting enlightenment through the concrete block known as a man's head.

Help end the wage gap by looking at your own paycheck. Make sure women doing the same job at work are getting paid the same as you. Participate in Equal Pay Day, usually held in early April on the day that marks the point in the new year when a woman has finally earned the wages paid to a man in a comparable job during the previous year. Contact fairplay@aol.com for more info.

And you can join in the effort to push Congress to pass two pieces of national legislation affecting equal pay. The Fair Pay Act would allow women to bring suit based on the principle of equal pay for equal work and would allow employees within a single company to sue if they believe they are being paid less than someone with an equivalent job and equivalent training. The Paycheck Fairness Act provides for higher damages in these types of lawsuits and protects employees who share salary information. The Center for Policy Alternatives has been working for pay equity for the past twenty-five years. To find out more, go to www.cfpa.org, or contact them at 202-387-6030.

Finally, join a union—or try to start one. According to

the AFL-CIO, a thirty-year-old female union member making $30,000 a year stands to lose about $650,133 over a lifetime because of unequal pay. If she's not a union member, on the other hand, she'll lose about $870,327. If you convince the other men on the job to unionize the establishment, then you'll have greatly improved your female coworkers' lives, and your own.

how women can survive without men

1. Visit a Sperm Bank or an Adoption Agency. Most communities have adoption agencies or sperm banks available for women who would love to have children but, for whatever reason, want to do it without a man. It's good for kids to have two parents (and easier for the parents, too!), but everything you've heard about how damaged children turn out to be if they were raised by a single mother—well, that's one of the Big Lies of our culture. In his book *The Culture of Fear,* Barry Glassner points out that "those raised by single mothers had income and education levels roughly equal to those raised by two parents. Research shows that as a group, children of single moms tend to fare better emotionally and socially than do offspring from high-conflict marriages, or from those in which the father is emotionally absent or abusive."

2. Learn Where to Buy a Stepladder. There are many fine brands, sizes, and styles available at affordable prices. Try

Home Depot at www.homedepot.com. And for further information about this revolutionary invention, go to the American Ladder Institute website at www.americanladder institute.org.

3. When All Else Fails, Love Yourself. Some folks who can lend a hand (so to speak):

By phone or online:

Good Vibrations
800-289-8423 or 415-974-8990
www.goodvibes.com

The Pleasure Chest
800-753-4536
fax: 323-650-1176
www.thepleasurechest.com

Xandria
800-242-2823 or 415-468-3805
fax: 415-468-3912
www.xandria.com

Retail stores:

Good Vibrations
2504 San Pablo Avenue
Berkeley, CA 94702
510-841-8987

The Pleasure Chest
7733 Santa Monica Boulevard
Santa Monica, CA 90046
323-650-1022

Xandria
1210 Valencia Street
San Francisco, CA 94110
415-974-8980

While the author has made every effort to provide accurate telephone numbers and Internet addresses at the time of publication, neither the publisher nor the author assumes any responsibility for errors, or for changes that occur after publication.

lacking harriet

jesse green

I KNEW which window was his, or was supposed to be: the one in the peak of the boathouse across the river. He was some sort of coach there (sports escape me) and apparently was permitted to live in the attic. Could he see, beneath his window, the name of his club spelled out in shingles on the Victorian Gothic façade? The name was Victorian Gothic, too: Vesper. At evening, year-round, the building, like all its boathouse neighbors, blazed with Christmas lights that out-lined the eaves and gables, the windows and walls, rendering it a child's flat drawing of itself. I used to think those lights must have been horribly annoying to the shadowy man who lived inside, even as I appreciated how they had been strung for the benefit of commuters who, driving home from Philadelphia to the suburbs, might wish to muse on the pa-cific yet manly art of the scull, the prettiest of all exertions.

Needless to say, it wasn't as a rower that I knew him. Whatever he was by dusk, Mr. Orr (as I might as well call him) was by day my tenth-grade English teacher. Shaggy, electric, enigmatic, lean, he was a figure from a racy yet literate novel; not, alas, a novel of my invention. He was rumored to smoke pot behind the football field, and make out with female students there—but only the best female students. He was high-minded. He wore little round glasses, taught *Dune* as a parable of human domination, and had terrible handwriting. One day, a substitute teacher, consulting the impenetrable seating chart Mr. Orr had provided, determined that my name was Chuck. "How could you write so badly?" I protested upon his return from whatever charming illness had kept him from shaving for two days. "Anything's possible," he answered, laughing. He seemed to find the mistake hilarious; in any case, he promptly started calling me by the ill-fitting name. I secretly loved it. With its allusions to ball-playing and drill bits—not to mention its harsh ictus and dirty rhyme—Chuck seemed like a taste of sex to me, who at fifteen had had none.

They don't call it a crush for nothing. It may seem like a feeling you hope to express—push out of yourself—but it's really a feeling you hope to be pushed down by. In the heart's eye, it comes from above. Prominence of any sort will suffice. Mr. Orr's was a literal prominence (that attic room) but it was also more. Handsome and young and heterosexual, he was at the pinnacle of society's erotic pyramid; as such, he had nothing to hide. He was a kind of full-time spiritual erection, unafraid to advertise his truth in the soft-sell flutter of sleepy eyes, or the billboard wallop of tight jeans. Everyone knew it, those bright, "mature" girls especially, but I'm sure we proto-homosexuals felt it more urgently. However much sense it has made throughout history for students to have crushes on teachers, it made even more sense, in those particular dark ages, for students like me: gay boys with no way to think of sexual love but as a thing that comes from the powerful to the powerless. Only the luckiest of us have crushes on peers who might return the feeling, or even recognize it. For everyone else, to love a man "that way" could only have meant loving someone who was indisputably in charge. How else could it happen? Ravishment came into it.

Mr. Orr liked me—if not in "that way," then in *some* way. He was writing a paper for a criticism class he took in the evenings. "Did you see the movie *Zardoz*?" he asked once, during a free period.

"Uh, Sean Connery?" I ventured.

"It's about this barbarian whose virility is the only hope for reinvigorating an effeminate, hypercivilized race of the future. Let me read something to you." Mr. Orr's paper examined the movie's sexual imagery. As I recall, it went on for some ten thousand words like this: "Penis, penis, penis, penis, penis, penis, penis, penis, penis, penis . . ." By the time he was finished reading, and looked up from his manuscript with hoarse self-satisfaction, I had made an imaginative leap from my own frozen embarrassment to that of the male organ, which (it had never occurred to me before) perhaps grew stiff and red not from pleasure but from pure mortification.

I sat there, open-mouthed, as if I had been slapped out of the blue by a friend. Not quite out of the blue. After all, we both knew what he was doing.

"What do you think of that, Chuck?" asked Mr. Orr,

taking off his glasses. I did not have to reread *Dune* to get the message that humanity progresses by the exertion of dominance. Or see *Zardoz* to know what men do.

IF, INFAMOUSLY, we love whom we love, the less publicized corollary is that we are who we are. For gay men, this can get to be a fairly knotty problem.

I am far older now than Mr. Orr was then, and never saw him again after high school. But he set, or confirmed, a pattern of erotic expectation that lasted for many years. The men for whom I conceived a sexual interest were almost always older or more powerful than I. They knew things about the world, about handling people, about sex itself. They would save me from the burden of having to decide what I actually wanted, because their own preferences would be so clear and peremptory. I could not be embarrassed by a desire I did not have to name. It did not occur to me that, in their blinkered certainty, they might be feeling exactly the same way.

They were exciting in proportion to their opacity, these men; their lack of apparent introspection commandeered one's gaze. But when I imagined, as I lay spent and beard-bruised between passions, a life that included a permanent partner, it was never with a Mr. Orr or his descendants. Such a man would not in any case hang around long enough to be ensnared. And while I might desire bodily preemption, I required free rein elsewhere. This was a paradox that could not be resolved even imaginarily; my fantasy marital life thus lacked particulars, especially in contrast to my fantasy material life, which was kitted out to the last fish fork. All I could see of a future partnership amounted to this: an apartment, where we would be apart. But where would we be together? I'd see a sheet wafting neatly onto the bed, of its own accord; I'd see meals float midair in procession from the kitchen to the table; I'd see a bathroom recently used (*Ah! His toothbrush!*) but immaculate. The agent of all this domesticity was missing. Our lives were skew. He was there but in abeyance, like a housekeeper whose hours are carefully calibrated never to intersect with her employer's.

He was a wife.

It had been my mother's lifelong struggle—she married at twenty—not to model that kind of wifeliness. Once my brother and I were old enough, she went back to school and then into full-time work. Yet even when she had attained a high level of respect and responsibility in her professional life she could not leave the house without making all the beds. She would stay up late into the night doing laundry, and cook quarts of spaghetti sauce on weekends for us males to defrost on weeknights. Then, one day, I was shocked to find the house untidy when I got home from school in the afternoon. Not knowing what else to do, I made the beds and cleaned the breakfast dishes. I didn't mind doing it, but I was dismayed by my belated realization of the immense burden of "women's work" my mother had engaged herself to. She would eventually say, when asked what she wanted in order to make things easier, that she wanted a wife.

I, too, was discovering that I wanted, at least in my domestic fantasies, a wife—and a husband in my erotic ones.

But I did not really consider what I offered these stereo-typed figures. My mother knew all too well what she of-fered my father. But boys are never asked, the way girls constantly are, to translate themselves into the dominant language, to make their offers legible, to change their very names so as to enlarge someone else's. And while men have supposedly become more sensitive to these inequities (but was not my own name changed, to Chuck, by a man?), sen-sitivity in many of them is a stylistic affectation, like wearing a beret. It was not as an act of feminist solidarity, but as a gesture of one-downsmanship, that men who participated in the (hetero)sexual revolution of the Sixties—and in its freedoms—asked to be seen, just like women and blacks, as chattel suppressed by an establishment culture they unironi-cally called "The Man." One need only look at the way they treated the women they loved to realize that nothing had changed but the rhetoric.

As it turned out, my own sexual revolution, two decades later, made the same point: Boys will be boys. I could not see it in my relationships with other men, which were still largely notional or fleeting, and were thus as unenlightening as looking in a mirror. But any woman I dated or (I suppose I should say) led on, could have told me that despite what-ever public demurrals of dominance or private struggles with erotic indifference, I was a man, too. I was concerned with my needs in a way that was not mere youthful selfish-ness but recognizably male, whether you favor a nature or a nurture argument to explain it: What a woman wanted was her own business, and intimacy was a door that opened only from my side. As the "woman" in that scenario just a few years earlier, I was now shocked to find myself reading from Mr. Orr's side of the script. The penis, even when it isn't a weapon, is a flagpole, and for the diffident gay man no less than the strutting straight one, access to the arsenal of male privilege is unimpeded. I am ashamed to say that when an ex-girlfriend used the word "fag" once too often, I hit her.

AT FIRST I didn't notice, when I met the man who would become my life partner, that he resembled Mr. Orr rather closely. Andy, too, had been a high school English teacher (but had now escaped the classroom); he'd once had shaggy light brown hair; he wore little wire-rimmed glasses and liked science fiction. Eight and a half years older than I, he could even have been the same age as Mr. Orr, though what seemed an unbridgeable chasm of time to a teen was now, at 37, no more than a brook, delightful to cross in bare feet.

Whether because of that slight generational difference, or because of the larger difference in personality between us, Andy brought to our shared cosmos a much longer comet trail of past involvements, with both men and women, than I did. Joining our orbits in 1995 was therefore more a matter of my merging into his than vice versa, just as my mother had come into marriage in 1951 with little besides a sharp eye for observing the onslaught of my father's friends and kin. But Andy brought something even more consequential and coercive than auld acquaintance to our marriage: He brought a child. Andy had adopted his first son about a year before we met; his second would arrive nine months into our relationship. By then, that baby was not *his* but *our* second, though "ownership" of the boys would turn out to be a human real-estate transaction that raised in each of us the dread specter of an inner Donald Trump.

Eight years later, that transaction long since ironed out (neither of us owns the boys; they own us), we are "four men living all together"—though two of us enact a masculinity still defined by knights, superheroes, and furtive, contraband weapons. I can't speak to the way my relationship to Andy might have proceeded had there been no children involved, or had they come along after a decorous honeymoon of several years. What I can speak to is the way two adults, under the stress of living together and raising young boys, enact *their* masculinity. It is not always a pretty sight. Not so much in practical matters, like divvying up chores, which actually goes more smoothly than in many male-female relationships. We choose who will make the beds—or, for that matter, pump the gas—as a matter of taste and ability, not because one is a woman's job and one a man's. Perforce freed from the prison of established gender roles, we inhabit a domestic world in which masculinity is, in that sense, meaningless. A job not done by men simply does not get done.

But there is more to a marriage than the chores. There is, for example, how you *do* the chores. I was astonished and frustrated to learn, in our first year together, that not everyone naturally bows to the obvious superiority of my method of loading the dishwasher—or folding the laundry or balancing the checkbook. And even more astonished to find that I, the soul of easygoing indulgence, could be the source of an equivalent frustration in Andy. It had seemed sufficient that our division of labor was egalitarian, but it turned out that our habit of dominance was not. This is partly the result of having met as full-fledged adults, already set in our ways; it's easy to be easygoing when one has not yet formed tastes, or when one lives alone. But I came to feel that the habit of dominance was more directly the result of resurgent maleness, which does not begrudge shared work nearly as much as shared control. And so, when Andy and I say (as we often do) we want a wife, it isn't seriously because we want someone to take the "wifely" chores off our hands, though that would be nice. It's because we want someone around who will graciously, or at any rate silently, defer to all our certainties.

For the thing about a gay male relationship is that— surprise!—it involves two men. Despite stereotypes, neither is a wife or wants to be. Just watch a Bette Davis movie (and make the appropriate substitutions) to see how brutal an old-fashioned fairy can be. At home, even florists and hair-dressers fight like cats and dogs.

The assimilated gay man is haunted by those stereotypes, and yet I liked those men, whose steely masculinity was at odds with their feminized presentation. The year before my crush on Mr. Orr, I had a geometry teacher who wore pink-tinted glasses and plaid bow ties. He required his students to prove the Pythagorean theorem in crewelwork, and got a great deal of pleasure at the sight of thick-fingered jocks, otherwise so dominant, despairing to wield the dainty needles. "I hope you hit better than you knit," he lisped to one hapless lug whose hypotenuse was flaccid.

The bitchiness of pre-liberation homosexuals, depicted so enjoyably in incorrect works like *The Boys in the Band*, has often been posited as a kind of emotional camp: the record of a failed experiment in personhood. I'm not sure that's right. I think the Dr. Jekyll and Miss Thing bipolarity of gay men actually had less to do with the disaster of being gay in a straight world than with the simple fact of being male in a gay world. Segregated by gender, like prisoners, all men enact arcane struggles for dominance, and the home-made knives come out. If simple repression were the cause, the style would have disappeared by now, a full generation after Stonewall. And yet the style persists; many of the men in newfangled gay partnerships are every bit as fey-ferocious as Paul Lynde, sneering and sibilating in his center Hollywood Square. However they express their nonheterosexuality—whether by armoring themselves with muscle at the gym or by plucking every last hair from their bodies (or both)—gay spouses each expect to lead and be deferred to, exactly as if they were married to Harriet Nelson. Lacking Harriet, something's got to give. Mr. Orr could have taught me that lesson: With both men pulling on the same side, a two-man scull will only move in circles.

NO WONDER Andy and I sometimes get dizzy. An issue requiring resolution arises; it may be as trivial as what time to have dinner or as momentous as moving. More typically it will lie between those extremes. Which extracurricular activities should the boys take on? Can we afford a new car? A "conversation" ensues, in which the merits and conse-

quences are thoughtfully examined without their ever alter-
ing, or much revealing, our impervious foregone conclusions.
We each believe the other has understood our position, but
he has done no more than view that position at close range
through the wrong end of a telescope, leaving it smaller
than it was to begin with. One of us thus moves forward
with the false sensation that he is acting on a joint decision;
when the other howls, it is with the self-inflicted wound of
having assumed his position had naturally prevailed. How
could a privileged man assume otherwise?

It's no accident that the question of dominance arises
most regularly in our attempts to make decisions about the
boys; each of us being the younger of two brothers, we instinctively see our sons' struggles in the light of that experience. Sometimes it seems as if we therefore live in a house
of mirrors, each reflection squabbling with the next for purchase on a swatch of authority. Indeed, it is the sight of the
boys enacting their miniature versions of our masculine ar-
guments that most painfully pulls us up short. Sometimes
they would rather play no game at all (or watch no video or
share no dessert) than agree to each other's preference.

This is hardly our peculiar gay dilemma; every family
faces these disputes, and most settle them more or less sanely.
Nor are all gay male couples, with or without children, engaged in a bristly war dance. (Some seem as calm and cooperative as quilters.) No doubt there are lesbians, too, who
crave a mouse-killing man around the house while wran-
gling with their lovers as fiercely as we do. But as a laboratory for studying the state of contemporary masculinity, you

could hardly do better than the stainless-steel kitchen of Homo Americanus at the turn of the twenty-first century.

Unless it would be in the Formica ghost of his parents' kitchen. For if some gay couples don't fit the pattern, it is also true that many heterosexual couples do. And the way they do is telling. The father of the bride at a recent wedding we attended made a rueful toast in honor of his late wife: "At the beginning of our marriage," he said, "she told me that since I was a man and a lawyer, I should handle all the big things in our life together, while she would content herself handling the small. In fifty years," he concluded, "there was never a big thing."

The laughter was explosive. At the start of what everyone hoped would be a new, more just kind of union, the subterfuges by which the old kind maintained a semblance of equilibrium had to be honored and exorcized. I laughed, too, but with a pang of recognition, and not just because my own mother had mastered the same playbook. I was playing from it now. Was it the triumph of feminism that a gay man could use old-fashioned feminine machinations to achieve dominance? No. It was another sign that feminism, like gay liberation, is still radically incomplete.

For you can hire a housekeeper, if you've got the money, to make the beds (my mother eventually did); you can purchase spaghetti sauce by the vat; you can drive right up to the full-service pump if you don't like the smell of gas. But you cannot thereby escape the growing obligation of a would-be fair society to accept how little it means to be a man—or a woman. It is as individuals we must fare, without recourse to the traditional perquisites (or perceived limitations) of our gender. This is a bitterer pill for men than it is for women, who have nothing worth keeping to lose; how much bitterer still for gay men, whose maleness may be the only taste of supremacy they've had.

Our family is a laboratory for that as well, since our boys are the leading edge of what it will one day mean to be male. By then, Andy and I may be bickering over whether to keep the seat up or down on the toilet at the rest home, and they may have spouses of their own to torment with *their* impervious foregone conclusions. But it seems clear to me—for they are boys who, however aggressive, nevertheless elect to take sewing class after school, or fold origami fowl for their friends—that our little unisex commune has taught them something good. After all, there are more meaningful ways of defining difference (and sameness) than by the tired and coarse old dichotomy of gender. Should our boys marry women some day, those wives will undoubtedly be grateful for husbands who, whatever their failings, haven't a clue what women's work is.

Children are not an experiment, though, and in any case I sometimes think they change us more than we change them. But they *are* a puzzle, as difficult as any calculus. Alter one variable, and who knows what you get? Andy and I are gradually learning that our rubber-stamp alternativity as gay men does not magically satisfy our duty as partners: to bend, to meld, to lay down arms. We must show our boys that men need not call out the emotional artillery (or raise the drawbridge) every time they disagree. And though we are far better at it now than we were when we started, the boys have been watching intently from day one. If they are freer by our example to conceive of maleness in myriad ways, perhaps, by the same token, they are even more firmly cemented in the fact of maleness than we were. Despite all our female friends, whose breasts they leer at like little Dean Martins; despite their beloved (and, without exception, female) teachers; despite my mother, who at any rate died before handing over the secret of her balancing act; despite all the gentle womanliness in their lives, they are far more boyish than we ever were. How could it be otherwise? They have not had to read *Dune* to get the message that humanity progresses by the exertion of dominance. Or see *Zardoz* to know what men do.

multi-tasking man
rachel lehmann-haupt

FEMINISM'S FIRST SUPERMODEL was an ancient goddess. As the story goes, Mahisa, a rebellious and greedy god, seized the celestial kingdom when his creator, Brahman, denied him immortality. The gods became so incensed by this tyrant that in order to win back their kingdom they combined their powers to produce a divine force in the form of a beautiful woman. Durga was a shapely siren with eight wild arms wielding deadly weapons.

Whirling her mighty arms, Durga sought Mahisa and seduced him. When he fell in love with her, she smiled, batted her wide eyes, and whispered that she could only marry a man who could defeat her in battle. Mahisa was charmed by her challenge, and so sure that he could beat a woman that he took her on.

Their battle was fierce. Mahisa, slick and focused, maneuvered in between and around the swipes of Durga's weapons. The goddess struggled, but didn't give up. When Mahisa was convinced that he had won, she suddenly overwhelmed him with the whisk of her arms and won the battle with a deadly blow to his heart.

In 1972 this multiarmed goddess appeared on the premiere issue of *Ms.* magazine. This time she juggled new weapons: a telephone, a steering wheel, an iron, a clock, a feather duster, a frying pan, a mirror, and a typewriter. There she was in high gloss, with her head tilted in a luring glance, dainty smirk, and demure eyes. She was no longer delivering blows to the ancients, but a modern media message to thousands of housewives and husbands of post–World War II America. A woman's ancient power to juggle multiple tasks, she declared, was the key to the economic power that would free her from cloistered suburbia, housebound ennui, and Freudian shackles that held that anatomy is destiny.

Helen Fisher, the feminist anthropologist, in her book *The First Sex*, says that a woman's skill to juggle multiple tasks evolved out of men and women's naturally separate worlds—and naturally different brain structures—that date back millions of years to the sunburnt plains of East Africa. The women of the tribal village were responsible for gathering more than half of the meal, taking care of the children, watching out for wild animals, and managing the social and marketing networks of the village. The village men were responsible for focusing on the hunt.

"As our male forebears tracked warthogs and wildebeests," Fisher writes, "they gradually evolved the brain architecture to screen out peripheral thought, focus their attention, and make step-by-step decisions." Women's brains, she argues, evolved to handle many tasks at the same time; what she calls "web thinking." There is even scientific

rachel lehmann-haupt

evidence from studies that the corpus callosum, the bundle of millions of nerve fibers that connects the two hemispheres of the brain, is larger in women, and therefore allows for greater communication between each side.

By harnessing these ancient juggling powers, the second wave of feminism was supposed to wash away the wife's troubles and empower her from the bedroom to the boardroom. Rather than husbands and wives operating in separate fiefdoms, pulling their weight at the office and the home, respectively, women could liberate themselves by dominating both environments. Ms. Durga's many arms meant that the modern woman could have it all. She could be the working woman, the housemaid, and the sexy goddess, and her gallant god in shining gray flannel stability, unchanged, would still love her.

Thirty years later women have indeed come a long way. Women managers still make 76 cents for every dollar earned by their male counterparts, but women now account for almost half of the labor force. And that number is rising. The majority of men and women no longer live in separate and isolated worlds. Technology and the global economy have connected us together both at work and in our homes, and there are now ways for each sex to play more equal roles in each realm. Home offices and telecommuting options, on-line grocery shopping and home delivery services, high-speed breast milk pumps and web cams in day care centers allow us all to toggle more efficiently between the duties of work and home.

These profound cultural changes have created an opportunity for traditional gender roles to break down and evolve. Now that Ms. Durga has tipped the scales, for better or for worse, isn't it time for her to put down her weapons and take the focus off trying to hold it all? Isn't the next step a new and altogether different feminist supermodel? What about a multi-tasking man?

Despite feminist progess, the majority of modern men are still focused solely on the hunt. "My career, not my home life," as one young technology entrepreneur in his twenties, who works at home, put it. "The hunt is not the nest. It is the hunt."

TODAY AMERICAN MEN are still only doing a fraction more of the work in the home than they were thirty years ago. A 2002 report by the Institute for Social Research at the University of Michigan found that American men are doing a mere four more hours of housework a week than they were in 1965. Women aren't doing as much house-work, but they are still doing 27 hours more a week than men are. The nanny/housekeeper may act as a bejeweled arm for many upper-income goddesses, but then we must ask, how many of these appendages of privilege are men?

While the traditional corporate wife of the '50s has be-come all but obsolete, the corporate husband has yet to re-ally define himself. There are now the few corporate superheroes such as Hewlett-Packard CEO Carlton Fiorino, who boasted in a 2002 *Fortune* magazine story that the stay-at-home husband is "The New Trophy Husband." The reality, however, is that most American women feel more overworked than men because the brunt of multi-tasking is not equally distributed.

It may simply be a communication problem. Women, in their quest to figure out how to have it all, may have lost track of the conversation with men. In the 1970s the ideal feminist woman became the tomboyish Charlie perfume girl. She didn't ask her man to change. She merely untied her apron strings and took long strides of bold suited confidence that told us that she bought her own seduction potion rather than waiting for that special gift from her man. In the 1980s she wore broad shoulder-padded suits, took the train to Wall Street, and competed with high-octane men, all without asking her man to make a similar conversion. He was still the head of the household, still the stoic Marlboro man at the center of every scene. He might have moved over a bit to share his office with the broad in the pants, but it was still his world. Despite a few sensitive moments, he was still focused mainly on the hunt. "We saw women as equals," said a lawyer in his forties. "But it was still about the boys' network and a female secretary who supported you."

As it turned out, women did not really resemble the cool and confident Charlie girl. They were exhausted, anxiety-ridden and over-burdened. By the end of the 1980s women were suffering from what Arlie Hochschild, a sociology professor at the University of California–Berkeley, called "the stalled revolution." In her book *The Second Shift: Working Parents and the Revolution at Home*, she argued that men and the organizations that they worked for weren't helping take on the weight of domestic labor. "Workplaces have remained inflexible in the face of family demands of their workers," she wrote. "At home most men have yet to really adapt to the changes in women."

In the 1990s the "stalled revolution" in some ways got worse. Men and women became even more alienated from each other. Women gained more economic power and more confidence about their innate feminine powers. Many even argued that a woman's natural abilities to multi-task gave her an advantage over men in a new technology age where everyone was bombarded from all directions with the web, instant messages, and cell phone conference calls from offices around the globe in an ever-growing—and feminized— service economy.

Ms. Durga transformed from the shoulder-padded career woman to the post-feminist power girl who could grace- fully toggle between work and home; talk of politics and nail polish; Madeleine Albright's weapons strategy and Monica's thongs. Men were suddenly "stiffed," as Susan Faludi observed. They may have learned that it was cool to tap into their more gentle side, carry the Baby Björn, and push the stroller with both hands. They may have traded the bachelor party entertainment of silicon-enhanced strippers for silicon-enhanced facials, manicures and massages at day spas. They also lost track of what it meant to be men.

Many men reacted by running away to pound their chests in the woods. They became cigar aficionados. They joined Promise Keepers meetings in baseball stadiums. They did everything to grasp the last hold on traditional manliness. "That means Russell Crowe. Someone who has steely clear, focused confidence. Someone linear and ballsy. A brute. A guy who can fix things," said a writer in his thirties.

.   .   .

AT THE TURN of the twenty-first century American women are still sent happy-ending messages through the media—and all the fairy tales that we read as kids—that we need a prince who will let us let down our hair and save us—both financially and emotionally. Many women still want this image, or at least are sexually attracted to it. They want "a man."

But rather than a half-liberated prince in a gray Armani suit, what women really need is Durga's twin brother. A multi-tasking mensch. A man who can take some of the weight off women's many arms by bringing home the bacon, frying it up in a pan, without ever letting us forget that he's "a man!" The problem with this vision is that anatomy may be destiny. Men might not have the neurological wherewithal to deliver. "I can see how it would make my relationship with a woman easier, but it's just not natural for me to multi-task," says a New York editor in his thirties. "I know women think I'm just being stubborn, but when I try I feel like the slow kid in the fast class."

In 2001, Alladi Vankatesh, a sociologist at the University of California at Irvine's Center for Research on Information Technology, began studying this very issue by looking at how traditional gender roles are shifting in the information age. Vankatesh, a soft-spoken Indian man in his mid-forties, spent a year in the sprawling suburban homes of Los Angeles observing the different ways men and women respond to computer technology. After interviewing close to seventy families, he discovered that not much has changed in a million years. When men use computers, they tend to focus on a single task or an immediate goal. Play game! Win game! Find information!

Women on the other hand, he says, think about how the

computer integrates into the rest of their lives. How it can help them toggle between working at home and maintaining a connection with their children's school and other parents in their community, for example. "The good news is that because computer technology does seem to be saving women time, they are feeling less pressure about the work of home," he says. The fact remains, however, that men are overwhelmingly still focusing on the hunt.

THE HUMAN BRAIN has not changed significantly in twenty thousand years. As Helen Fisher explains, even if women in the nations with the highest birth rates, such as Africa and India, begin to select partners who are inclined toward more feminine behavior—including multi-tasking—it's going to take a long time before an actual hard-wiring evolution occurs. A new breed of super multi-tasking man is not arriving any time soon.

Maybe the optimal partnership will be have to be more like the Wonder Twins, the characters in the '80s television cartoon *The Super Friends*. Zan and Jayna were from the planet Exxor. Zan, the boy, had the power to change spontaneously into any water-based form. Jayna, the girl, could become any animal. In order to activate their shape-shifting powers, the twins needed to touch hands. "Wonder Twin Powers, activate!" they would shout. When fighting a villian, Jayna would shout "Shape of the Sphinx!" and Zan would yell "Form of an Ice Shovel!" The Sphinx would then hit the villain over the head with the ice shovel. Their super powers worked only when they combined their different strengths.

Clinging to evolutionary determinism, however, could also thwart social progress. As women's salaries become necessities for survival of the modern family, men, despite ill-wiring, can no longer afford to focus solely on the hunt. Many modern men, especially those of the generation who were nurtured in Ms. Durga's multiple arms and grew up in the multi-tasking world of computer technology, have therefore begun to adapt.

Even in the most neo-traditional households, where the husband still takes the train to the organization and the wife has set up her office at home in order to manage the house and child care, a new multi-tasking masculinity is beginning to emerge. "Fathering is all about multi-tasking," said a writer in his thirties. "Just last night, in fact, I was swinging my daughter in the car seat to try to coax her to sleep, while at the same time I was downloading music into our computer, checking e-mail, reading a Philip Roth novel, and tinkering with an upcoming article. I only have two hands but sometimes I feel like an octopus. I have literally begun to undertake certain tasks with my feet.

"I also do almost all the cooking," he continued. "That said, my father was fairly shocked when he came to visit, because he saw me doing a lot of things that he never had to worry about—and I think he found that somewhat inappropriate." For men of generations X and Y, the social effects of feminism are slowly taking hold, but the pressures for more change are mounting. As women become more economically independent, they are staying single longer, choosing to rely on their social networks of friends for support rather than settling for a male partner who may not necessarily meet their standards of companionship. A higher divorce rate is forcing more men to live alone, care for themselves and develop the skills of the home front that traditionally have fallen to women. As liberated gay couples become more prominent, gay men, who either through biological or social wiring fall into more traditionally feminine roles, are becoming new social role models.

Most major corporations still lack in-house day care. Most men are still not granted paternity leave. There are still strong cultural pressures on men that make them feel that if they scant their jobs in favor of the work of home and child care, they might appear wimpy or uncommitted. Despite these obstacles, men are progressing in the direction of Durga's twin. If the conversation continues, the balance of roles will improve even more.

There may even be the possibility for change in men's brain circuits. Eric Kandel, a neuroscientist at Columbia University, won the first Nobel Prize in medicine of the twenty-first century for his seminal work with the sea slug aplysia. By studying the way the slug's nerve cells respond to chemical signals that produce changes in its behavior, Kandel and his colleagues discovered that learning can produce physical changes in the brain by strengthening connections between nerve cells.

Men aren't sea slugs, but it could be that the more they multi-task between the work of the home and their work, the more their brains will learn and change. It could be that once upon a time in the future, Durga's multi-tasking twin in shining armor could come to her rescue, overthrow the tyranny of the pressure for her to do it all, and prove that anatomy isn't destiny, experience is.

the limit

christian wiman

I don't understand anything...and I no longer want to understand anything. I want to stick to the fact....If I wanted to understand something, I would immediately have to betray the fact, but I've made up my mind to stick to the fact.

—Fyodor Dostoyevsky, *The Brothers Karamazov*

I WAS FIFTEEN when my best friend John shot his father in the face. It was an accident, I'm certain, and but for the fact that I'd dropped a couple of shotgun shells as I was fumbling to reload, the shot could have been mine. I sometimes wonder what difference that might have made.

We were dove-hunting, catching them as they cleared the edge of the small tank on John's family's property outside of town. Surrounding the tank was a slight rise of brush before the fields, and John's father, a country doctor who shared a small practice with my father, had wandered off through the brush behind us to check the fenceline. I was close to my limit that afternoon, which I'd never gotten, wearing one of those hunting vests with pockets big enough to hold a dozen or so birds. I remember the full feel of it, reaching in every so often to touch the little feathery lumps as they cooled. It was nearly dusk, my favorite time in West Texas, the light like steeping tea, shadows sliding out of things.

I'd been hunting for a couple of years. It seems odd to me now that I was allowed to have a gun, as my family's history was not a placid one, and I myself was prone to sudden destructive angers and what my grandmother would call "the sulls." I have more than one vivid memory of being in my bedroom as one of these angers subsides, books and clothes scattered on the floor, a chair and dresser overturned. I take the shotgun from under my bed and pump a shell into the chamber—roughly, so everyone in the house is sure to hear. No one comes. No one ever comes. I set the stock on the floor, lean my chin on the top of the barrel, stretch my arm down toward the trigger I can't quite touch, and wonder if this is something I'll grow into.

Theatrics, that gun aimed at my parents more than myself, with a kind of calculated malice that, twenty years later, makes me wince. My mother was terrified of guns. That my brother and I weren't allowed to have toy guns as we were growing up, yet both got shotguns as gifts in our early teens, is ironic, I suppose, though in that flat world of work and blunt fundamentalism in which I was raised, where in grade school county history lessons I learned the virtues of a man who'd slaughtered three of the seven white buffaloes known to exist, where one branch of my family had spent their happiest years in a town called Dunn, it has only a sad sort of retroactive irony.

My mother's hatred of guns was something more than the expression of a delicate feminine sensibility. Her own mother had been murdered in front of her and her two brothers when she was fourteen. The killer was her father, about whom I know only that he was compulsively itinerant, almost certainly manic-depressive, and for the month or so prior to the act had been living apart from his family. He walked in the back door one evening and killed his wife as she was cooking dinner, waited while his children ran out into the fields, then laid down beside her in some simulacrum of spent desire and shot himself in the head.

This was just a story to me, less than that, really, since it wasn't so much told as breathed, a sort of steady pressure in the air. I don't remember it ever being mentioned, and yet I also don't remember a time when I didn't know about it. It had more reality for me than the night in my infancy when my father, who was also given to the sulls, went into his room and didn't come out for several months, for I have no memory of this and didn't learn of it until after I'd left home; but less reality than the aunt, Opal, who'd committed suicide before I was born. Supposedly, the whole extended family had conspired for a time to create their own private climate of calm, eradicating all hints of darkness from their lives like a country rigidly purging its past, steering conversations toward church and children, hiding the knives. It was hunting, as one might imagine, that proved most difficult in this regard, though Opal's husband was very careful to make sure their two sons kept their guns "hidden" under the beds, the shells all locked up in a little chest to which he had the only key. It seems not to have occurred to anyone that they might simply stop hunting and get rid of their guns. It was Texas. They were boys.

My family was so quiet about these matters that I thought they were something we were supposed to be embarrassed about. I learned early and no doubt too well that only certain kinds of violence were acceptable, both as topics of conversation and as actions. I loved the story of the uncle who, frustrated by a particularly recalcitrant cow, slammed his fist into its skull so hard that the cow dropped immediately to its knees like some ruined supplicant. I loved my immense, onomatopoetic uncles, Harley and Burley, who'd storm into town after months on offshore oil rigs, the nimbus of gentleness around each of them made more vivid and strange by their scars and hard talk, the wads of cash they pulled from their pockets like plunder.

And though I was mildly, reflexively disciplined by my father after the one truly serious fight I had growing up, when I was consumed with an anger that still unnerves me and continued to beat a cowboy I'll call Tom even after I'd broken bones in my hand and every blow was doing me a lot more damage than it was doing him, I was alert to the tacit masculine pride. Even the principal who meted out our corporal punishment for fighting on school grounds whipped our backsides with a kind of jocular aggressiveness that amounted to approval.

But anything that suggested madness rather than control, illness rather than health, feminine interiority rather than masculine action, was off-limits. Or perhaps not so much off-limits as simply outside of the realm of experience for which we had words, for I don't remember resisting discussing these things, really, or having them deflected by adults. Later, when I would begin to meet other young writers who, like myself, generally had more imagination than available experience, the events of my family's history would acquire a kind of show-and-tell exoticism, little trinkets of authenticity brought back from the real world. That it wasn't a real world, not yet, that it had no more reality for me than what I read in books, didn't seem to matter too much at the time.

Now it does. At some point I stopped talking about my family's past and began reinventing it, occasionally in what I wrote, but mostly just for myself, accumulating facts like little stones which I would smooth and polish with the waters of imagination. I chose them very carefully, I realize now, nothing so big that it might dam up the flow, nothing too ugly and jagged to be worn down into the form I had in mind. Psychoanalysis is "creating a story that you can live with," I have been told, and perhaps that's what I was doing, though in truth I think I wanted less a story I could live with than one I could live without, less a past to inhabit than some recreated place I could walk finally, definitively away from.

The bullet hole between my grandmother's shoulder blades, then, and the way she crumples faster than a heartshot deer. I can see my grandfather stepping away from the door, can see the look in his eyes, which, I know, is meant to assure his children as they back slowly out of the room that he is as baffled and saddened by this as they are, that they needn't be afraid, that he would never, never hurt them. He walks heavily across the room, steps over his wife, and, in some last gasp of that hopeless hardscrabble sanity his children will inherit and pass on, turns off the stove so the dinner won't burn, then lies down beside her on the floor.

I can see my Aunt Opal, too, gathering the laundry, humming something, deciding at the last minute to wash the coats. She is not beautiful but there is something of the landscape's stark simplicity about her face, a sense of pure horizon, as if what you saw were merely the limit of your own vision, not the end of what is there. As she shakes out her husband's coat, a single forgotten shotgun shell falls out of the pocket onto the floor. I can see the dull copper where the light dies, the little puckered end of the red casing. Oh, honey, she says as she picks it up, bemusement changing to concern on her face, concern to pain, it's not your fault. It's no one's fault.

Lately, though, more and more, it's John I see, standing stolid and almost actual in his boots and hunting vest, lifting his shotgun to his shoulder and laughing as I fumble to load mine. He is physically very similar to me but at ease in his body in a way I'll never be. He does not yet inhabit that continuous present that precludes remorse, but already he is all impulse and action, whereas I am increasingly deliberate, increasingly interior. There is some inner, inarticulate anger we share, though, and recognize in each other. When John's begins to slip out of control, the results for the people around him will be immediate, palpable, and utterly disastrous. My own implosion will be no more noticeable to the people around me than something I've imagined.

The gun that goes off in my ear now is a fact. It is muted by all the intervening years, by all that has happened, both internally and externally. Still, the authority of its report surprises me, as does the strangely muffled shout that seems to occur at almost exactly the same time, as if the dove, which once again John has not missed, which as I look up is plunging downward, had a human cry.

I DON'T WANT to kill myself. I never have, though for a time not too long ago the act emerged in me like an instinct, abstractly at first, and with a sort of voluptuous, essentially literary pleasure. (Nietzsche: "The thought of suicide is a powerful solace; it enables a man to get through many a bad night.") Gradually the thought became more painful as it became more concrete, more dangerous as it became more familiar, more alienating as it became more my own. I thought of it as a kind of cancer in my mind, because eventually no matter what I was doing—teaching a class, sitting at a dinner party, trying to write, waking every hour of every night to check the clock—that was what I was doing, attending to that slowly clarifying imperative that beat itself out inside me as steadily and ineluctably as my own pulse.

I told no one. I couldn't. On the couple of occasions when I'd made up my mind that I would tell friends what was happening, my heart began to race, I had difficulty breathing, and I simply had no language for what I needed to say. Also, even during the worst of it, I always doubted the validity of the feeling, suspected that, like the impersonal stories I used to tell about my distant familial history, it might just be a bit of disingenuous self-dramatization. Despite the fact that I've had relatives on both sides of my family commit suicide, despite my knowledge that my father has resisted the impulse all his life, and my sister has twice attempted the act, I suspected I might be faking, using the thought of suicide as a way of avoiding the more mundane failures of my life. I wasn't going to tell anyone until I was sure. But how does one prove such terror is real except by committing the act itself?

My father knew, not definitively, perhaps, but with something like that visceral sense by which an artist comes to recognize the flaws in anything he's made. Our relationship is as fitful as ever—we go months without talking to each other—but there is more ease between us now, more forthright affection and trust. I think this has more to do with him than me. During the fifteen years or so when our relationship consisted of little more than holiday exchanges of information, he endured a divorce, bankruptcy, the loss of his medical practice, the death of his second wife, divorce again, back surgery, an almost fatal rattlesnake bite, a heart attack (from the volume of serum given to counter the snakebite), cancer, a plane crash, alcoholism, the estrangement and self-destruction of his children, and no doubt several other calamities which he's managed to keep secret. It was a run of luck that would have mellowed Caligula.

During the approximately six months that I was—what to call it?—thinking, sinking, we talked on the phone twice. On both occasions he asked me, out of the blue, and with a sort of mumbling quietude that I've begun to recognize in my own voice at emotional encroachments, "Do you ever think of doing away with yourself?" That's just the way he said it, "doing away with yourself," which led me to make a snide, annihilating comment about the linguistic imprecision and general uselessness of psychiatry, because in his late forties that's what my father had become, a psychiatrist living on the grounds of a state hospital, where suicide was as ubiquitous and predictable an impulse as hunger, where even the doctor whose place my father had taken, whose office he used and whose bedroom he slept in, had "done away with himself."

Some families accumulate self-consciousness in the way that others accumulate wealth (and perhaps one precludes the other). A man who eats and works and copulates all with same bland animal efficiency somehow sires a son who, maddeningly to the father, pauses occasionally in the midst of plowing to marvel at the shapes in the clouds, or who sometimes thinks fleetingly that perhaps there is an altogether different order of feeling than the mild kindliness he feels toward his wife. He in turn has a son who has the impulse to be elsewhere—geographically, sexually, spiritually—but not the wherewithal to wholly do so, who lives the impulsive, appetitive lives of his own children in the fixed world of his parents, and destroys both. A person emerging from the wreckage of this—and many simply don't—is likely to be quite solitary, given to winnowings and adept at departures, so absurdly self-aware that he can hardly make love without having an "experience." He might even be, maddeningly to all concerned, a poet.

That I should have turned out to be a poet seems strange to me for all sorts of reasons—I don't relish poverty or obscurity, to name just two—but my background has never seemed one of them. Bookless though it was, my childhood, with its nameless angers and solitudes, its intimate, inexplicable violence, seems to me "the very forge and working-house" of poetry. Tellingly, my father, though he certainly never read poetry, is the one member of my family for whom my becoming a poet never seemed at all odd or surprising. I begin to understand this now. He knew—taught me—love's necessary severities, how it will work itself into, even be most intense within, forms of such austere and circumscribed dimensions that, to the uninitiated, it might not seem like love at all.

I am eight years old. My mother has been scratched by the kitten we've had for a month or so, and there has been a flurry of panic and activity as she has had the beginnings of a severe allergic reaction and been rushed to the hospital. I don't know where my brother and sister are, or why I've come home with my father, or if my mother is all right. I'm sitting on the couch, staring at the television, though it's not on. My father is looking for something in a kitchen drawer, now he's back in the bedroom looking for something else. My face is boneless, ghostly on the black screen. I'm hardly there. He walks past me with the kitten in one hand and a hammer in the other, opens the sliding glass door to the porch, closes it behind him. I shut my eyes, will myself away.

It's eight years later. My father is having an affair. He and my mother are at the edge of what will be a nasty, protracted, ruinous divorce in which their children will be used as weapons. It's the middle of the afternoon on a school day and I'm stoned, maybe on speed as well, I forget. Some little argument cracks the surface of civil estrangement we've tacitly agreed upon, and out of that rift all the old anger rises.

I begin to curse at my mother in a way I've never done before or since, now I break something, now something else, and she's scared enough to call my father at the hospital and leave the house until he rushes home.

They come in together. I am sitting in the living room, seething, waiting. My father stands over me and quietly—guiltily, I realize, the first flaw in his hitherto adamantine authority—asks me what is going on. I tell him I'm ashamed of him. I call him a liar. I curse him in the harshest and most profane terms I can muster. He hits me open-handed across the face—hard, but with a last-minute hesitation in it, a pause of consciousness that seems to spread like a shadow across his face and, as he sinks into a chair, is to this day the purest sadness I have ever seen.

I stand up slowly. I am vaguely aware of my mother yelling at my father, of my sister in the doorway weeping. I am vaguely aware that our roles have suddenly and irrevocably reversed, that he is looking up at me, waiting for what I'll do. I hit him squarely between the eyes, much harder than he hit me. He does nothing but cover his head with his hands, doesn't say a word as I hit him again, and again, and again, expending my anger upon a silence that absorbs it, and gradually neutralizes it, until the last blow is closer to a caress.

That was the end of my childhood. My father moved out within a month or so, and around the same time I gave up drugs (well, close enough), began the exercise regimen that I've maintained for twenty years, and started assiduously saving for the tuition for my first year of college, to which I was suddenly determined to go, and which I would choose entirely on the basis of its distance from Texas. Once there I sometimes went months without talking to any member of my family, whose lives seemed to me as dangerously aimless and out of control as mine was safely ordered and purposeful. I began to read poetry, which I loved most of all for the contained force of its forms, the release of its music, and for the fact that, as far as I could tell, it had absolutely nothing to do with the world I was from.

And then one night John killed a man outside of a bar. I'd kept up with him somewhat, had been forced to, in fact, since in a final assertion of physical superiority he'd ended my lingering relationship with my high school girlfriend by impregnating her. I knew that he'd gone to work in the oil fields, and that he was deep into drugs. Our friendship had fallen apart before this, though, a slow, sad disintegration that culminated in a halfhearted, inconclusive fistfight on a dirt road outside of town. I forget the reason for the fight itself, and anyway it wouldn't be relevant. What we were trying to do, I think, was to formalize the end of something that had meant a great deal to both of us, to attach an act we understood to a demise we didn't.

My mother called to tell me about it. John had gotten in an argument with a stranger that escalated into blows. They had been thrown out of the bar by bouncers and continued the fight in the street. In front of some thirty or forty people John had slowly and with great difficulty won the fight, beating the man until he lay on his back gasping for air. And whether the pause I've imagined over and over at this point is something that came out in the trial, or whether it's merely some residual effect of my friendship with John, my memory of a decent and sensitive person to whom some

christian wiman

glimmer of consciousness must surely have come, what happened in the end is a fact. At nineteen years old, with his bare hands, in front of a crowd of people who did nothing, and with a final fury that must have amazed that man who was only its incidental object, John destroyed him.

Hanging up the phone, sitting there in my dorm room of that preposterously preppy college fifteen hundred miles away from my home, it all came back, the guns and the fights, the wreckage of my family, my friendship with John, the wonderment in his voice in the hours after that hunting accident when he kept saying, I shot my father, I shot my own father, as if he were trying out the thought, trying to accommodate it in his consciousness.

I did what I always do: I went for a run, thirteen miles through the hills of Virginia, much farther than I usually ran, but without difficulty, my heart a steady thump-thump-thump in my chest. It was not release. It was the same thing as my precipitous decision to get out of Texas, no different from what poetry would be for me for years, until I would finally find myself back home one day, living on the grounds of that state hospital, collecting facts. It was what suicide would have been the final expression of: flight.

DR. MILLER'S FACE was obliterated. He walked out of the brush across from us and around the edge of the tank with the hesitant precision of someone making his way across a familiar room in the dark. Amid the blood and loose bits of skin there were clumps of pellets cauliflowering his cheeks and the sockets of his eyes, distorting his forehead and throat like a sudden, hideous disease, his dark shirt darker down his chest. His lips, too, were so misshapen that it was hard at first to understand the directives he was giving us, though he spoke calmly, deliberately, with the same west Texas mix of practical necessity and existential futility that no crisis could ever shock my own father out of.

He drove. I don't remember there being even a moment of discussion, though both John and I had our licenses by then, and though Dr. Miller had to lean over the steering wheel to see, wincing as the pickup jolted over the ruts and stones. I was sitting in the middle of the seat, John at the door. I kept trying not to look at Dr. Miller, kept thinking that his breaths were shorter than they should have been, that I could hear blood in his lungs.

There were two gates before we got to the road. At the first one, John simply leapt back in the truck as it was still moving, leaving the gate unlatched. Dr. Miller stopped, turned his head like some sentient piece of meat toward us, and said, "Close the gate, John."

At the second gate, after John had gotten out of the truck, Dr. Miller said without looking toward me, "You didn't fire that shot, did you?"

Could it be, in life as well as in writing, that our deepest regrets will not be for our lies, but for the truths we should not have told?

"He didn't mean to," I said, the words spilling out of me, "it was an accident, we thought you were in the south pasture, we didn't hear you, we ..."

"It's my fault," Dr. Miller said peremptorily, putting his hand on my knee. "I know that."

About halfway through the ride John began to weep. He was leaning over against the door, and as his shoulders trembled up and down, it seemed years were falling away from him, that if he were to reach out it would be with a hand from which all the strength was gone, if he were to speak it would be in the voice of a child. I looked out at the fields that had almost vanished, darkness knitting together the limbs of mesquite trees, accumulating to itself the crows and telephone poles, the black relentless pumpjacks which, when John and I spent the night out here, beat into our sleep like the earth's heart.

Dr. Miller drove himself straight to my father, who was still at the office. My father registered no more alarm for Dr. Miller's injuries than Dr. Miller himself had done, though my father did, I noticed, immediately and carefully touch my face, my shoulders and arms, as if to ensure himself that I wasn't the one hurt.

John and I waited in my father's office. I sat in my father's chair behind the desk, John in the chair across from me, looking out the window. This is when I remember him saying, "I shot my father, I shot my own father," not to me, and almost as if it were a question, one that neither I nor anyone else could answer. Not another word was said. I sat there watching the clock on the wall across from me, willing it to go faster, faster.

To be a writer is to betray the facts. It's one of the more ruthless things about being a writer, finally, in that to cast an experience into words is in some way to lose the reality of the experience itself, to sacrifice the fact of it to whatever imaginative pattern one's wound requires. A great deal is

gained, I suppose, a kind of control, the sort of factitious understanding that Ivan Karamazov renounces in my epigraph.
When I began to spiral into myself and into my family's history, it was just this sort of willful understanding that I
needed. I knew the facts well enough.

But I don't understand, not really. Not my family's history and not my childhood, neither my father's actions nor
his absence. I don't understand how John could kill someone, or by what logic or luck the courses of our lives, which
had such similar origins, could be so different. I don't understand, when there is so much I love about my life, how I
could have such a strong impulse to end it, nor by what dis-
pensation or accident of chemistry that impulse could go
away, recede so far into my consciousness that I could almost
believe it never happened.

It did happen, though. It marked me. I don't believe in
"laying to rest" the past. There are wounds we won't get over.
There are things that happen to us that, no matter how hard
we try to forget, no matter with what fortitude we face them,
what mix of religion and therapy we swallow, what finished
and durable forms of art we turn them into, are going to go
on happening inside of us for as long as our brains are alive.

And yet I've come to believe, and in rare moments can
almost feel, that like an illness some vestige of which the
body keeps to protect itself, pain may be its own reprieve;
that the violence that is latent within us may be, if never altogether dispelled or tamed, at least acknowledged, defined,
and perhaps by dint of the love we feel for our lives, for the
people in them and for our work, rendered into an energy
that need not be inflicted on others or ourselves, an energy

we may even be able to use; and that for those of us who have gone to war with our own minds there is yet hope for what Freud called "normal unhappiness," wherein we might remember the dead without being haunted by them, give to our lives a coherence that is not "closure," and learn to live with our memories, our families, and ourselves amid a truce that is not peace.

I hear my father calling me from what seems a great distance. I walk down the hall of the office that has long ago been cleared out and turned into something else. But here are my family's pictures on the walls, here is the receptionist's window where my sister and I would play a game in which one of us had some dire illness which the other, with a cup of water, or with some inscrutable rune written on a prescription pad, always had the remedy for. And here is John, small and terrified, walking beside me.

Dr. Miller is sitting up on an examining table, his face swathed in gauze, his shirt off, revealing a sallow, soft, middle-aged body. Its whiteness shocks me like a camera's flash and will be the first thing I'll think of when, within months, John tells me that his father has left for another woman. We stop just inside the door, side by side. My heart seems almost audible.

"Well now," my father says, smiling slightly as he looks to the table then back to us, "did you boys get your limits?"

Dr. Miller laughs, and John moves toward him.

He is all right. Everything is going to be all right. I stick my hand in my pocket full of cold birds to feel how close I've come.

binuclear man
ruth bettelheim

with m. flaming and a. flaming

I AM SITTING in my office, in the afternoon; warm summer sunlight streams in through the windows. The two other people in my office have come to seek advice from me, a psychotherapist, because they are struggling to deal with their son who is misbehaving. They are divorced parents, ex-spouses who share custody of the boy.

I tell them that they need to set boundaries for their son: they need to make it clear to him that if his grades do not improve—he's currently getting D's and F's—he will not be allowed to use the phone or watch TV. The boy's parents, however, are violently opposed to the measures that I suggest. They believe that their son is not really responsible for his own misbehavior and bad grades: he is a victim of divorce. They believe that their divorce damaged their son, possibly in irreparable ways. They feel that they need to indulge their son to make up for all the wrongs which they have inflicted on him by divorcing and subjecting him to a joint-custody life, and cannot bear to deny him any plea-sure. How can we take these things away from our son, they ask, and still have a loving family? They fear that he will be angry and full of hate if he is deprived of his pleasures and social life.

I tell them that children need to have limits of behavior set and enforced in order to feel loved and secure. To children's minds, if their parents can't be bothered to stop them from doing something it is either because their parents don't care or because it isn't really important that they stop. As I say all this, I think of my own son and daughter, both now adults and also "victims" of divorce. I think of the people they are today—successful, happy, and autonomous individuals—and the ways in which growing up in a nontraditional family shaped them as individuals.

"I would never suggest anything that I would not apply to my own children," I tell the distraught parents.

I REMEMBER my son coming home from school. It is Fri-day, and his father is picking the children up to take them to his house for the weekend. My son remembers to pack his backpack, and then has time to play a video game. His sister, five years younger, does not remember. She is deeply en-gaged with her Barbies. Suddenly, the doorbell rings: Dad has arrived, and he is in a hurry to leave immediately to avoid the rush hour.

My daughter must stuff her bag as quickly as she can as her brother rushes out the door, not wanting to displease his father. He yells at his sister to hurry up! She is struggling to remember what she needs. I come in to say goodbye and give each of them a hug. Meanwhile, both children know that Dad is waiting. They want to get out the door as fast as possible, but they do not want to let me down. And they cannot afford to leave anything behind that they might need for school on Monday. My son hugs me and runs to the car—my daughter clings to me a few moments longer, filled with conflicting feelings, before running after her brother.

In the car, my daughter remembers that she has forgotten the things she needs for a project due on Monday. She tells her father, who by now is quite irritated, and her brother, not wanting to bear their father's anger, teases her. She runs back to the house, trips on the stairs, and skins her knee. She has no time to be in pain or deal with it: she gets her stuff and runs back to the car.

Sometimes it is my son, sometimes it is my daughter who has forgotten something or is late. Both children are caught by conflicting loyalties and under pressure: they long to please both parents, and they have to remember every single thing that they will need for the three days that they are spending with their father. This is emotionally charged multitasking of the most demanding sort, and it is repeated twice a week with each transfer from one parent's house to the other. Equally difficult is their sense that there is Mom's time and Dad's time, which are determined by the custody schedule, but there is no time that is just for them. This creates the feeling that their lives are not their own, and enhances their sense of obligation to meet others' needs. For them, it is a given that they must do so.

My son describes his life immediately prior to and after

the divorce as being like walking on a narrow bridge across the sea. The tides, his parents' moods, needs, and desires, and the tensions and conflicts between them threatened to pull him down and drown him on either side. He needed to become exquisitely aware of what each of us was feeling, how each of us would react to things said or done, in order to protect himself from being emotionally swamped or just kept from a desired activity like guitar lessons or a trip to the beach. As a result, he became immensely intuitive about what others are feeling, deeply empathetic and a superb diplomat able to soothe the most fraught situations: these were the skills that he needed in order to make life less dangerous for himself. He learned these things out of self-protection first and foremost, and secondly out of loyalty to both parents. And he is not alone.

Study after study, even those conducted by the most vocal critics of divorce, have found that adult children of divorce are more empathetic and have a greater devotion to honesty, kindness, and integrity in relationships than their peers. Although these lessons are often painful for children, and although it is natural for us to regret their suffering, it is also unjust to the children of divorce to remain blind to what they have gained. Rather than writing them off as damaged, we can learn from their ability to blossom under adversity.

THE PARENTS in my office are not alone in their beliefs about the destructive effects of divorce on children. The last two decades have produced a tidal wave of divorce hysteria, and many divorced parents feel deeply stigmatized and guilty as a result. In particular, divorce is blamed for the troubles of young men; the feeling is that if boys today are "in crisis," this must have, at least in part, to do with the ravages of growing up in a nontraditional family, without the benefit of traditional parental roles. And it is certainly true that divorce is not without its costs, but it is also not without its benefits—particularly for boys.

How can I convey this to the parents in front of me? How can I help them understand that instead of feeling guilty they need to cultivate and encourage the positive aspects of their situation? How can I help them see that their son can suffer the problems of coming from a "broken home" and still arrive at adulthood a better person than he might otherwise have been? Do I give them the details of my son's life? Or those of other children who have been my patients? If I tell such stories, I have to be very careful about the details so as to avoid breaking anyone's confidentiality. The stories are too vague and general. They aren't believed. And anyway, the mother says, "What's that got to do with our boy?" They are afraid of losing their son's affection. He has been lying to them quite regularly, skipping school and growing and selling pot behind their backs. This somehow does not relate to the lack of a meaningful response on their part. So I let my mind drift back to my son, to see what I can find there that I can tell them and that might help.

IN GENERAL, parents don't divorce unless there are deep unbridgeable differences between them. In my case, I married, full of idealism, a man from a radically different religious and cultural background. I came from a family of intellectual Jewish refugees. He came from a Mennonite family who eschewed cars and plowed their small farm with a horse; his father barely completed the fourth grade. Still, we felt at first that we had so much in common that these things were insignificant. We felt the bond of being raised at least partly in other cultures, mine Viennese, his Mennonite. However, problems arose between us over our ways of responding emotionally and what we needed and wanted both out of life and a relationship. These fundamental differences led to silent but deadly conflict.

I recount this to illustrate what is true of all parents who divorce: there are deep, profound, and irrevocable differences between them. That is the reason they divorce. Parents want to avoid divorce for many reasons. They do not want to admit failure as partners or as parents, or harm their children by "breaking up" the home and family, or risk losing contact and the bond with their children. They do not want to lose control over their children and of course there is also money; neither wants to suffer the lowered standard of living, which seems inevitable if the pie has to be divided to support two separate households. Only very profound differences could overcome all of this resistance to divorce. When they divorce, parents are finally free to live out those differences, rather than to try to hide or deny them as they did while they were married. Thus, the new homes they create after the divorce reflect these differences.

After the divorce, differences are allowed out of the closet and flourish. That is what the parents needed. But for the children, another problem is created. Children no longer live in a world where there is one agreed-upon set of rules, values, or beliefs. Suddenly there are two of all of these. Two sets of rules about bedtime, bath time, homework, TV, movies, video games, hugs, table manners, good behavior and bad behavior. In one house you must attend church, in the other religion is disregarded. In one you must always say please, thank you, hello, goodbye and ask permission to go out. In the other these things are undesirable. In one house it is a sign of being a "goody-two-shoes" to worry about being on time to school and getting each assignment in on time and done well, in the other these are required behaviors. The two homes are in fact two different cultures, and because of this children in binuclear families become adept at living in two worlds. They are forced to recognize that there is more than one right way to do things and that they had better learn very quickly what the rules are in each so as not to upset either parent or get in trouble.

I remember my son as a boy. There he is, 12 years old. He is faced with conflicts of loyalty that permeate his life on a daily basis. He is faced with shifting from one set of rules and expectations to another every week. It takes a huge toll on him. Each time he changes households, every week, he goes through a period of adjustment, which causes him to be irritable, as we all are when we travel from one culture to the other and must adapt quickly to the new cultural rules to succeed. Businessmen are provided with guides to the basic rules of behavior in each culture. Children are not. They must figure it out themselves, and frequently the adults even deny that such a problem exists.

Of course this process is painful for children, but if skill-fully negotiated by attentive parents, what is the end result of this harsh learning about living in two cultures? Practically, the differing cultures of binuclear families teach both survival skills and attributes that are usually described as "masculine" and those that are usually described as "feminine" to children of both sexes. Both boys and girls in post-divorce families must learn to be diplomatic, sensitive to others' needs, empathetic, nurturing, multitasking, resilient in new situations, independent, and self-aware. For my son, it means he likes living abroad from time to time and enjoys traveling. He has no trouble adapting to new cultures, whether at college or at the in-laws' house, abroad or in the workplace. New jobs, with different demands and work-place environments, are quickly and easily negotiated. It is second nature to him to quickly read and assess the situation he is in, figure out how it works and to become a valued as-set in it. Like so many other children of divorce, he is suc-ceeding where our culture expects him to fail.

Additionally, in my experience and that of researchers across the ideological spectrum, living in two divergent cul-tures with loyalty to both causes children to become very self-reflective and autonomous thinkers. Each parent's point of view must be considered and evaluated. They are often at odds with each other and both can't be right. So the child very quickly learns that there are at least two valid points of view on almost every aspect of reality and it is up to him to decide which one makes the most sense. Such children are forced to develop ethics and opinions of their own, based on their own perceptions and experiences. They must develop identities that are their own as well. They are most likely viewed and evaluated in very different ways in each parent's household, as each parent values traits differently, and the children naturally respond quite differently to each culture they live in. A mother might regard her children as cold and uncaring, while at the same time a father sees them as kind and empathetic. Because children can't be both, they must figure out for themselves who they are.

Since these children are independent thinkers and self-defined persons, they do not accept authority without question. This can be particularly problematic for boys. Because they are taught from an early age that being able to confront others is a sign of masculinity, boys tend to be much more direct in their challenges to authority than girls.

For example, after my divorce both my son and my daughter had to take a chemistry class in school, a class that both children found repetitive and boring. Both of them easily grasped the material; they felt that the homework and class presentations did not contribute anything to their understanding, and that they could get A's on their exams simply by reading the textbook. My daughter reacted to this situation by immediately proving to the teacher that she was a good student: she turned in all her work promptly, was polite and charming, and contributed regularly to class discussions. After she proved herself this way, later in the semester the teacher was happy to excuse an occasional absence or missed assignment.

Like most boys, however, my son took a more direct approach. After getting A's on the first few quizzes, he tried to discuss his objections to the homework directly with the teacher. The teacher insisted that all the homework had to be completed promptly and fully. My son responded by not doing any homework while continuing to get A's on his exams, to demonstrate to the teacher that he was right. After being scolded by the teacher, he began cutting class: angry about what he saw as the teacher's arbitrary authority, he wanted to show her that he could "ace" the final simply by reading the textbook at the end of the semester. Sure enough, he did "ace" the final—but ended up receiving an F in the class anyway for not turning in his homework and being absent. My ex-husband and I were called into the school counselor's office where we were told that our son was "troubled." Like many boys in divorced families, he was labeled as having an attitude problem or being emotionally disturbed because of his efforts to develop a uniquely autonomous identity. This is a tragic irony, considering that most parents wish for children who question assumptions and feel comfortable with their individuality, and that as adults these traits—creative thinking and independence—are highly sought after.

One of the major ways in which adults impact children is by their beliefs about them. If the people that children love and respect, their parents, grandparents, and teachers, believe that they are damaged due to divorce and treat them as damaged or defective, they must struggle against the weight of these convictions. There are studies that demonstrate that when teachers and counselors are told that the child they are watching on a videotape is from a divorced family, they see the child as having significant problems. If they are told that the child comes from a traditional home, they find the same behavior by the same child unproblematic. This is especially true of boys.

Children on the receiving end of this bias end up being treated by parents, teachers, and others as problem children, when in fact they are perfectly normal. If we believe that children are helpless victims, we force them to respond—often in negative ways—to this depiction of themselves. On the other hand, if we believe that they are successfully solving important problems and gaining valuable new skills and abilities, we make it easier for children to have confidence in themselves and their ability to overcome obstacles.

THE MOTHER SHIFTS uncomfortably in her chair. The father stiffens, his posture indicating his displeasure with what I am saying. They are too polite to say so, but it rankles them. They are committed to the idea of their guilt. The guilt has become a habit for them, part of their identity as parents; it also takes the responsibility for misbehavior off their son. He is a good boy, they agree, who has been let down by the adults in his life. He is floundering because he lacks a full-time father, a role model for how to be a man. And yet, if handled properly divorce may force both father and son to become a new kind of man: a kind of man that is uniquely needed in, and suited to, contemporary culture.

I realize that in many ways my son is a very different man from his father, or either of his grandfathers. My ex-husband and I both had very old-fashioned fathers. They were not involved in day-to-day child rearing. Occasionally they disciplined us or tried to teach us something about the

world or life or some skills, but both men subscribed to essentially nineteenth-century roles as fathers. Before the divorce, my ex-husband and I also delegated household tasks
along traditional lines. I was in charge of caring for the children, cooking meals, etc., while he did house repairs and
yard work. To our children, my ex-husband was a relatively
distant figure who had little to do with their day-to-day
lives—not because of lack of love or caring, but because
that was how he was taught to be a father.

All this changed with the divorce. For the first time my
ex-husband was confronted with being a parent who was
responsible for all aspects of the children's lives. This was
not easy for him. He had absolutely no role models or background or training for this. He wanted badly to be fully engaged in the children's lives: take them to school, help with
homework, provide meals, and so on. But he had to invent
the whole thing from scratch. As a devoted father who was
determined to maintain his relationship with the children
and to provide for their needs, he had to struggle. At first the
task was overwhelming, but gradually he found a way to be
a different kind of father than he had been. Although certain kinds of empathy and nurturing behavior are still difficult for him, he learned to meet many of the children's
needs that had previously been out of his sphere.

From this example, my son learned how to be a parent in
ways that his own father was never taught as a child. Unlike
his father and both of his grandfathers he has had a role
model of a father who is hands-on and a primary caretaker.
He has, in addition, developed attributes that are usually
considered feminine: adaptability, empathy, emotional hon-

esty, intuitiveness, and nurturing as a direct result of living in a binuclear family. He has deep in his innermost recesses the desire and all of the capacities to be the very father that young women seem to long for in a partner. Boys like mine, who grew up in binuclear families, have been forced to develop differently.

THE PARENTS before me do not yet see these things in their son. They are still concerned. I suggest that if they are unwilling or unable to deprive him of any pleasures, perhaps they should send him to boarding school or to live with another family member. They are unconvinced. I warn them that the boy's behavior will escalate until they are prepared to do something. Not responding to small gestures of delinquency will cause him to up the ante until their hand is forced. They leave dissatisfied.

Four months later, they make another appointment to see me. Their son has escalated his acting out: he has started running away. At first it was only for a night or two, and they found him at his friend's house. Then he disappeared for a week. Now he just returned after having been gone for over two weeks. They are desperate, and ready to listen. They agree to try to become more authoritative parents. I emphasize the need for the rules to be few but important and that the consequences must be previously established, and ones that make sense to the boy. If schoolwork isn't done, he will not be allowed to do other activities; if he is not a good family member, he will have to do his own laundry, prepare his own meals, take public transportation to get where he wants to go, and so forth. On the other hand, any and all progress toward these goals, even the smallest, must be noticed and praised by the parents. Each parent has concerns: that this will make things worse, that the other parent will not follow through. I tell them that they both don't have to do it the same way or even have the same rules, and that even if only one parent becomes authoritative, it will be enough to make a difference. They leave full of doubt.

RESEARCHERS of all stripes have found that most, if not all, of the problems attributed to divorce (other than those caused by poverty) are attributable to a lack of warm, attentive, authoritative parenting. In order to maintain a child's self-confidence and teach the self-control that children need to thrive, parents must set and enforce boundaries; this is particularly true for boys, who often have greater difficulty learning self-regulation than girls. It is self-control and self-confidence that underlie the capacity to make creative and productive use of the skills taught by growing up in a binuclear family.

After the parents leave my office, I reflect on their situation. Like many families, they have been paralyzed by their negative assumptions about divorce and their feelings of guilt. It is not that they are wrong to believe that divorce has been a painful experience for their son: divorce is difficult for most, if not all, children. The problem is that they have forgotten what their son needs—for in many ways, children in divorced families need the same things from their parents as children in every other kind of family: caring, love, structure, clear boundaries, and the belief of their parents that they are not damaged individuals.

Given these things, children and particularly boys who grow up in binuclear families gain a unique opportunity. Our society is changing at an ever-accelerating pace, and we now live in a global service economy. Many have documented the attributes needed to excel in such a society; borrowing from the work of researcher and cultural commentator Daniel Goleman, these traits include empathy, emotional awareness, self-confidence, self-control, social deftness, persuasiveness, resilience, cooperation, and adaptability—a list that encompasses both traditionally "masculine" and "feminine" attributes.

This set of competencies closely matches those learned by boys growing up in binuclear families, especially those fortunate enough to have warm, caring, and also authoritative parents. Given the premium on these abilities, boys from binuclear families are often at an advantage in later life. They have been forced to develop a skill set which will enable them to be uniquely competent partners, parents and professionals. Their future can be bright—not in spite of, but because of, what they have endured.

war is obsolete
choyin rangdrol

TEARS SPRANG from my eyes, loosening hardened emotion from my face like stones easing down a cliff in driving rain. It was a moment of lucidity in which, for the first time, I felt cleared of a choking obstruction of my humanity. A heavy psychological burden had been dislodged and peace came rushing in to take its place. Until that moment my life had been gripped by the crippling effects of war, even though I had never been a soldier.

My father spent his entire life in a veterans' hospital after returning home deranged from World War II. I never met him nor felt a single touch of his embrace. Nightmares of soldiers chasing me from home and into a breathless abyss haunted my childhood dreams. The experience of being a "latchkey" only child in a single-parent household was a war of inexpressible loneliness. The suburban neighborhood that shrouded my childhood was mired in sporadic death, including news of schoolyard friends who escaped the hood only to be killed in Vietnam. Wars on drugs and poverty raged around me as teachers taught us to "duck and tuck" in case of nuclear attack. As a young African-American male, my fate was suspended in a chrysalis of endangerment, violence, drugs, and the looming threat of incarceration.

The notion of achieving personal peace was not a consideration until well into my adulthood. Yet after many years of personal suffering as well as causing suffering in the lives of others, my life changed forever. I found an imperturbable peace that is now what I call "who I have always been."

In order for me to find stable peace my life had to undergo a transformation that I could never have planned. It began rather innocently in the form of an experience I can only describe as hearing a distant calling from within. It was a peculiar remembrance of inner peace almost too nebulous to discern. I had felt it all my life and yet in that moment of tearful realization it was as though I had never heard it before. We all have this calling, but it becomes muted by the clamor of ideas and views we are imbued with as children by the adult world. This inner yearning for peace haunts us when we become exhausted with the misery of our own suffering or that of our fellow human beings. Our ability to intellectually desensitize our emotions fails us and we are left with an insistent pang in our gut. While clenched in my tearful moment of emotional seizure, a part of me simply shut down in woeful fatigue. I can't say whether it was the violent deaths of my childhood friends, the death of my mother, the chronic ill effect of knowing that war had stolen my father, or the continuous aggravation of witnessing the evildoing in the world. But deep in the recesses of my psyche a gentle voice pierced the clamor and appeared as a familiar whisper of inner sanity. It suggested that inner conflict is the result of a failed process even a child knows to avoid.

We all have this inner voice and its message is the same. Deep in our hearts an indestructible primordial message resonates that aggression and killing are wrong. In its simple eloquence our heart knows that war is inconsistent with the deepest aspirations for human survival. Every human being in the world has this profound voice of inner yearning. It is beyond politics, beyond wealth, beyond power.

No human being in the world wakes up in the morning with a desire to kill. Even executioners do not revel in their grisly task. Mothers want their babies to live. Parents in general want their children to live in peace. Children want their parents to live long and healthy lives. We want these things because it is our nature. We know it because despite all the concepts we may hold and actions we may do to the contrary, our inner voice remains unstained and powerful. In this way those who endorse aggression and those who do not are both united in a mutual aspiration of peace for themselves if no one else.

In a single instant I realized that this fathomless declaration of peace was a part of me yearning for expression like a child being held against its will. In what is retrospectively perhaps the most courageous act of my life I allowed myself to be open to what I now know was the voice of my indwelling humanity. You see, our desire for peace among human beings is not a learned concept, but something we are born with. It is not like the art of war, which must be taught. Immediately after birth infants instinctually seek peace in the bosoms of their mothers. Even witnessing this instant of connection between infant and mother brings tears to the eyes of most human beings. What sane person can think of war or killing at such a moment? No one, because even as adults we know that the miracle of a human life emerging into the world is a symbol of humanity's greatest aspiration for peace on earth.

One need only watch children at play to witness the natural affinity of human beings to peacefully abide. With very little direction children tend to easily adopt compassion, patience, and tolerance toward one another. Racial differences, language barriers, cultural proclivities, wealth, social status, privilege and so on subordinate with relative ease to children's desire for harmonious play. Every human child demonstrates this sophistication. It is the evidence that inner peace is not learned, but dwells within.

This same voice of peace is within you and me. Unlike our physical bodies that must be compatible for the mutual exchange of an organ, our inner voice is without such limitation. Each of us can clearly see it in the other despite being conditioned to ignore it. We have been taught to view it as childish and weak. Yet when we consider the extent human beings must constantly be convinced of the necessity of aggression, it seems as though our yearning for peace almost stands on its own. Aggressive adults often have to bolster their deeds with alcohol and drugs. Gangs "beat" their new members into their social order. Soldiers must be booted through camp and ordered to kill under threat of punishment or death for disobeying. Yet, all one has to do is sit still for a while and peace naturally arises. Our natural proclivity for peace can also be found in the fact that even in the heat of battle great warriors yearn for victory so that peace can prevail. To overwhelm an enemy without giving or taking casualties is considered the ultimate battle. This too is an expression of the nobility of peace. Why? Because our humanity drives this knowing that we are better off when peace abounds.

When this voice pierced the shell of my hardened heart it was the first time in my life I had recognition that the disgruntled nature of my life was not the way of the world. I began to consider the possibility that my perception of continual aggression in the external world was emanating from inside of me rather than outside of me. I can only describe this as a spontaneous awakening to an understanding that I was projecting my inner turmoil onto the great movie screen of life. This was a frightening realization because if I was doing it that meant that many other people must be doing it as well. What does it mean if, for example, a person is unaware of his or her inner turmoil while instructing others in life-threatening circumstances? Who would want to be operated on by an angry doctor? What is the potential outcome of an angry peace leader? To be unaware of one's own inner turmoil is a form of blindness that is dangerous to self and others.

My question to myself was, How had I come to be in a state of embattlement at the core of my being? How does this happen to any of us? No one seeks inner conflict yet we arrive there anyway. For me, the answer lay in better understanding how my mind and heart had come to oppose one another without me realizing it.

First, I had to admit that my absent father, ignorance of life, black rage, and a host of other learned behaviors appeared in my mind as rites of passage into adulthood. In retrospect I now realize my mind had been traumatized in this way from a very early age. I accumulated mental baggage that I used to intellectually justify my anger, hatred, and ill will toward others. I had successively desensitized myself, as many people do, to accept aggression, harm to others, and killing as an unfortunate but legitimate problem in a malevolent world. I felt that violence was just a hard fact of life that befell unfortunate people. It was a kind of mindless acquiescence to a perception that some bigger scheme of circumstances must be in play when suffering or destruction is brought to bear on human life. It was not my problem nor did I perceive I was involved in its perpetuation.

The pivotal new understanding came when I accepted my inner voice's affirmation that indifference to aggression was inconsistent with my basic nature as a human being. It was not merely an issue of morality because morality often falls into a realm of intellectual debate. The voice of our humanity is non-debatable, non-negotiable, and unrelenting in expressing our yearning for human survival on earth. Recognition of our basic affinity for peace is beneficial in our homes, communities, society, and world. When any of us chooses to live our life from the basis of our peaceful birthright, he or she instantly becomes a better mother, father, sister, brother, son, daughter, teacher, community leader, and so on in a way applicable to that individual. Understanding this, in my heart I knew what every human being inherently knows, that violence is wrong.

The problem is that as we grow into the constraints of racial, cultural, societal, and religious adulthood, we lose our connection to other human beings. We become disconnected from those who do not look, act, think, or believe as we do. Then, in contrast with our childhood ease of accommodating differences, we intellectually give ourselves permission to do to others what we would never want to have done to ourselves.

We further distance ourselves by using time, space, and direction as wedges between our shared aspirations. Young people see their interests as distinct from the interests of old people. The past, the present, and the future become potential points of contention serving as sticks to be thrown on the fire of separation. The quick-witted people separate themselves from those who are slow on the uptake. The people of the north find conflict with those from the south. The lower class yearns with envy for the privileges of the upper class. The people of the east take issue with those in the west. The upward-moving people come to resent and separate from the downward-moving people. Finally, the entire cosmos appears to be filled with displays of separateness and potential for aggression. The railroad tracks of division seem to appear everywhere. Individuals as well as humanity in general begin to feel surrounded and respond to potential aggression ubiquitously. Everyone becomes endangered by what others suspect may be an intent to commit an act of aggression.

The core problem for most of us is that we don't understand that this preoccupation with conflict and division runs contrary to what we feel in our hearts. By entertaining ideas of conflict in our mind we set up a contradiction with the peace that eternally dwells within us. Our minds become conflicted with our hearts. The war outside our bodies becomes the war within. We become ravaged with emotions and fears as though we have swallowed a spiritual poison. The war we unwittingly ingest to the core of our being can cause us to view even our most precious loved ones as potential enemies at the slightest disagreement. Families become torn, friendships are strained, communities become fractured, societies fall into discord, and the whole world becomes threatened with annihilation. Cumulative human discord arises in the world as an aggregate expression of the internal war within individuals manifesting unimpeded.

In my tearful moment of truly listening within, like a flash of lightning I realized that my perception of hate and anger in the world was inseparable from my own inner disquietude. I realized I was constantly confirming and reconfirming my own inner war by pointing out strife in human relations around me. It was like a person watching a movie and all of a sudden realizing he is the projector and screen as well. This is not to say I believe that by changing myself the world would necessarily change, too. Rather, it meant the amazing discovery that my personal peace was separable from what was going on in the world around me. I could be free.

. . .

OUR STRUGGLE today is against the belief that interpersonal and collective aggression has been with us since the dawn of humankind and will forever remain a part of our fundamental nature. This is incorrect and suggests that human beings are incapable of evolving beyond mass murder as a problem-solving strategy. Humanity's habitual revisitation of lethal conflict is only an expression of our misunderstanding about the mechanism that creates inner turmoil and how it evolves from one person's disquietude into a massive collective act. War begets itself like cancer spreads in the body. The character of aggression is to replicate itself while simultaneously destroying its host. Until we understand the genesis of inner conflict the most we can hope for is periodic remission of a terminal disease.

Conflict is an exercise of the intellect. It is a rational message of concepts that leads one to believe that the other person is an adversary. I had become conflicted by judging the conduct and behavior of those around me. Unwitting judgment unimpeded in one's inner being can be addictively hypnotic. One can become mesmerized by the cycle of recurring aggression in a way that makes being more aggressive seem like a way to break the cycle. This is like a mouse on a treadmill that thinks it can get off the treadmill by running faster.

People obsessed with judging others while making no effort at introspection cultivate a zombie-like view of self-imposed suffering. In this way I realized that holding on to negative ideas about other people never gave me a sense of wholeness. I unknowingly allowed judgment to play a crucial role in the drama of continually nurturing my resentment and anger. I accepted given notions that the "enemy" was clearly defined before I was born and that society was capable of defining my adversaries for me. I, like many others, felt that this was enough to act upon with continual intellectual malice as well as justify physical violence towards others.

But the inner voice I am speaking of stood in contrast to this habitual disregard for the deep connection I have with other human beings. In retrospect I understand that the arising of this voice was the arising of my humanity. That is, it was the part of me that continually dwells in peace, compassion, tolerance, and love like children playing together on a summer afternoon. When I finally came to know the essence of what I've written here tears leaped from my eyes. I was both elated and profoundly saddened. I was elated to have found the meaning of liberation from a lifetime of self-imposed suffering. Although I still had years of work to do before being able to live from the confidence of indwelling peace, I, for the first time in my life, could see how this understanding could release me from the cycle of conflict at the core of my being.

With due respect for those who risk their lives on behalf of innocent others, I acknowledge the courage it takes to confront aggression with aggression. However, I maintain that peace takes even greater courage. True peace can be defined as unshakable nonviolent courage in the face of lethal aggression. The works of Gandhi, the Buddha, and Martin Luther King, Jr., exemplify the sophistication of peaceful engagement in the face of aggression. As the world grows increasingly dangerous the resourcefulness of peaceful reso-

choyin rangdrol

lution must be pushed to genius in a way that is understand-
able to the laity. This genius must first be settled in the process of inner transformation.

The only way to create lasting peaceful outcomes is to
pursue such a goal based in the deep and abiding sense of
peace that dwells within all of us. This is the only option
whose basis, means, and end has the power to relegate the
aggressive basis of war into obsolescence.

afterword
howard zinn

IT IS A TRIBUTE to the achievements of the "women's movement" of the last few decades that, as in the preceding pages, we can have the intensely personal, honest testimonies of men and women about their most secret fears and longings. Reading their stories, one must marvel at the sheer variety of human experience, usually concealed from us as we are taught to see others in the simplistic categories cherished in a myopic culture.

The dominant culture, narrow-minded, suspicious, insists that we answer the questions on all the bureaucratic forms we encounter in the course of living the modern life: Are you male or female? Are you black or white? Are you a citizen or foreign-born? The people in Rebecca Walker's book defy those questions.

There is something comparable in the history examinations given in schools all over the country: Answer this question, true or false. What is false is the idea that human behavior can be forced into such narrow channels, compelled to make choices that violate our natures.

Many of the testimonies in this book rebel against society's insistence on a clear-cut distinction between men and women, on preconceived ideas of what is "masculine" and what is "feminine." All of us, the dominant culture declares, must choose one or the other, or rather, have the choice made for us, on the basis of a biological distinction that allows no deviation and remains fixed for the rest of our lives.

Once we have been thus branded and herded into one corral or another, we are expected to behave like everyone else in that corral. And so women are to be compliant, sexually and ideologically, while men are to be strong and dominant, in an artificial division of labor that demeans both sexes.

We are given arbitrary definitions of what is "normal," ironically, in a society that pretends to sanctify individualism while not allowing the individual self-determination. Indeed, a government that claims to care about human rights punishes those who want to be themselves. As one of the writers here points out, the construction of artificial social differences amounts to a violent maintenance of the status quo.

The trick played on men is that while they are supposed to relish their strength, the reality is that they live in a hierarchical world in which only a small number of men have power over the rest: can exploit them economically, can send them off to war. The trick played on women is that their presumed natural delicacy is under constant attack by a world that limits their possibilities for a full life. While pretending to revere them as mothers, this world puts impossible economic pressures on their ability to raise children, and then takes these children, when they are grown, off to die.

Men and women are set against each other as handy in-house enemies while the larger society rules both groups from afar. The challenge then, as Rebecca Walker reminds us, is for men and women to find their purpose in life independent of what the dominant culture has ordained for them. We must not let the rulers of society define us, because if left on our own, we may find that we define ourselves solely by our capacity for love and connectedness, and not by our allegiance to artificial ideals of masculine or feminine.

Perhaps the most pernicious of these artificial definitions is that which says men are naturally violent and women, as bearers of children and supporters of men, will therefore be willing accomplices in this violence.

If this were so, political leaders would not have to work so strenuously to inculcate "patriotism" from the time little children are taught to salute the flag and pledge allegiance and adore military heroes. They would not have to use the most sophisticated propaganda tools to persuade the population that a war is necessary for "freedom" or "democracy" or "national security" or "to end all wars." They would not have to entice young men into military service with promises of economic security, nor have to work hard to convince their mothers and wives and sweethearts that they are doing something noble, "for their country."

I like the story in this book about a father who has to counter the idea in his children that "black manhood" demands physical prowess and military heroism. Years later, his son, the writer of the essay, is told by a spiritualist about Tehuti, a deity who says that we should be neither warriors nor victims. The person to be admired is one who does not fight, but who watches and waits, analyzes and documents. "They are the ones who remain long after the battlefields are paved over with asphalt and strip malls. And then they tell their tale."

The power holders in society will try to divide us by gender or race or religion or national boundaries. But we will continue to resist that, will continue to insist on crossing all those boundaries. We do this because as human beings we have a common interest in peace and love, and we know that it is only the recognition of this common interest that can save us.

contributors

Ruth Bettelheim has been a practicing psychotherapist for forty years, and has taught at Claremont Graduate School, California School for Professional Psychology, and the Center for Early Education Teacher's College. She has served as a mental health consultant and parent educator for numerous public and private schools, as well as for UCLA and the University of Chicago.

Born and raised in Baton Rouge, Louisiana, **David Coates** survived a career in business only to realize that the ladder of success he was struggling to climb was leaning against the wrong wall. David is now near completion of his master's degree in integral psychology at the California Institute of Integral Studies in San Francisco.

Meri Nana-Ama Danquah is the author of *Willow Weep for Me: A Black Woman's Journey Through Depression*. She is also the editor of two anthologies, *Becoming American: Personal Essays by First-Generation Immigrant Women* and *Shaking the Tree: A Collection of New Fiction and Memoir by Black Women*.

Michael Datcher is the author of the critically acclaimed national best seller *Raising Fences: A Black Man's Love Story* (Riverhead)—a *Today* Show Book Club selection. He has written for *The Washington Post,*

Los Angeles Times, Vibe, Ladies' Home Journal, and *The Source.* He is a frequent news commentator on BBC Radio in the UK and has appeared on *Nightline* and *Dateline* as an analyst. His essays and poetry are widely anthologized, and he is the coeditor of *Tough Love: The Life and Death of Tupac Shakur* (Alexander Publishing). Datcher teaches English literature at West Los Angeles College and UCLA Extension, and is the director of literary programs at the World Stage Writers' Workshop in Leimert Park. He is a board member of PEN USA.

Jay Ruben Dayrit's work has appeared in several literary journals and anthologies, including *The Minnesota Review, Nexus, Sycamore Review, His 2, Brilliant New Fiction by Gay Men* (Faber & Faber) and *Contemporary Fiction by Filipinos in America* (Anvil). He works at *Wired* in San Francisco.

Jesse Green is a regular contributor to *The New York Times Magazine* and, on radio, PRI's *The Next Big Thing.* His articles, essays, and profiles have appeared in many other publications including the *New Yorker, The Washington Post, New York, Premiere, The Yale Review,* and *GQ.* Green is the author, most recently, of *The Velveteen Father: An Unexpected Journey to Parenthood,* which was named one of the best nonfiction books of the year by the *Los Angeles Times Book Review* and was the recipient of a 1999 Lambda Literary Foundation prize. His first novel, *O Beautiful,* which *Entertainment Weekly* called "one of the best five novels of the year," was reissued by Ballantine in June 2000.

Rachel Lehmann-Haupt writes about culture and gender politics. Her work has appeared in *The New York Times, The New York Observer, Wired, Vogue,* and *New York.* She lives in Manhattan.

Peter J. Harris is producer/host of KPFK's *Inspiration House: VoiceMusic for Whole Living,* Mondays 10–11 P.M., 90.7 FM; publisher of *Drumming Between Us: Black Love & Erotic Poetry,* a Los Angeles magazine; and author of *Hand Me My Griot Clothes: The Autobiography of Junior Baby*, which won the Oakland PEN Josephine Miles Award in 1993.

Born and raised in the nation's capital, **Kenji Jasper** is a regular contributor to NPR's *Morning Edition* and has written for *Savoy, Essence, Vibe, The Village Voice, The Charlotte Observer*, and Africana.com. He is the author of three novels, *Dark, Dakota Grand,* and the forthcoming *Seeking Salamanca Mitchell.* Jasper is now at work on *The Lone Ranger and the Marlboro Man*, a double memoir about his grandfathers.

Michael Moore is the author of the number-one *New York Times* bestseller *Stupid White Men* and the bestseller *Downsize This!* His film *Bowling for Columbine* won the Academy Award for Best Documentary and holds the box-office record as the most successful documentary of all time. He is also the creator of the classic documentary films *Roger & Me* and *The Big One,* as well as the Emmy Award–winning *TV Nation* and the highly acclaimed television series *The Awful Truth.* Moore lives with his wife and daughter in Michigan and New York City.

Jarvis Jay Masters is a Buddhist writer living on death row in San Quentin prison. His stories and essays have been published widely. He is the author of the book *Finding Freedom: Writings from Death Row.* A growing international movement is seeking to overturn his wrongful conviction.

Tajamika Paxton's work is a unique blend of expression. She is a noted film producer, writer and the owner of Good Karma Yoga, a yoga and wellness studio in Los Angeles.

Choyin Rangdrol is a Lama in the Vajrayana tradition of Tibetan Buddhism. He is the founder of Rainbow Dharma, an organization devoted to ensuring the inclusion of African-Americans in the spread of Buddhism in the West.

Caitríona Reed is a poet, hypnotherapist, and teacher of meditation practices for awakening to the spiritual and global emergency of our times. She has been leading workshops and retreats for adults and young people in the U.S. and Europe for twenty years. She is cofounder of Manzanita Village, a Buddhist retreat center in Southern California.

Douglas Rushkoff is the author of ten books on media, values, and popular culture, translated into over twenty languages. His social commentaries appear on NPR's *All Things Considered, CBS Sunday Morning,* and the back page of *Time.* His latest book, *Nothing Sacred,* presents Judaism as the process by which we get over religion and start acting nice to one another.

Malidoma Somé is a fully initiated Shaman and elder of the Dagara tribe of West Central Africa. Malidoma's mission and spiritual vocation is to bring the Wisdom of Africa to the West. His name, Malidoma, in Dagara means "he who makes friends with the stranger/enemy." At the request of the tribal elders, he has undertaken to make friends with the world by sharing many of the previously secret Wisdom teachings of his tribe, including knowledge of the fivefold African Wheel. To fulfill his spiritual vocation, Malidoma immersed himself in Western culture. He has earned three master's degrees and two Ph.D. degrees—one in political science from the Sorbonne in Paris, and the second in world literature from Brandeis University in Boston. Malidoma travels and teaches throughout the world. He makes his home in central California.

Martha Southgate is the author of two novels, *The Fall of Rome,* which was named one of the best novels of 2002 by Jonathan Yardley of *The Washington Post,* and *Another Way to Dance,* which won the Coretta Scott King Genesis Award for Best First Novel. She received a 2002 New York Foundation for the Arts grant and has received fellowships from the MacDowell Colony and the Virginia Center for the Creative Arts. Her nonfiction articles have appeared

in *The New York Times Magazine, O, Premiere,* and *Essence.* She lives
in Brooklyn.

Bruce Stockler's humor pieces have appeared in publications including *The New York Times,* the *Los Angeles Times, The Philadelphia Inquirer,*
and *The Christian Science Monitor.* A regular contributor to *Esquire,* he
has also been a joke writer for Jay Leno. He and his family live in the
suburbs of New York City.

Anthony Swofford is the author of *Jarhead.* He served in the United
States Marine Corps from 1988–1992. His writing has appeared in
The New York Times, The New York Times Magazine, Harper's, Details,
and other publications. He is an assistant professor of English at Saint
Mary's College in Maraga, California, and he lives in Oakland. He
currently is working on a novel.

Christian Wiman is the author of two books of poems and numerous
essays and reviews. His work has been published in *The Atlantic
Monthly,* the *London Review of Books,* and elsewhere. He has taught at
Stanford University and Lynchburg College. Wiman is the editor of
Poetry magazine and lives in Chicago.

Howard Zinn was a shipyard worker and Air Force bombardier before
he went to college under the G.I. Bill and received his doctorate
from Columbia University. He taught at Spelman College and
Boston University, was active in the civil-rights movement and anti-
war movement, and has written many books, including *A People's
History of the United States* and his memoir, *You Can't Be Neutral on a
Moving Train.*

credits

"Sanctuary," "Pablo's Wish," and "A Reason to Live," from *Finding Freedom: Writings from Death Row.* Copyright © 1997 by Jarvis Jay Masters, Padma Publishing. Reprinted by permission of the author.

"The End of Men" from *Stupid White Men . . . and Other Sorry Excuses for the State of the Nation!* by Michael Moore. Copyright © 2002 by Michael Moore. Reprinted by permission of HarperCollins Publishers Inc.

"The Limit," by Christian Wiman from the Fall 2001 volume of *The Threepenny Review.* Copyright © 2001 by Christian Wiman. Reprinted by permission of the author.